FRITZ B. BURNS
and the
Development of Los Angeles

Fritz B. Burns, 1957, Honolulu, Hawaii.

Fritz B. Burns Collection, Loyola Marymount University.

Fritz B. Burns
and the Development of Los Angeles

**The Biography of a Community Developer
and Philanthropist**

James Thomas Keane

The Thomas and Dorothy Leavey Center for the Study of Los Angeles
Loyola Marymount University
and
The Historical Society of Southern California

Los Angeles, California 2001

Contents

Illustrations

Foreword

Founders of great cities can frequently be found in the private sector. Not until recently, however, have historians paid adequate attention to such private-sector figures, preferring instead to chronicle the lives, fortunes, and misfortunes of public-sector figures, politicians especially. Of late, however, historians have been giving increasing attention to the role played by bankers, developers, and other members of the business community in creating not only the physical fabric of the American city, but its social and institutional life as well.

In no city is the drama of private sector creativity more important than in Los Angeles. From one perspective, in fact, the entire history of the City of Angels—indeed, the entire history of Southern California—could be written in terms of its land-use patterns and real estate development, as historian W.W. Robinson has proven in his many worthwhile monographs. The central story of Los Angeles and Southern California, after all, is the story of how people flocked into a near-empty landscape and created, virtually overnight, an intricate array of cities, towns, and suburbs. In this regard, figures such as Abbot Kinney, Gaylord Wilshire, Harry Culver, Alphonzo Bell, A.W. Ross, Ole Hanson, even Edgar Rice Burroughs, developer of Tarzana, must be considered not only as business entrepreneurs, but as social and cultural entrepreneurs as well. In one way or another, the developers and homebuilders of Southern California were orchestrating a most powerful cluster of value and symbol—

those relating to place, community, home—and in so doing were helping to create the social, psychological, cultural, even the ethical fabric of the cities, towns, and suburbs they were bringing into existence. The developers of Southern California, including the developers of Los Angeles, were entrepreneurs concerned with the bottom line, true; but they were also orchestrators of the deepest possible instincts and hopes of human beings to find their place in the world, which is to say, to find their home.

And now, thanks to the scholarship and narrative skills of historian James Thomas Keane and the support of the Thomas and Dorothy Leavey Center for the Study of Los Angeles at Loyola Marymount University and the Historical Society of Southern California, the previously untold story of one of the founders of Los Angeles, developer Fritz B. Burns, now stands revealed in all its historical and paradigmatic significance. This biography is of historical significance because Fritz B. Burns helped create Los Angeles, the Westside and the San Fernando Valley especially, as a human community in time and space. Burns' life is of paradigmatic significance because in just about every phase of his life—his Midwestern origins, his migration to Los Angeles in the 1920s, his capacity for self-invention and self-actualization, his combination of show biz salesmanship and a deep hunger for personal and public culture—Fritz B. Burns not only helped bring Los Angeles into being, he incorporated into the very fabric of his life the dynamics and ambitions, the DNA code, if you will, of the emergent city.

Los Angeles in the 1920s was the Great Gatsby of American cities: the product, that is, of its own imagined identity, brought into being through sheer force of will, energized by the influx (eventually) of some 1.5 million new residents. An inland city transformed itself into a deep-water port. A semi-arid city reached across the desert to appropriate the waters of the Owens, and later, Colorado Rivers. A city somewhat

delayed in its institutional development now created or
expanded its colleges and universities, brought into being a
new downtown, constructed a new City Hall, hotels, two
football stadia, and expanded its industrial infrastructure.
But most of all, a city that was still, as of the First World War,
largely comprised of semi-arid steppes, empty arroyos, graz-
ing pastures, scratch properties of various sorts, sandy knolls,
and lima bean fields, subdivided itself into a glorious future
and began to emplace on each portion of these subdivisions
homes, homes, and yet more homes. Here was a kind of fast-
forwarded instant history: the creation, the self-invention,
the overnight actualization of an urban fabric that in other
times and places had taken centuries to create.

Like so many of the Americans coming into Los Angeles
during these Great Gatsby years, Fritz B. Burns was a Midwesterner, a Minnesotan, with his Army service behind him.
Burns brought to Los Angeles a haphazard (due to his other
pursuits) education at the University of Minnesota and the
Wharton School of Finance, a buoyant optimism, a belief
that he could sell anything to anyone, and a conviction that
Los Angeles, where he was now choosing deliberately to
make his home and his fortune (a millionaire by thirty, he
promised himself), was the best possible place to make all
dreams come true. In his novel *The Boosters* (1924), Mark Lee
Luther caught this mood of Los Angeles at the time that
Fritz B. Burns was arriving: its sense that anything could be
done, that the City of Angels was on the cutting edge of
American destiny, that all one had to do was to roll up one's
sleeves and bring the City of Angels into existence.

Like a Gold Rush pioneer a half-century and more earlier,
Fritz B. Burns literally lived in a tent—for some five years!
—pitched on the Westside of the city he was helping to
develop. A millionaire by thirty, as he had promised himself,
he lost his wealth in the Depression; but no matter, this was
but a momentary setback, and the tent at Playa del Rey soon

became the mansion in Hancock Park and by the late 1940s, in partnership with Henry J. Kaiser, another larger-than-life figure, Burns was developing homes by the hundreds, then the thousands, in west Los Angeles and the San Fernando Valley.

Once again, Fritz Burns was making history and incorporating its dynamics within his own life. A Midwesterner in the boom of the 1920s, he became the recovered entrepreneur of the embattled 1930s; and when an entire generation who had trained in or passed through California during World War II returned to California after the war to make a new life, Fritz B. Burns, in partnership with Henry J. Kaiser, was on hand to welcome them with an entirely new genre of affordable housing. Thanks in part to Burns, Kaiser, Ralph and Goldie Lewis, David D. Bohannon, Henry Doelger and the other California developers of the late 1940s and 1950s, millions of ordinary Americans, including millions of Californians, now found themselves housed as no other generation of working people had ever been housed in human history. True, as critics have more than once pointed out, there was a certain conformity to this housing, which had to be mass-produced at a rapid pace; but there was also the individualizing possibility of home ownership, which for millions of Americans was a first-time experience. When that job was done, or at least well-started, Burns headed even further west, to Hawaii where, once again in partnership with Henry J. Kaiser, he helped create the built environment of yet another developing American place.

As might be expected, Fritz B. Burns made millions in the course of this activity. He also gave significant amounts of it away. Among other philanthropies and causes, he must be considered one of the founders of Loyola Marymount University. He led, in fact, the parade on groundbreaking day for its new campus flamboyantly mounted upon a spirited horse. Intelligent and curious, Burns found time in the midst of his busy life to read—if not omnivorously, then certainly with an intensity beyond that expected of a busy entrepreneur—and to write poetry up to the time of his death a few months short of his eightieth birthday.

So then: while historians continue to chronicle the politicians, engineers, artists, trial attorneys, and other expressive personalities of a city, including the City of Angels, let them also remember, as James Thomas Keane has remembered, those flamboyant and ever-hopeful salesmen-entrepreneurs known as developers. They, too, were founders of the city; for not only did they build homes and meet markets for housing, they also answered dreams: the hopes and dreams of hundreds of thousands of Americans who were coming into the City of Angels in search of a better life. They are still coming to this day, and this biography leads us to hope that on hand to greet them will be the successors of Fritz B. Burns, welcoming the newly-arriving citizens of the city to their new lives and to their new homes.

Dr. Kevin Starr
State Librarian of California

Acknowledgments

Fritz B. Burns was fond of noting to reporters that, left to his own devices, he would have come to nothing in life; his achievements were the result of a careful habit of surrounding himself with persons of strong character and extraordinary talent. The same can be said of this biography. While the responsibility for any omissions or shortcomings is mine, a great many individuals deserve credit for its substance.

First and foremost are Joseph E. Rawlinson and Ken Skinner of the Fritz B. Burns Foundation, who contributed time, effort, and resources to produce this biography in numerous interviews and meetings. They also provided an invaluable resource for the project through their personal remembrances of a man who was their friend and coworker before he was an historical figure.

The Historical Society of Southern California provided timely aid and oversaw publication of the manuscript. I am in debt to Thomas Andrews, Executive Director of the Society, as well as to Martin Ridge, former President, whose careful commentary and suggestions have been an important influence on the book's style.

Numerous individuals at Loyola Marymount University and the Thomas and Dorothy Leavey Center for the Study of Los Angeles at Loyola Marymount University contributed valuable time, effort, and advice to this project, including the President, Robert Lawton, S.J., Fernando Guerra, Mara Marks, Veronica Galvez, Danitza Pantoja, and student research assistants Adam Nicolai and Denis Delja.

John and Frances Morehart welcomed me into their home and provided me unrestricted access to Fritz Burns' personal notebooks, as well as to their private pictures, news clippings, and memories of Fritz Burns. Many of Burns' former friends and business associates also willingly sacrificed time for interviews, including Gregory Dillon, Richard Dunn, Jacqueline Sanborn, Winifred Cockey, and Herbert Lightfoot.

While the bibliography provides a complete list of the libraries and archives utilized, a number of individuals at those institutions provided ready assistance far beyond the call of duty. I owe a special debt of gratitude to Dace Taube of the University of Southern California Regional History Center, Genevieve Troka of the California State Archives, Martin Hackett of the University of Pennsylvania, Donna Reichle and Adrienne Ash of the National Association of Home Builders, Jennifer Watts and Erin Chase of the Huntington Library, and Mary Lou Crockett of the Westchester/Playa Del Rey Historical Society. Thanks are also due to Errol Stevens, Neil Bethke, Cynthia Becht, and Clay Stalls of the Charles Von der Ahe Library at Loyola Marymount University, all of whom consistently offered their expert assistance, patience, and genuine enthusiasm for the project over the course of many months.

Valuable assistance also came from staff members of Charles Von der Ahe Library at Loyola Marymount University, the Bancroft Library at the University of California at Berkeley, the Management Library at the University of California at Los Angeles, the McHenry Library at the University of California at Santa Cruz, the University of Minnesota, the Los Angeles Public Library, the Paul Ziffren Sports Center Library in Los Angeles, and the Westchester/Playa Del Rey Historical Society.

A number of other valuable contributors include Michael Collins, FSC, Dana Cuff, Greg Fischer, Judson Grenier,

Greg Hise, Jeff Kearns, Gary Lease, Julie Lugo-Cerra, Ron Marasco, Lynne Marlow, Donald Merrifield, S.J., Thomas Owenson, Joseph Schulte, Sarane Van Dyke, Coral Von Zumwalt, and Frank Wilkinson. I also owe special thanks to my parents, Robert and Maureen Keane, who offered constant encouragement and support during the past year and the many preceding it.

Finally, this book is the result of the extraordinary efforts of Michael Engh, S.J., whose diligent labors to direct, edit, and shepherd the manuscript through to completion should not go unrecognized. It is regrettable that, were I to credit this modest man properly for his essential role, he would promptly edit it out. Equally important as his material contribution has been his positive example, and his presence as an editor, mentor, and friend has proved to be a remarkable blessing throughout.

Preface

For half a century, Fritz B. Burns achieved remarkable success as a land developer and salesman, yet he failed to complete one of his most important projects—the telling of his own story in the housing of America and the creation of modern Southern California. He planned an autobiography and assembled the notes, but discovered he possessed neither the skills nor temperament for self-promotion. His talents lay in buying property, constructing homes, and developing communities. From the early 1920s until his death in 1979, Fritz Burns subdivided land and pioneered housing construction practices quickly copied by developers throughout the country. Burns left a legacy of things built, not words written.

James T. Keane shows us the content, character, and contributions of Fritz Burns, who tied his career to the growth of Los Angeles. He follows Burns the land developer who promoted the mass construction of homes, engaged in the "hard sell," and prided himself on the communities he created. As the people's builder, Burns lived by the salesman's creed, "know me by my products, not by my word." He erected houses, hotels, and shopping centers, first in California, then in Hawaii. Through Keane's biography we discover a builder with powerful behind-the-scenes influence, a man who created a place for himself within the business and political establishment of modern Los Angeles. By including accomplishments alongside blemishes, such as the sprawl of suburbs in Los Angeles, Keane reveals the multifaceted dimensions of this flesh-and-blood man. He also introduces Burns the family man, the lifelong poet, the book-devouring reader, the loyal business associate, the inveterate risk taker—the story of a life worth knowing.

Throughout his life, Fritz B. Burns formed many profitable partnerships, so he would appreciate the collaboration that produced this volume. The Historical Society of Southern California, known for a century of printing the best in local history, welcomed the opportunity to join with Loyola Marymount University in sponsoring this book. In this endeavor, the University honors its longtime patron and the charitable foundation he established. The school's Thomas and Dorothy Leavey Center for the Study of Los Angeles undertook this project, and, with this volume, inaugurates scholarly publishing about this modern metropolis. The teamed efforts in this joint venture would have pleased Fritz Burns, just as the candor of this volume would appeal to him. The Historical Society of Southern California and Loyola Marymount University are proud to present a work that significantly advances our understanding of the history of modern Southern California and the creation of the suburban American West.

MICHAEL E. ENGH, S.J.
Loyola Marymount University

CHAPTER ONE

"I'll Be A Millionaire By Thirty"

"A period of development is at hand greater than our most sanguine dreams."   *Fritz Burns, 1928.*

In the winter of 1934, a lonely, battered tent claimed sole occupancy of the beach at Playa Del Rey. Used by builders to shelter workers and store supplies on-site during construction projects, the shabby structure was just large enough to sleep two adults comfortably. Its canvas walls served as a feeble buttress against the unceasing wind that blew cold over the ocean and kicked up a steady cloud of sand. The tent was surrounded on either side by miles of eerily deserted beach, and opened toward the waves of the Pacific Ocean a hundred feet away. Behind the tent rose imposing bluffs crowned by elaborate homes, the largest residences of a failed resort subdivision called Palisades Del Rey. Atop the highest summit, commanding an unmatched view of the Pacific Ocean from three sides, stood an Italianate mansion faced in Utah granite.

The contrast between the weather-beaten tent on the sand and the palatial home atop the nearby bluffs was only enhanced by their unique surroundings. No more luxurious mansion existed for many miles, and no accommodations could be more spartan than the interior of that lonely tent below. The two structures nevertheless shared a common purpose. They were, respectively, the former and current homes of a thirty-five-year-old real estate salesman by the name of Fritz Bernard Burns.[1]

As vice president and sales manager of the real estate firm of Dickinson & Gillespie in 1925, the twenty-five-year-old Burns had used the construction of the mansion to advertise his sales program at Palisades Del Rey. Photographers had documented each stage of the home's construction, and elaborate brochures for Palisades Del Rey included the mansion as an example of the attractiveness of valuable homes in the subdivision. Burns hosted elaborate dinner parties for prospective home buyers and visiting dignitaries alike. The enormous size of the house far exceeded the needs of a newlywed couple and an infant son, but Fritz Burns' home at 200 Waterloo Street was much more than a place of residence. For a self-assured young man fond of boasting "I'll be a millionaire by thirty," the mansion was visible proof that he had reached his ambitious goal. Gazing out from his upstairs sunroom at the attractive homes rising under his direction, Fritz Burns in 1925 could consider himself the master of his destiny.[2]

Known to the few locals as "Moonstone Beach" for its semiprecious stones, the Playa Del Rey shoreline occupied the midpoint of Santa Monica Bay in Los Angeles. Anyone still fortunate enough to possess an automobile in the lean year of 1934 could visit the area via Del Rey Boulevard, if careful to note where the asphalt of the road ended and the sand began. A second option was a trip on the Pacific Electric passenger trains, the "Big Red Cars." Both the "Redondo Beach-Del Rey Line" and the "Lagoon Line" stopped at the foot of the bluffs at Trolley Way. An occasional beachgoer might disembark at the Del Rey stop, but otherwise Playa Del Rey served as little more than an underused transfer point in 1934.[3]

To the north of the trolley stop was the Del Rey Beach Club, skirted by stacks of bundled umbrellas and folded beach chairs. The club was so bereft of members or activity that it appeared to be closed entirely. Nearby were a few makeshift volleyball courts and an abandoned pier slowly

Aerial View of Palisades Del Rey, 1924, before construction of homes. The Pacific Electric trolley tracks are visible along the base of the bluffs, and the Del Rey Lagoon (foreground) is still open to the sea. Dickinson & Gillespie planned to turn the lagoon into a yacht harbor. The fields in the rear of the picture are now Los Angeles International Airport.

Fritz B. Burns Collection, Loyola Marymount University.

surrendering to the pounding of the waves. Bordering the trolley line sat a few rows of tiny wood cottages of simple construction, their status as newcomers to the beach evidenced by their lack of plumbing, insulation, or electricity. Screen doors swinging in the wind betrayed them as abandoned vacation rentals, deserted in the winter months.[4]

The mansions rising from the bluffs above the beach had reached their heyday in the late 1920s as a prestigious neighborhood for Los Angeles' newly rich. Early buyers included movie stars and entertainment industry moguls. By 1934, most of the homes were unlighted and abandoned, though curbed asphalt roads, lined with elaborate light standards, wound through the rolling hilltops. The Great Depression had bankrupted the majority of owners and residents, who had long since moved on to seek their fortunes far from the remote streets of the failed resort town.

Looming over the tract was the Italianate mansion on Waterloo Street. Built in 1925 at the summit of the highest hill in Palisades Del Rey, it included fireplaces of Batchelder tile in ten rooms spreading over six thousand square feet. From the leaded glass windows of its forty-foot ballroom, no structure blocked sightlines that reached the whole of the Santa Monica Bay, from Malibu to Palos Verdes. The mansion's splendor led to rumors in later years that it had been built for Cecil B. DeMille, and that Ronald Reagan and Jane Wyman were married there.[5]

Four years after he moved into his new home, Fritz Burns had bought out his three partners in Dickinson & Gillespie and had become president of the company. Justin Dickinson, Clifford Gillespie, and Burns' uncle, William Schreyer, had chosen to dissociate themselves from an increasingly unpredictable real estate market, where sales depended more on speculation than perceived value. Burns did not share their concern. Since moving to Los Angeles in 1921, Dickinson & Gillespie had become a multimillion-dollar operation that sold out dozens of subdivisions and reaped huge profits for its four partners. Burns saw no limit to the company's spiraling profits and rapid growth, particularly in Los Angeles, where real estate prices knew no direction but up. In 1927, Burns and other area real estate magnates arranged for two universities to move to the Del Rey Hills, and the City of Los Angeles picked the area for a municipal airport. Events seemed to justify Burns' growing optimism for the future.[6]

Two years later, when the stock market crashed and the real estate market collapsed, the new owner of Dickinson & Gillespie found events beyond his control. Lot buyers in Palisades Rel Rey reneged on contracts and defaulted en masse. Banks demanded payment on loans taken out to finance improvements in the subdivision. Fritz Burns' extensive land holdings became virtually worthless with the advent of the Great Depression. Within the year, creditors foreclosed on his loans, and Burns was forced to abandon his mansion on an aptly named Waterloo Street. Determined to hold on to his remaining properties and business in Palisades Del Rey, Burns adapted a construction tent to his suddenly diminished needs. He took up residence on Moonstone Beach, only a few hundred feet from his previous home. As he had predicted, he had become a millionaire by thirty. He had not foreseen, however, becoming all but destitute by thirty-one.[7]

For the next five years, the tent served as both his home and his office, and the exigencies of an austere existence rarely took him far from its flapping confines. Upon waking with the sunrise every morning, Burns swam in the rough surf a hundred feet from his bed. In the afternoons, he would join students from nearby Loyola University for volleyball games on the sand. He ate what he could afford, which meant in large measure that he survived on cottage cheese, supplied by a former employee of Dickinson & Gillespie. Visitors included his brother, Robert, a law student who dropped in regularly to attempt to persuade Burns to sign papers declaring bankruptcy, and the occasional member of the Del Rey Beach Club, which Burns owned and operated for the scant dollars it brought in every month.[8]

Afternoon trips for mail revealed a never-ending stream of letters from creditors that announced his default on outstanding loans or demanded payment for services provided. To hold his creditors at bay, Burns partially paid those bills that could not be ignored and promised future payment on the rest. He also set aside a portion of his income for a few low-cost business ventures. The shacks lining Trolley Way were the remnants of the 1932 Los Angeles Olympic Village, purchased after the Olympics for $140 apiece and dragged by mules to Playa Del Rey. Burns rented the rickety two-room structures as summer cottages. He had also formed a partnership with a local oil wildcatter, Sam Herndon, to prospect for oil in the Del Rey Hills. Any strike on Burns' land entitled him to two percent of Herndon's profits.[9]

Despite his losses in 1929, Burns also began to frequent tax sales for property in the Del Rey Hills. The County of Los Angeles had seized huge swaths of privately held land in the early years of the Depression through liens on unpaid property taxes. The long-departed owners had either gone bankrupt themselves or had abandoned hope that any of the land would ever again be worth its appraised value. To acquire title to such properties, Burns needed only to pay off the accumulated taxes. Though these relatively paltry sums were often beyond Burns' financial reach, whenever possible he purchased property throughout the area.[10]

The devastating losses suffered during the Great Depression had severely battered both Burns' pocketbook and his personality. These travails should have been enough to send him home to Minneapolis and to redirect him to an existence more placid and predictable than that of real estate salesman. Nevertheless, at the onset of the winter of 1934, Fritz Burns sat alone in his little tent on the sand and began engineering an improbable comeback.

What possessed Fritz Burns to continue his lonely vigil among the remnants of his past? What burning vision kept him warm in that tent against the never-ending chill of the wind whipping off the surf? How many nights of doubt followed an optimistic purchase of yet more worthless land at the western edge of Los Angeles?

Over the next half-century, Burns would return from destitution and rise to national prominence as a housing pioneer and a master builder. He would help to reshape an entire country's way of life. His powerful convictions and leadership ability would make him the leading voice of the private housing industry across the nation. His accomplishments during a world war and in its aftermath would transform him into an outspoken and powerful public figure in Los Angeles. Through homebuilding operations over several decades, he would construct total communities out of empty farmland and erect over twelve thousand homes. Ventures in tourism and commercial properties would result in groundbreaking transformations of those industries. A lifetime of giving, perpetuated after his death by a foundation bearing his name, would translate his financial successes into a generous philanthropic mission to needy organizations throughout southern California.

Such a litany of success warrants attention, even in a city with a famous capacity for rebirth and new beginnings. When considered as the endeavors of a penniless man who witnessed the sun rise on his thirty-fifth birthday from the open flap of a canvas tent, the story becomes all the more noteworthy. The obstacles he faced were immense, his financial resources were few, the prospects for success were limited. Fritz Burns possessed, however, the uncommon drive and eternal optimism befitting a master salesman. The story of his life is a testament to the power of both, from the success of his early years, to his lonely vigil on the beach, through the decades of remarkable undertakings that followed.

CHAPTER TWO

"The Knock-Em Cold Kid"

"Under all is the land. Upon its wise utilization and wide-spread ownership depend the advancement of national well-being and the perpetuation of the free institutions that go to make the American way of life."
Preamble, Realtor's Code of Ethics

"Frankly, I never felt I was cut out to be a salesman. I was too backward and hesitant about brushing up against the public." Fritz Burns, 1952.[1]

Fritz Bernard Burns was born October 9, 1899, in Minneapolis, Minnesota, the older of two sons born to Patrick Henry Burns and Marie Elise Schreyer. His father's family had been farmers in Ireland and in various spots throughout the United States, while his mother was a German immigrant who moved to the United States with her family at the age of eight. The couple owned and operated a small women's-wear factory in Minneapolis, and while not wealthy people, made enough to provide a decent living for themselves, Fritz, and his younger brother, Robert.[2]

The diverse backgrounds of his parents are perhaps what one should expect of the ancestors of a man with the uncommon name of Fritz Bernard. Patrick Henry Burns was the son of an Irish immigrant, Bernard Burns, born in Carrickmacrosse, County Monaghan, one of three brothers who came to America in 1847 in the Irish Diaspora from the mass starvation of the potato famine.[3] Bernard Burns eventually settled in St. Mary's, Minnesota, a small enclave of Irish farmers fifty miles south of Minneapolis. The surrounding townships were filled with more typical Minnesota residents of the time, Swedes, Norwegians, and Germans, and in that third group was the family of Fritz Schreyer, a German immigrant who had first settled in New York City before moving to Minnesota with his wife, daughter Marie Elise, and newborn son, William "Billy" Schreyer. Fritz Schreyer's father had fought in the Franco-Prussian war and been awarded an Iron Cross, a source of great pride for the family, and his son took the family back to visit their home in Germany on eight separate occasions before they moved to Minnesota. After Patrick and Marie were married, their firstborn son was given the names of his two grandfathers, Fritz and Bernard.[4]

Patrick and Marie's clothing factory in Minneapolis was by the nature of the business a low-margin endeavor. Years later, Fritz Burns would recall his mother's admonition not to cause trouble with the landlord's son for fear of eviction from their rented flat, as well as the constant debates over sales, discounts and percentages in the factory. Marie researched, designed, and sketched out the products, while Patrick served as the "cutter," rolling out the thick fabric and cutting patterns six at a time. Oftentimes Marie would go "window-shopping" to keep up on the latest fashions, standing before Minneapolis department store windows and meticulously copying new product lines for duplication back at their little factory.[5]

Patrick died in 1905 and left Marie in a precarious financial position. Fritz was six years old; his brother Robert was only two. She kept the clothing factory operating, but eventually had to send young Fritz to live with her parents, who owned and managed an apartment building in Minneapolis. To what must have been the sheer delight of their grandson, they also owned a candy store. In grammar school in Minneapolis by this time, Fritz was also put in charge of keeping the hallways and stairs of his grandparents' four-flat apartment

Marie Schreyer Burns with her
first child, Fritz Bernard Burns,
shortly after his birth
in 1899 in Minneapolis.
*Fritz B. Burns Collection,
Loyola Marymount University.*

building clean. Among his other chores was a task typical for
the time: emptying the collected water from the pan under
the icebox every day. He always remembered his grandparents as extremely traditional people, and at mealtimes his
grandfather ate alone, before Fritz and his grandmother.
Though born and raised in Germany, his grandmother eventually picked up enough English to check on Fritz' home-
work and help him with his studies.[6]

A good student as a child, Fritz soon began devoting
almost all his time outside the classroom to his early entre-
preneurial efforts. While still in grade school, he picked up
work delivering papers and watering and cutting lawns, and
at the age of eight took an after-school job with Dickinson &
Gillespie, a Minneapolis real estate development firm in
which his uncle, William "Billy" Schreyer, was a partner.
Burns began as one of a fleet of bike-riding youngsters who
delivered handbills around Minneapolis, all of them adver-

tising lot sales in various new subdivisions around the city. His pay was seventy-five cents a day.[7]

His friendship with Billy Schreyer would grow into an important one for Burns over the years. Schreyer fulfilled the role of a male authority figure in Burns' life, but still always remained an associate and confidant. Billy was Marie Schreyer's younger brother, had been born in the United States, and was only eleven years older than Burns.[8] When apart, the two kept up a close and lively correspondence that sheds light on their unique relationship. Among Burns' extant personal papers is a letter he wrote to Schreyer in December of 1919 upon hearing that Schreyer's wife, Gerda, had suffered a miscarriage. "If anybody has any idea of how good a father you would have made, it is me," Burns wrote. "You have been a father and then some to me, Bill, and don't ever forget that I realize it. I consider myself the most fortunate kid in the world to have an uncle like you and I'm going to do my damndest to show that I appreciate my opportunities and know how to take advantage of them."[9]

Upon finishing public grade school, Burns enrolled at De La Salle Institute, a Catholic high school run by the Christian Brothers on Nicollet Island in Minneapolis. For several months every year, he was able to walk directly to the school across the frozen surface of the river. Catholics were a distinct minority in Minneapolis, and Burns later recalled well the looks of his grammar school classmates when he announced he would be attending the "Brothers' School."[10]

While he claimed in later years that he attended De La Salle in order to take advantage of their three-year business course, "in preference to a public high school, where I would have to take courses not related to business," his academic transcript reveals as much of a classical education as it does financial or business training. Courses included Catechism, Spelling, Bookkeeping, Common Law, English, Geometry, English Classics, Phonography, and Typewriting. Fifth in his class his

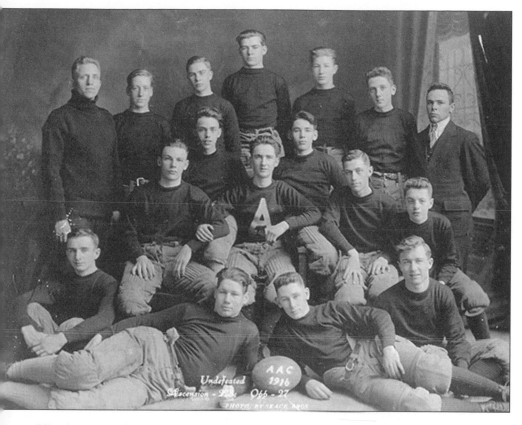

The Ascension Athletic Club, Fritz Burns' parish football team in Minneapolis,
Minnesota, in 1916. Burns, 17 years old, is at the far left of the second row.
Fritz B. Burns Collection, Loyola Marymount University.

first year and showing excellent grades, he quickly exhibited
the ambivalence towards formal education that would mark
his coming college experience and dropped down to a "C"
average. His extracurricular activities were somewhat limited
because of his after-school jobs, but he played on his parish
football team despite a general and lifelong disinterest in most
sports. Burns often joked in later years that he had "never let
education interfere with my business."[11]

It was during high school that Burns also first became a landowner. With the help of Billy Schreyer, he purchased two plots of land in the suburbs of Minneapolis from Dickinson & Gillespie. Payments on his new property were one dollar a week, which he paid directly to Schreyer out of his Dickinson & Gillespie earnings. At sixteen, Burns also made his first real estate deal, selling a partially completed house for $1,850, with a $50 down payment. He was working at the time at Dickinson & Gillespie as an office boy and rent collector, and sales crews sometimes took him along on out-of-town trips to "break him in." On one such occasion, the sales team was marketing a subdivision in St. Cloud, Minnesota, sixty miles north of Minneapolis, when a violent rainstorm broke out. Sure that no prospective buyers would venture out to their temporary sales office, the salesmen put Burns in charge and left. When two men arrived to look at lots in the subdivision, Burns took them out in the rain and mud himself. The sale amount had to be negotiated, since the penciled prices on the lot map had been badly blurred by the rain. Burns made the sale, earning a commission of ten dollars in the process.[12]

At the time, Dickinson & Gillespie was subdividing and marketing large parcels of land in the rural areas surrounding Minneapolis. The subdivisions existed for the most part only on maps, because the actual land was usually little more than slightly graded hills cut through with gravel streets made passable by a light sprinkling of oil. Dickinson & Gillespie marketed them via mass-produced sales brochures and postcards with such colorful names as "Minnetonka Manor," "McNair Manor," "Superior Boulevard Gardens," "Nokomis Knoll," and "Lake Nokomis Shores." Individual builders were recruited to build homes on empty lots. This flair for marketing and promotion did not go unnoticed by young Fritz, and it reappeared years later in much more extravagant form in countless brochures and newspaper advertisements for Burns' own developments in Los Angeles.[13]

Upon graduation from De La Salle in 1916, Burns enrolled at the University of Minnesota. Because he had completed only a three-year high school curriculum, he was required to enroll in a special program intended to cover gaps in his education while still allowing him to attend college. His academic career at the University was both painful and short, and he compiled a poor academic record in his only year. In the meantime, he joined a fraternity, Zeta Psi, and earned a reputation for lackadaisical military drill performance besides.[14]

The United States entered World War One in 1917, and soon after Burns, then eighteen years of age, enlisted to become a "Sixty Day Lieutenant" in the Student Army Training Corps, an accelerated program designed to turn college students into officers in two months. He was assigned to Fort Sheridan, Illinois, and joined the regimented life of the army. His letters to Billy Schreyer told that "the moon is still shining when we get up in the morning" and that daily drill, training in marching, signaling, and shooting, occasional parades, and classroom time combined to make it "certainly an arduous life." The officers-in-training were expected to complete training in a third of the time normally allotted during peace. They were given a half-hour of personal time each night and an occasional weekend off. Burns would try to get to Chicago to see a show or would remain on the base to catch a boxing match, one of his few sporting interests. "I ought to be as hard as nails when I get away from here," he wrote, "and in good condition to go back to school, if I do go back."[15]

Assigned to clerical work because of his typing ability, Burns was presented with a unique opportunity to direct the course of his military training with a clever bit of subterfuge. When the assignment cards for the next phase of their training arrived in the office, he noticed that he had been assigned to a base in Kansas. Furthermore, the assignments were alphabetical, and the T's were going to Camp Martin, a base outside New Orleans. Preferring the excitement of New Orleans over Kansas, he crossed his fingers, switched his card, and "sweated it out the next day when the names were all called out alphabetically except mine. 'Threadgill. . . 'Thompson'. . . then 'Burns!'"[16]

Hostilities in Europe came to an end soon after Burns' arrival in New Orleans, leaving him untouched by the war but also disappointed at the prospect of returning home to Minneapolis. His mother, who had married a local brewer named Al Theilen, wanted him to return immediately to continue his studies. Burns had other plans, to travel and to get some exotic experiences under his belt. Al Theilen had also brought into the family children of his own from a previous marriage, and Fritz felt that for him to return home and become a student again would be an unnecessary burden on his mother and her new family.[17] "The big question in my mind now is what to do when I get discharged," he wrote to Billy Schreyer at Christmastime, 1918. "I tried to get confidential with Ma and let her know about some of my plans . . . I would like your advice in the matter, Bill. It looks like this is a mighty good time for me to get a little experience and see something of the world. It was a great disappointment not to have gotten overseas."[18]

Burns also confessed to a bit of vanity in his decisions: "I know damn well that the Theilen family would be tickled to death to see me come trailing home after all this big talk." All the enlisted men had been sent home, while Burns and thirty-five other officers were awaiting their discharge and enjoying themselves in the streets of New Orleans. "If it weren't for the uncertainty of my future, I would be having the time of my life down here," he wrote. "New Orleans is a good town for a good time."[19]

When his discharge finally came, Burns decided against the northbound trip up Highway 61. Now nineteen and possessed of a restless spirit, he headed for the New Orleans docks instead, and signed on as a mess boy on the "Santa Christina," a thirty-foot wooden ship headed for South America. He spent several months at sea on trips to Cuba, Venezuela, and Colombia. While he had finally gotten his chance to see something of the world, it could have been under better conditions. The work, which included cooking and cleaning for the crew, was hard and demeaning with little in the way of reward. Upon his return to the United States, he decided to give his education another try and enrolled at the prestigious Wharton School of Finance at the University of Pennsylvania, in Philadelphia. Until classes began in September 1919, Burns worked for Dickinson & Gillespie on a traveling sales crew, selling subdivisions throughout the western states. He found upon his arrival at Wharton that the personal style of a traveling salesman was not quite the same as that of a business student. "I had been selling real estate in Cheyenne, Wyoming," he noted years later, "and arrived 'on campus' in a pink and white pin-stripe silk shirt and a check suit, which was hardly in keeping with the conservative Philadelphia atmosphere."[20]

His time at Wharton proved a pleasant experience for Burns, who quickly took to the marketing and finance curriculum and found himself one of the top students in his class. "I am more of a student than I have ever expected I could be, and I can truthfully say that in all my classes I rank with the 'foremost few'," he wrote to Schreyer.[21] Years later, he gave much of the credit for his lifelong marketing skills to walks with a professor down Chestnut Street in Philadelphia, studying the pros and cons of each business and its presentation and marketing strategy along that mercantile stretch. Burns' roommate in Philadelphia, Cosby Byrd, was an architecture student at Penn. "He was studying architecture, had peculiar habits of working better at night than in the daytime, and we got along very well together," Burns remembered years later. "In fact, I think I enjoyed his architectural endeavors more than some of my more prosaic studies."[22]

Burns also became something of a bon vivant during his time in Philadelphia. He asked Schreyer and Dickinson & Gillespie to loan him money for expenses, and offered various reasons for his profligacy: "I have got a few girls here in town that I step out with occasionally, but I always restrict those activities to weekends!"[23] A few years later, when his brother, Bob, had followed him to Wharton and also found himself in financial straits on account of his lifestyle, he wrote Fritz asking for a loan. With customary humor, Fritz replied, "I really can't understand how it is that you're unable to get along on $50 a month. The cost of living certainly must have gone up tremendously in Philadelphia, because when I was there four years ago I got along quite easily on $300 a month."[24]

After his year at Wharton, Burns rejoined Dickinson & Gillespie. The company had expanded its operations substantially beyond the suburbs of Minneapolis, and Burns headed up a sales operation that traveled the country buying up and subdividing real estate parcels. Often, the company would buy land before even visiting an area. Burns would then travel by train to the nearest town, advertise in the local paper, set up lot signs, hire a team of salesmen, offer picnic lunches and "tent-talks," and use his speaking ability to persuade prospective buyers to purchase lots. His tactics were simple but effective. A favorite approach was to board a crowded streetcar in a targeted area with tract maps and blueprints sticking out of his pocket. Eventually, someone on the car would inquire as to their purpose, at which point Burns could launch into his prepared sales pitch. A more fantastic stunt he once used to great effect was erecting a tower next to a road adjoining a subdivision, then hiring a man to stand atop the tower doing gymnastic stunts. Passing drivers were helpless to resist, and every one that pulled over was given a sales pitch and a taste of the Fritz Burns charm.[25]

The company purchased open land wherever a streetcar line or a road passed near, as far east as Brockton, Massachusetts, and throughout the western states, including North and South Dakota, Wisconsin, Montana, Wyoming, Oklahoma, and Texas. Nor did they limit themselves to areas suitable for housing or business developments. Dickinson & Gillespie also subdivided land into one- to three-acre lots, advertising them as "exactly suitable for chicken raising, truck gardening, fruit growing, fox farming, bee culture, [and] greenhouse location."[26]

Buoyed by their profits—by late 1920, the company's assets had grown to better than $300,000—J.W. Dickinson, Clifford Gillespie, Billy Schreyer and Burns turned their eyes towards Los Angeles. Burns had proved himself to be an extraordinary salesman, and Los Angeles was the mother lode of real estate investment at the time. "I presume we should call you the 'knock-em-cold kid' and that congratulations are in order regarding your Oklahoma sale," Clifford Gillespie wrote to Burns in 1921. "I have no hesitancy in saying that you will carry out your instructions for Los Angeles in the same manner and I feel confident that every lot there will be sold. If such should be the case you would make a pretty piece of 'jack,' which I only hope will come true...such being the case, we have only success ahead of us. Failure is impossible."[27]

Between 1880 and 1921, Los Angeles had been the locus of several feverish land speculation booms that drove the growth of the area from a sleepy township of 11,200 in 1880, almost all clustered around a downtown center fifteen miles from the Pacific, to a wide-ranging metropolis of over a million residents by 1920.[28] Central to the growth of the city was the presence of the vast Pacific Electric streetcar system built by railroad and real estate magnate Henry Huntington, who controlled a trolley system that encompassed more than a thousand miles of track and carried over 250,000 passengers daily. He also controlled the Huntington Land Company, which turned immense ranchland holdings into prime real estate simply by pushing through new streetcar lines and subdividing the suddenly accessible land surrounding them. The engine of the city's growth for forty years, real estate became an all-encompassing craze by the early 1920s. For example, more than 1,200 real estate offices were open for business in Los Angeles in 1921, and real estate sales, speculation, and development constituted a major part of the city's economic activity throughout the decade.[29]

Backed by the finances and faith of his fellow Dickinson & Gillespie officers, Burns and a sales force of almost one hundred salesmen set up offices in Los Angeles in 1921. They began the process of buying, subdividing and selling large undeveloped chunks of the city and the surrounding area, concentrating particularly on the San Gabriel Valley and neighboring communities.[30] At the time, subdividers saved money by making scant improvements to the purchased land. New tracts of land for sale needed only a gravel road for access, and subdividers were not responsible for sidewalks, curbs, or pavement.[31] Burns needed to do little more than make certain an area was connected by road or trolley car to the rest of the city in order to offer plots for sale in a new subdivision. Fred Marlow, Burns' partner in later Los Angeles real estate developments, was an early subdivider in the San Fernando Valley, selling ten to thirty acres at a time in Reseda, Glendale, Burbank, North Hollywood, and Owensmouth (now Canoga Park). He commented on the standard practices of subdividers of the time: "In those days there was no control by any planning or zoning agency, and all we did was file a record of the survey map, crown up the streets with a blade pulled by mules, and sprinkle a little decomposed granite on the roads. The land boom was on, and we were out to make profit. It was a seller's market, and none of us bothered to put in any curbs, gutters, or sewers."[32]

Like almost all real estate subdividers of the time, Dickinson & Gillespie never built actual homes on the lots sold in Southern California. Local builders could be invited in, or new owners would be encouraged to build their own home on the site. Inevitably, many of the lots in any subdivision were purchased by investors with no intention of building a home or living on the land. They bought on speculation with every expectation they could unload the land once the continuously spiraling value of the property reached their desired selling point. In order to reassure buyers looking for a home, Dickinson & Gillespie followed the standard real estate practice of including a number of protective restrictions on each project. Restrictions might cover anything from the allowed height and width of homes, the size of a garage, the minimum distance allowed between the house and the street, or even the architectural style allowed in a certain neighborhood. For example, "Hollywoodland," the famous development that gave Los Angeles its emblematic "Hollywood" sign, required all homebuilders to take their plans before an architectural review board, "thus assuring attractive homes." Racial covenants, which restricted property ownership to whites only, were widely used by subdividers throughout Southern California, including Dickinson & Gillespie.[33]

Because most subdivisions would inevitably look rather bleak and lonely while the actual physical lots were being sold, the sales teams relied on far different tactics from the "model home" real estate sales approaches of later decades. "I'm sure old-time realtors in the city of Los Angeles will remember that lunch and lecture methods were used in the early twenties," Fred Marlow later commented. "This was to escort a prospect out to the property with a continuous line of sales talk. Then we gave him a cheap lunch, after which he was compelled to listen to a lecture with pictures about the prospect of making money in Los Angeles. He was then shown a lot or two, ushered into a 'closing' office and subjected to a high-pressure sales talk. This resulted in a confused and befuddled prospective purchaser giving up a check as a deposit on the purchase of a piece of property which would make him a fortune. In the absence of getting a check the closing salesman would sometimes accept a diamond ring as a deposit."[34]

To these high-pressure sales tactics, Burns introduced a number of innovations. One of his first moves was to purchase a number of surplus World War One airplanes from the Army for barnstorming and promotional purposes. In the uncrowded skies of Los Angeles at that time, a biplane roaring by with "Dickinson & Gillespie" on its side would cause quite a stir. In 1923, Burns, an amateur pilot, flew parallel to a Los Angeles-bound train in a biplane for over a hundred miles. Gillespie reported back that "it had the passengers of our train all worked up, as well as the people at the stations along the way."[35] To lure crowds out to the subdivisions, lot buyers were offered a "free ride in a sturdy airplane." Dickinson & Gillespie gave away presents by the hundreds, and occasionally contests were held in which a lot buyer could pick the name of the development itself.[36]

No number of stunts or contests matched for creativity the endless pamphlets and brochures Burns produced for his subdivisions. Based on the elaborate (and oftentimes wildly hyperbolic) Dickinson & Gillespie brochures that Burns delivered to homes in Minneapolis as a boy, these new brochures and pamphlets were brightly decorated, intricately illustrated pieces of art. Filled with catchy slogans such as "The Fortune Spot," "Where Nature Smiles Her Sweetest," "Where Health, Prosperity, & Contentment Are Partners With You," and "The Residential Wonder," they included

Fritz Burns' airplane, circa 1925. Burns purchased the plane in San Diego from the U.S. Army after World War One for Dickinson & Gillespie promotions. He also offered free rides to prospective lot buyers.
Fritz B. Burns Collection, Loyola Marymount University.

maps listing major roads, trolley lines, and timetables for Pacific Electric cars. Lots were generally advertised at prices between $600 and $1,495, although Dickinson & Gillespie offered terms as low as fifteen percent down, with considerable discounts for those willing to put down a large cash payment. The end result of this masterful sales job was a new real estate record for Southern California. In thirty-six months, Burns and his salesmen sold out thirty-six subdivisions. Bedecked with fanciful names such as "Hollydale Gardens," "Alta Manor," "Orange Blossom Manor," "Poppyfields," "Highway Highlands," and "Hollywood Laurelgrove," all are now neighborhoods in the various communities of the San Gabriel Valley, including Pasadena, Alhambra, and

Altadena, as well as North Hollywood, Hollywood, Burbank, and Glendale.[37]

By 1924, Fritz Burns was indeed making "a pretty piece of jack" as a result of his record-breaking performance as a real estate salesman, and his correspondence reveals a degree of personal growth to match his new success and responsibilities. He took a prominent role in his younger brother Robert's life and education, arranging for "Bob" to follow in his footsteps at Wharton and paying his tuition and expenses. When Robert followed a bit too closely in those footsteps by flunking a number of courses, Fritz commented dryly, "it is very nice to learn of the progress you're making along social lines, but I don't think you will be able to cash in on it after you get out of school." He added in a more serious tone that "it is sufficient to say that I feel that it isn't necessary for you to go two thousand miles from home to go to school in order to produce this kind of stuff." He also confessed to his family that he was doing well financially, and joked that his new accoutrements were of the type he had always associated "with lounge lizards, knickers, and Hollywood, and I hope that I am not in that category yet." At the same time, his confidence in his own abilities as a businessman had soared, and he picked up the dangerous habit of promising to friends and associates, "I'll be a millionaire by the time I'm thirty."[38]

In his personal life, Burns fell in love with a woman by the name of Lucille Robinson, whom he had met through her sister, Gladys Morse. Both Lucille and Gladys worked for Dickinson & Gillespie at the time as secretaries. Fritz and Lucille were married in Los Angeles in a civil ceremony on June 10, 1924, and on May 12 of the following year, Lucille gave birth to a son.[39] He was given the names of his father and grandfather, Fritz Patrick Burns, though he was known throughout his life as Pat. Fritz and Lucille's marriage lasted little more than three years before it ended in divorce. Fritz gave Lucille generous financial support throughout her life, and she remained close to Burns and his relatives. Both Lucille and Gladys Morse worked as army switchboard operators during World War Two, and after the war Gladys Morse worked for Burns for four decades as an apartment manager. Pat lived with his mother throughout the remainder of his childhood, and shared a home in the Hancock Park area of Los Angeles with her for many years.[40]

Along with his new family life and a hectic work schedule, Burns also found time to invest in a new sports venture, the first National Football League franchise in Los Angeles. Along with actor Lew Cody and a few small investors, Burns owned the Los Angeles Buccaneers, who entered the NFL in 1926. The team played all its games on the road and compiled twelve victories and four defeats. The Buccaneers' record becomes more impressive when one considers the squad kept only fifteen players. Coach and star of the team was three-time collegiate All-American, Harold "Brick" Muller, a California football legend for his Most Valuable Player performance in the 1921 Rose Bowl, where California trounced Ohio State, 28-0. Other players included former USC superstars Johnny Hawkins and Henry Lefebvre, as well as Burns' recruits from both the University of Pennsylvania and the University of Minnesota.

Because college football held an iron grip on the imagination of football fans in the 1920's, the National Football League of 1926 was a far cry from the multibillion-dollar industry it is today. The league featured twenty-two teams, including such colorful and unlikely entries as the Maroons from Pottsville, Pennsylvania, the Duluth Eskimos (with Ernie Nevers), the Providence Steam Rollers, and the Hartford Blues. Some NFL legends were well in the making. Jim Thorpe already had his Canton Bulldogs, and Harold "Red" Grange was adding to his considerable collegiate reputation in a pro career with the Chicago Bears.

The Buccaneers had limited financial resources, and

although Muller was paid the princely sum of $15,000, most of the squad was paid between $80 and $150 a game. Years later, guard Don Thompson reminisced about a particularly rough game in Pottsville, a mining town in the heart of Pennsylvania coal country: "There was a quarter of an inch of ice on the puddles in the playing field that had to be broken before the game. The spectators stood on the sidelines and threw chunks of coal at us through the entire contest." Every player on the squad played both offense and defense, and several times ringers had to be picked up to play on days when injuries left the team short too many players.[41]

Ultimately, the team's financial losses became too onerous to bear, and in 1927 Burns and his fellow owners declined to field a team. "Brick" Muller went on to become a physician, and much of the staff went back to their day jobs as salesmen for Dickinson & Gillespie. Los Angeles would remain without professional football for twenty more years, until the Cleveland Rams arrived in 1946. The Los Angeles Buccaneers were Fritz Burns' only venture into professional sports.

The Dickinson & Gillespie syndicate, now featuring Clifford Gillespie as President, Justin Dickinson as Vice-President, Burns as Vice-President and General Manager, and Billy Schreyer as Secretary-Treasurer, decided in 1924 to purchase a large expanse of bluffs overlooking the Pacific, south of Venice, and named it "Palisades Del Rey." With business in Southern California going so well and with the Los Angeles real estate craze becoming ever more heated, J.W. Dickinson and Clifford Gillespie had moved the entire company to Los Angeles earlier that year. The year before, 714 new subdivisions had been registered in Los Angeles, comprising over 86,000 lots.[42] Furthermore, with beach property fast becoming the crown jewel of local real estate, it appeared the Los Angeles coastline would soon be completely under development.

The subdivision included the townsite of Playa Del Rey, the bluffs fronting the Pacific (including a smaller Dickinson & Gillespie luxury subdivision, "Surfridge"), and the Del Rey hills, which sloped from the reverse side of the bluffs towards Inglewood. While located only thirteen miles from downtown Los Angeles, the area was extremely isolated. To the north lay Ballona Creek and a large expanse of wetlands between Palisades Del Rey and Venice and Culver City, and to the south and east lay bean fields, hog farms, and scattered ranches. The major access roads to the area—including Jefferson Boulevard, Culver Boulevard, Manchester Avenue, and Century Boulevard—were as yet unpaved and barely passable during inclement weather, offering little more than rutted dirt tracks for much of the journey.[43] A Pacific Electric trolley line offered interurban rail access, with a stop at the base of the Palisades Del Rey bluffs on "Trolley Way." Downtown Los Angeles was a forty-two minute ride away on the trolley, a reasonable commute in Los Angeles today but a considerable trek in 1924. Despite these obstacles confronting Dickinson & Gillespie at Palisades Del Rey, the syndicate forged ahead with their ambitious plans and made another fortune.[44]

Once again, as with his record-breaking performances in other Los Angeles subdivisions, Burns handled the sales and marketing operations. Every morning he held a sales meeting on the beach, and began each with a mandatory calisthenics session. Burns admitted years later that he did it largely to "get the men out of bed."[45] Exotic sales promotions included a treasure hunt for prizes buried in the beach sand. The five thousand contestants who showed up were given a shovel and various clues as to the whereabouts of the "hidden treasure." Dickinson & Gillespie also offered to pick up prospective buyers at their homes and drive them all the way out to Palisades Del Rey, free of charge.[46] In contrast to earlier developments, which were oftentimes sold without improvements, Palisades Del Rey lots were sold as a luxury development. Every new owner received a written promise that Dickinson & Gillespie would install water mains, gas lines, sewers, curbs, sidewalks, and surfaced roadways in the development. Discounts were offered for residents who built homes instead of holding empty property as a speculative investment.[47]

The subdivision's most attractive feature was its physical location overlooking the Pacific. Dickinson & Gillespie had the foresight as well as the good fortune to be selling out Palisades Del Rey at a time when the Los Angeles shoreline was becoming not only a prime location for real estate, but also a symbol for California and Los Angeles itself. The residents of Southern California's beachfront movie colonies and resort communities represented the area as an American Cote d'Azur, with the attendant high prices and scarcity of open land.[48] Exploiting this perception, Burns claimed to reporters that he had walked the California shoreline from Malibu to San Clemente to survey beachfront property, and proclaimed Palisades Del Rey to be "The Last of the Beaches."[49] Burns' sales brochures for the development further exploited, in breathless terms, the notion that Palisades Del Rey represented one last chance to get in on a land rush approaching its physical limitations. "Today Palisades Del Rey is a living, vibrating reality—the consummation of an ideal born of public demand—a dream transformed into a positive actuality in the almost unbelievably short space of but a few months," Burns wrote. "And, for all time to come, it will occupy an irreplaceable niche in the hearts of those fortunate enough to procure through it the realization of their inherent longing to live at the sea."[50]

Palisades Del Rey differed from almost all of Dickinson & Gillespie's other developments because it was intended and marketed as an exclusive, wealthy community. Burns stressed in sales brochures that fully 93 percent of the Los Angeles coastline had been developed and that Palisades Del Rey offered the "last three miles of the shore contiguous to Los Angeles." The four senior partners, as well as a number of sales associates who had become wealthy in the previous three years of rich profits and high demand, built huge mansions for themselves atop some of the highest points on the bluffs as examples of the possibilities open to new buyers.[51] Highly optimistic Dickinson & Gillespie "maps" were drawn to show a huge (nonexistent) yacht harbor where the Del Rey lagoon and a series of marshes lay beneath the bluffs. Whereas a subdivision map for "Highway Highlands" or "Poppyfields" in the San Gabriel Valley featured sixty by one hundred foot lots, Palisades Del Rey offered much larger parcels for mansions and estates. Lot prices were accordingly higher, and began at $2,995, fully five times the beginning prices in other Dickinson & Gillespie developments.[52] Burns also emphasized the area's appeal to movie stars, producers, directors, and various other Hollywood celebrities who lived in the area, especially after the 1927 opening of the MGM Studios in Culver City. Advertised residents included Louis B. Mayer, "Hopalong" Cassidy, Douglas Fairbanks, Sr., Lew Cody, and King Vidor, among others.[53]

For the first time at Palisades Del Rey, Dickinson & Gillespie abandoned its previous practice of forsaking building in favor of subdividing only. The four partners invested over $400,000 to build a private beach club on the shoreline next to the Pacific Electric trolley stop. The investment was to be recovered through the sale of one thousand exclusive yearly memberships at $400 each, along with one hundred life memberships at $1,000 each. Finally, to create the appearance of a complete community and to bring news to a subdivision far from the city center, the company ran its own biweekly newspaper, the *Palisades Del Rey Press*, that offered serious news, company propaganda, sports coverage, and gossip. Editorials addressed such compelling beach-town topics as the scandalous new bathing suits seen on the Palisades Del Rey beach and the "semi-nudity" they might suggest from their wearers.[54]

The officers of Dickinson and Gillespie had bolder improvements in mind for Palisades Del Rey. In May 1927, Fritz Burns, Justin Dickinson, Clifford Gillespie, and Billy Schreyer worked with Harry Culver, real estate magnate, Los Angeles Realty Board president, and founder of nearby Culver City, to arrange for a local investment group, the Blankenhorn Syndicate, to donate eighty acres to build a campus for Los Angeles Lutheran University. The acreage was located in the Del Rey hills, east of Dickinson & Gillespie's holdings, and immediately west of what is now Lincoln Boulevard. Dickinson & Gillespie donated twenty contiguous acres more to give the new university an even one hundred, enough to build facilities for five thousand students. Burns enthused in the *Palisades Del Rey Press*, "Great things are happening in Los Angeles. Great things are happening in Del Rey Hills. The strategic location of this area guarantees a city on this spot even in advance of this latest announcement. With a $5,000,000 university to be build here at once, a period of development is at hand greater than our most sanguine dreams."[55] Shortly after, Culver agreed to donate another hundred acres out of his own holdings across Lincoln Boulevard to Loyola College to built its own campus for five thousand students. The intent of these gifts of real estate was clear. Palo Alto had grown and thrived because of its proximity to Stanford, and in the late 1920s Westwood was experiencing a real estate and population boom because of the construction of UCLA. Burns and Culver expected two new universities to spur growth in the area and garner volumes of positive publicity for their nearby developments.

While Los Angeles Lutheran University never built on its hundred acres, Loyola College began construction the next May on its new campus and launched an aggressive fundraising campaign. Fritz Burns became a devoted benefactor of the fledgling Jesuit school, offering to serve as one of six "generals" heading up fundraising teams and eventually collecting pledges in excess of one million dollars.[56] The school's elaborate groundbreaking ceremonies featured Burns as a dashing figure, a self-assured twenty-seven-year-old millionaire riding on horseback in a solemn procession along with the Archbishop of San Francisco, the bishop of Los Angeles, and scores of public officials, dignitaries, and Los Angeles power brokers, including Harry Culver, Harry Chandler, Isidore Dockweiler, and Louis B. Mayer. While the calamitous events of the next five years would dash the University's hopes for the immediate future, it was the beginning of a philanthropic relationship between Burns and Loyola College (later Loyola Marymount University) that would last his entire life.[57]

In August 1926, Burns announced a doubling of his sales force and estimated the retail value of the company's acquired acreage at $12,000,000. The next year, home sites worth over four million dollars were constructed in the subdivision, and the average value of a home in Palisades Del Rey reached $20,000, a figure many of the owners would not see again for a full thirty years.[58] In a single week in 1927, Dickinson & Gillespie sold six hundred feet of oceanfront property in the development for $325,000. On April 1, 1928, just a few months after the announcements of the two universities for the Del Rey Hills, the Los Angeles City Council selected nearby Mines Field as one of three municipal airports to be upgraded in order to handle an increase in air traffic, with $2.4 million and 620 acres of land allocated for expansion within three miles of the two new schools. By the end of 1928, Angelenos had also voted in favor of Olympic Games bonds to pay for the construction of, among other big-ticket items, the first "Olympic Village" in the nearby Baldwin Hills.[59]

Burns was increasingly optimistic about the future of Palisades Del Rey and the surrounding area, as were many of his colleagues and the company's investors. In addition to the success of their own subdivision, they could point to two large universities, a municipal airport, and burgeoning development to the east as evidence of a bright future for a project they had boldly called "Building a City Where A City Belongs." When Justin Dickinson and Clifford Gillespie offered Burns the chance to buy out their interest in Dickinson & Gillespie early in 1929, it looked like the opportunity of a lifetime. He purchased both their shares of the company, and by the middle of the year was the new president of Dickinson & Gillespie.[60] He turned thirty a few months later, on October 9, 1929, and could honestly say his frequent boast had come true. He was a millionaire at thirty. Twenty days later, on October 29, 1929, the New York Stock Exchange suffered its infamous financial collapse, and ushered in the Great Depression.

The stock market crash was not the first and only indicator that the Los Angeles real estate market and the Southern California economy were in trouble. After record-breaking years for subdivision filings in the first half of the decade, Los Angeles experienced a sudden and ominous drop in applications for building permits from 51,000 in 1924 to a little more than 37,000 by the next year. Historians have estimated that Los Angeles in 1925 had over six hundred thousand subdivided lots standing vacant, and that the city was built for a demand of seven million residents a full fifty years before that number would live in Los Angeles.[61] Modern economists closely watch housing starts for signs of lagging or growing consumer confidence; in the late 1920s, the sudden slowdown in building permits in Los Angeles indicated that the massive real estate expansion had far outrun existing need and had turned into a speculative bubble ready to burst.

Much of Los Angeles' real estate activity in the latter half of the decade centered on the purchase (via loans from developers at interest rates of up to fifteen percent) of property for the purpose of a quick return on the investment through rapidly rising land values. This veritable Ponzi scheme required a steady flow of new investors as well as cheap and easy credit to perpetuate itself. Bank mortgages were short, between three and ten years, and required only the payment of interest for the duration of the loan. At the expiration date, the owner either had to sell to pay off the debt or take out a new mortgage, virtually *requiring* that property values spiral up at an unsustainable rate to keep the market afloat.

The collapse of banks and financial institutions after the October stock market crash meant an instant end to the real estate boom, because without mortgage loans to fuel speculation, the market for hundreds of thousands of vacant lots of land scattered throughout the San Fernando and San Gabriel Valleys and across the South Bay was gone. Between 1928 and 1933, the construction of new residences in Los Angeles fell by 95 percent.[62] Worse, the collapse of industrial activity (and the jobs it created) and consumer spending meant that suddenly bankrupt homeowners began defaulting on their homes at a ruinous rate. Even existing housing stock became financial quicksand, a phenomenon that repeated itself across the nation. In 1926, over 68,000 home foreclosures were reported in the United States; within six years, that number had more than quadrupled, eventually approaching the astounding total of almost a thousand non-farm foreclosures a day.[63]

The homeowners and investors of Palisades Del Rey were in a similar position. Many buyers, who had signed contracts but never put up the money to reserve particular lots, had either gone bankrupt or reneged on their deals. Burns was left with a huge development complete with miles of streets, water mains, electric and gas service, and even the Del Rey Beach Club on the Palisades Del Rey beach. In short, he owned all the luxuries one would expect of a wealthy seaside development, but had almost nothing in the way of buyers or residents.[64]

The next several years proved a tense and trying time, a pattern occurring with similar consequences across the nation, as one after another of his business partners abandoned the development or went bankrupt, including his younger brother, Bob, and his uncle, Billy Schreyer. Both spent the worst years of the Depression taking classes at Southwestern Law School to become lawyers in Los Angeles. Burns devoted his time to a desperate game of delaying tactics and partial payments of various debts, all while trying to regain title to as much of the virtually worthless Del Rey property as he could.[65]

The legendary Burns sales pitch which had sold out so many subdivisions was now a plea for time and understanding, redirected towards banks in Minnesota and New Hampshire which had advanced Dickinson & Gillespie the money to build Palisades Del Rey and were looking to foreclose on his properties. Burns struck various deals with the banks and offered to buy back foreclosed properties for ten cents on the dollar from organizations struggling themselves to stay afloat. While he was able to hold on to Dickinson & Gillespie's properties and pick up unimproved lots where banks had foreclosed, his own mansion at 200 Waterloo Street became too expensive to retain. Burns was forced to abandon the ten-room home overlooking the Pacific that he had built for his young family just a few years earlier. To save money, he moved an old Dickinson & Gillespie construction tent down to the beach at the end of Culver Boulevard and took up residence there.

Burns lived on the sand for almost five years while he consolidated his assets, fought off creditors, and survived under the constant threat of utter destitution. Bob Burns had actually drawn up the paperwork in 1934 for Fritz to declare bankruptcy, but he was always able to hold off his creditors for another day. His personal relationships suffered as well. Burns had separated from his wife, Lucille Robinson, and broke off contact with his longtime mentor Billy Schreyer after serious disagreements with Burns over investments and salary. Just a few short years after Burns had become the millionaire he had always predicted, the legendary businessman and determined young tycoon found himself all but bankrupt.[66]

Burns had an isolated existence in the tent, and began to develop a previously unseen poetic temperament. He was a voracious reader who had inherited a love of literature from his father's family, but not until he was thirty-five did he begin to save his own poetry. Burns continued to write privately throughout his life, and many of his favorites reappeared in speeches and sales lectures. His first dated poem, to an anonymous love interest in October 1934, reflected the solitude and loneliness of life on the beach:

> The mists cling close
> To the folds of the earth
> And the stars defiant shine through.
> And I long for a soul to share the fair sight
> And I know in my heart it's you.[67]

Several of the dominant personality traits that impressed Burns' colleagues throughout his life also began to emerge during his years in the tent. He exercised extreme caution in his financial affairs, a sharp break from both the highly speculative nature of his real estate business before the Depression and the free-spending lifestyle to which he had grown accustomed. He spent the early morning hours scouring the beach for glass bottles redeemable for pennies, a remarkable transformation for a man who had favored roadster convertibles and pinstriped suits in his twenties. Burns also developed an extraordinary work ethic that became cause for comment in every business venture he entered for the rest of his life. The Depression had cost Burns much more than just his fortune; it also eliminated any false sense of security he may have had in business affairs. "I was suffering under the hallucination that there was no such thing as a depression," he commented years later. "I thought I was a master salesman then, but I found out that in a depression, even a master salesman isn't master of his destiny."[68] Burns took the lesson to heart, and always kept close control over the financial details of his later projects.

The flow of business opportunities for a real estate developer of the time might have slowed to a trickle, but they never stopped entirely. Burns continued to strike business deals to improve his financial situation. He leased his Del Rey Beach Club to a local businessman for use as a public bathhouse and saved money on repairs by doing all the maintenance himself. A visitor to the club might well have found the president of Dickinson & Gillespie in a pair of rubber hip boots, wading through sewage with a plunger and a wrench.[69] A more lucrative deal came through in 1933, when Burns was able to lease the property at the base of the Del Rey bluffs to a group seeking to rent beach cottages. In 1932, Los Angeles had hosted the Olympic Games and pioneered the idea of a unified housing complex for athletes. The first "Olympic Village" consisted of compact cottages divided into two rooms each on undeveloped land at the edge of Baldwin Hills. Burns purchased many of the cottages in 1933 and brought them down to the beach at Palisades Del Rey, which he renamed "Olympic Beach." He wrote to his mother and new stepfather that he thought this new project would bring him up to date on his taxes and also provide the first step on the long road to economic recovery. Even in the most desperate financial straits, Burns retained a stubborn optimism. "It really makes quite an attractive appearance and takes a big load off our mind," he wrote of the beach cottages. "With the taxes being paid, everything is bound to work out alright, as this is a very valuable piece of property and should eventually sell for enough to pay off the noteholders. Everything is coming along fine and we are getting a fresh start and expect to be in high gear pretty soon."[70]

In possession of little more than some rental income and essentially useless property throughout the Del Rey hills, Burns then struck a deal with Sam B. Herndon, an oil wildcatter, and formed the Herndon Development Company. The new company set out to prospect for oil throughout the Del Rey hills. Their agreement stipulated that two percent of the proceeds from any oil sales resulting from a strike on his land would be returned to Burns. It was a galling moment for Burns, who years earlier had overseen the removal of oil derricks from the area, saying "(w)hile it may be true that oil is a maker of fortunes, it would be almost too much to expect that a field could be discovered sufficiently large enough to offset the detrimental effects its operations would have on the residential features and future of the community."[71] A few miles to the north of Palisades Del Rey was the visible devastation and environmental nightmare drilling had caused in Venice, and to the east Standard Oil had marred large areas of the Baldwin Hills with derricks, pumps, and prospecting equipment. Burns had little choice, however, with banks threatening to foreclose on his properties. He had a minuscule cash flow, and the prospect of a potential gusher was too tempting to pass up. He found the prospect of some verse on the subject equally tempting, as the following lines from "The Oil Strike" attest:

At Playa Del Rey
There's a new game they play called
Where is the bottom of the hole?
Where is the bottom of the hole?

The cores are all surprises
Everyone geologizes, but
Where is the bottom of the hole?
Where is the bottom of the hole?

The nodular is faulty
The sand is slightly salty
But where is the bottom of the hole?
Where is the bottom of the hole?

If you deviate but one degree
They'll have you up for larceny
Oh, where is the bottom of the hole?
Where is the bottom of the hole?

We use every kind of bits
But we're sure to get the schist
Down in the bottom of the hole
Where is the bottom of the hole?

It's too late for surveying
You'd better start praying.
Oh, where is the bottom of the hole?
Where is the bottom of the hole?[72]

His newfound and atypical pessimism notwithstanding, Burns was summoned one night in October 1934 to what is now the corner of Manchester and Delgany avenues in Playa Del Rey: Herndon's men thought they might have hit an oil deposit. Burns' longtime associate Dick Schulte remembered years later that Burns arrived on the scene just as the well blew in: "Black oil spewed all over the site, including Fritz and the drilling crew. Burns literally washed his face in what he called that 'wonderful black gold rain.'" A jubilant Burns mailed a picture postcard of the well to his mother and step-father, from whom he had been forced to borrow money to pay debts just a few short months earlier, joking, "[h]ere it is, Ma...I'll either get a new car or a fast motorcycle!"[73] By November, the discovery well was producing over fifty thousand dollars a month in oil sales, bringing in over one thousand dollars a month for Burns. It was a paltry amount in light of his pre-1929 fortune, but still more than enough to pay his back taxes, to satisfy the banks threatening to foreclose on his land, and even to purchase tax-delinquent properties throughout the area over the next several years. After the oil field was depleted, the Southern California Gas Company constructed a large facility in 1943 at the site of the original strike and used the emptied underground caverns to hold its reserves of natural gas.[74]

At the close of 1934, Fritz Burns would have had genuine reason to believe five years of privation, crushing disappointment, and humiliating financial losses were finally giving way to a new chapter in his life. No longer an arrogant young man filled with naïve optimism created by a decade of unexpected prosperity and contentment, no longer a man destined to be a "millionaire by thirty," he had witnessed, suffered from, and survived what must have seemed at times like an unending string of personal and financial setbacks. The man drawing up plans and formulating future advances at the end of 1934 had a fraction of the fortune he held in 1929, and owned as his primary asset a reputation as a genius for real estate in a time and place where real estate was of little worth. Armed with experience, tempered by sharp disappointments, and still possessed of the optimism and uncanny foresight that had brought him so far in his twenties, Fritz Burns at the close of 1934 began to build everything all over again.

CHAPTER THREE

"From A Beanfield To A Beehive"

"Don't hide your light under a bushel, smug in the fact that you are a very good salesman. Modern merchandising calls for more than this. You must analyze your market and then go out to meet it and encompass it. These are big days call-ing for the expansion of your biggest abilities."
Fritz Burns, 1941[1]

The financial windfall of the Del Rey oil strike allowed Fritz Burns to embark on several ambitious housing projects in the second half of the 1930s and establish himself as a major real estate developer in California. His new projects were dependent on several pieces of national legislation passed during the depths of the Great Depression. Soon after taking office in 1933, newly elected President Franklin D. Roosevelt proposed a new federal agency, the Home Owner's Loan Corporation (HOLC), to slow the avalanche of mort-gage foreclosures nationwide and protect homeowners with a standard structure for mortgage payments. Part of a flurry of programs created as part of the New Deal, the HOLC (and its sister program for rural foreclosures, the Emergency Farm Mortgage Act) was signed into law in June 1933. Both pro-grams implicitly recognized the federal government's inter-est in creating and protecting a nation of homeowners. They were also radical steps, ushering in a long-term transforma-tion of the American housing market from heavily concen-trated urban populations of renters to more thinly distributed suburban populations owning single-family homes.

The HOLC offered assistance to homeowners in two primary ways. First, it offered refinancing at low interest for tens of thousands of short-term (three- and four-year) mortgages in danger of foreclosure. It also offered owners who had lost homes through forced sale similar loans to regain their property. This put an end to the mass foreclosures witnessed during the tenure of President Herbert Hoover. Second, the HOLC introduced long-term mortgages of twenty and thirty years which amortized not only interest, but also the principal on a mortgage through regular (and equal) repayment schedules. Instead of seeking a new mortgage every few years and running the risk of losing one's home in economically difficult times, a home purchaser could count on a consistent monthly payment that would eventually result in outright ownership of the property. This new legislation also meant a property could be sold and the mortgage repaid before it ran its designated length, which allowed buyers to build financial equity in homes.[2]

The HOLC was closely followed in 1934 by a new initiative, the National Housing Act, which called for the creation of the Federal Housing Administration (FHA) and authorized it to insure mortgages issued by savings and loans throughout the country. In addition to standardizing the long-term self-amortizing mortgage, the FHA also spurred lending institutions to increase the average size of a mortgage from half of a home's purchase price to ninety percent by insuring the loan up to the latter amount. Because the federal government guaranteed payment on all approved mortgages, local lending institutions could safely offer loans to a whole new category of prospective buyers: workers who brought home a steady income but who lacked the wherewithal for a large down payment. In addition, this new financial security meant lenders could offer those loans at several percentage points less than the previous prevailing rate. With the introduction of the FHA insured loan in 1934, the interest rate on home loans in Southern California dropped from over eight percent to five percent.[3]

Intended initially to combat rampant unemployment in the building industry by spurring new home construction, the HOLC, the National Housing Act, and the FHA accomplished another goal far beyond their initial scope. Between 1933 and 1935, over one million mortgages were issued through these programs, and it has been estimated that forty percent of eligible Americans sought assistance through the HOLC. Upon the creation of the HOLC, the National Housing Act, and the FHA, a nation of urban renters began slowly transforming into a nation of suburban homeowners. Under many circumstances, it was actually cheaper to buy a home than to rent. Within three years, the construction industry began to reflect this transformation. In 1937, the market produced 336,000 housing starts, an almost fourfold increase from the low of 90,000 housing starts in 1933.[4]

This rebirth of the real estate industry was not without its pains. For example, when the FHA first announced that California lenders would be expected to abandon their short-term mortgages for loans with a maturity of twenty years and a sharply lower interest rate, it was met with what one developer called "a blank stare and a polite howl."[5] Not only did the program require that lenders pay the FHA an insurance premium of one half of one percent on every loan, but confidence in the federal government's ability to make good on its financial guarantees was understandably low after the banking collapse of 1929. Many California lending institutions, including banks, insurance companies, mortgage companies, and building and loan institutions, refused to cooperate. Only after Bank of America announced it would join the FHA program in August 1934 did the practice of issuing long-term mortgages with FHA insurance become standard in California.[6]

Home buyers were not the only beneficiaries of this new

legislation, as it also immediately created new opportunities in real estate practices for both developers and builders. Real estate developers, including Burns, had traditionally subdivided land strictly for the purposes of selling individual lots to builders or to new owners who would finance their own home construction or leave the plot empty as a short-term investment. This allowed for a quick turnaround between the purchase of new land and the sale of the individual lots, as in the case of Burns' previously mentioned record of thirty-six sold-out subdivisions in thirty-six months. It also forced the land developer, however, to assume an onerous financial burden. Beyond the initial purchase of the subdivision, the developer incurred costs grading the home sites and putting in improvements, including paved roads, curbs, electricity, and sewer and water lines. Fritz Burns' investment in Palisades Del Rey provides an example of the dangers to which this system exposed the developer. If a large portion of buyers were to default, the subdivider would be left with no income and heavy debt from the cost of improvements. Furthermore, to encourage construction firms to purchase plots and to build homes, the developer was often forced to offer concessions that ranged from an artificially low down payment to deferred monthly installments. To pay off this incurred debt, the developer was under heavy pressure to sell lots as quickly as possible to raise quick cash. In the 1920s, for example, Dickinson & Gillespie sometimes sold home sites in their subdivisions at auction. The potential loss of estimated value was outweighed by the necessity of covering the company's financial exposure in its initial investment.[7]

Insured mortgages through the FHA allowed developers to eliminate some of the financial risk of selling land to private builders and build new homes themselves in their subdivisions. By requiring buyers to gain FHA approval for their purchases, developers could guarantee ninety percent of their investment without fear of foreclosure. This steady cash flow allowed developers to contract local builders to construct homes at standard specifications set by the developer instead of the individual builder. Since the FHA had also set minimum guidelines for house size and structure, subdividers could even size individual lots to fit their selected home styles. This eliminated much of the guesswork caused by consumer choice in the selection of a unique home site.[8] Ultimately, the FHA and HOLC tolled the death knell for the practices of wild real estate speculation and the quick, haphazard subdivision and sale of empty land. In Southern California, where the real estate industry had been the catalyst for unprecedented growth in the 1920s and the cause of such widespread privation in the early 1930s, the era of the community builders was at hand, and Fritz Burns was in the vanguard.[9]

Oil money gave Fritz Burns the financial resources he needed to pursue further projects in the latter part of the 1930s, but even a master salesman needed assistance in those areas of community building with which he had no experience. These included the engineering skills to grade the land and prepare lots for development; the personal connections to bring in builders and lenders for large projects; and, most important of all, the financial and bureaucratic expertise to work within the guidelines of the FHA and to exploit this potential new bonanza for the real estate industry. He found all three in 1937 when he joined with Fred H. Marlow to form Marlow-Burns & Company.

Fred Marlow was a legend in Southern California real estate circles long before he met Fritz Burns. Born in 1899, nine months before Burns, the native of Pueblo, Colorado attended West Point, served in Europe immediately after the end of World War One, and then trained as an engineer at the Massachusetts Institute of Technology as part of the Army Corps of Engineers. He arrived in Los Angeles in 1920 as a "roper" who rode the city's electric car system and solicited clients for a real estate company. Soon after, he formed a partnership with Clifford F. Reid in a real estate development company that subdivided Owensmouth (now Canoga Park) in the San Fernando Valley. The two reaped large profits from the Los Angeles real estate boom of the early 1920s, and moved methodically through the San Fernando Valley, subdividing small chunks of undeveloped land in the present-day communities of Reseda, Glendale, Burbank, and North Hollywood.[10]

After his early success, a newly rich and increasingly brash Marlow became enamored of the real estate possibilities along the Los Angeles shoreline. In 1928, he and Reid arranged to buy six hundred acres from the Huntington Land Company on the Pacific Coast. The land lay between the Palos Verdes Peninsula, where Frederick Law Olmsted, Jr. was building a mini-city of his own, and Redondo Beach, the terminus of the same electric car line that serviced Burns' Palisades Del Rey development a few miles to the north. Less than a year after they began construction on their "Hollywood Riviera" development, the Great Depression eliminated the market for their resort, banks foreclosed on their property, and Marlow had lost his millions. "Let it be noted that at the time I was only 29 years old," Marlow later commented. "Getting into [the] big time, I thought my fortune was made for the rest of my life. I did not realize at that time that a big boom can often be followed by a big depression."[11]

During the Depression, Marlow worked for the New Deal's Civil Works Administration (CWA) despite his political affiliation as a "rock-ribbed Republican," and later with the Works Progress Administration (WPA). When the National Housing Act of 1934 called for the creation of the FHA, Marlow was appointed the first District Director for Southern California and Arizona because of his real estate and bureaucratic experience.[12] He spent the next four years immersed in the minutiac of credit appraisals, mortgage risk analysis, loan approvals, and negotiations with builders, developers, and government housing personnel. By the time he resigned in late 1937, he was an expert without peer on the subject of Southern California real estate. That expertise, in matters ranging from FHA loan approval to efficient construction methods and subdivision engineering requirements, made him an ideal partner to join Fritz Burns that same year in their new real estate venture.[13]

Burns and Marlow's first move as partners was to purchase twenty acres with an option on another hundred in the Baldwin Hills area of Los Angeles in 1937.[14] The largely undeveloped area, covering wide expanses of marshy land intermixed with low ranges of hills, was once part of the Rancho La Cienega and had been named for its onetime owner and figure of legend in Los Angeles, Elias Jackson "Lucky" Baldwin.[15] Baldwin's eldest daughter, Clara Stocker, had sold off various parcels of the original Baldwin estate when Baldwin's heirs divided up his holdings after his death. Large areas were set aside for oil drilling by Standard Oil, but residential developments by the Angeles Mesa Land Company still pushed steadily south from Los Angeles. Burns and Marlow acquired a portion of a tract that had been deeded to various charities, including orphanages, convents, hospitals, and maternity homes, known as the "Thirteen Stocker Charities," before liquidation.[16] Nearby was county-owned Ladera Park, as well as the residential communities of Leimert Park, a planned development built in 1928 by noted developer Walter F. Leimert, and Thousand Gardens, a subdivision near the site of the world's first Olympic Village, from the 1932 Los Angeles Olympic Games.[17] More importantly for Burns and Marlow, their new property was square in the path of Los Angeles' steady expansion to the southwest, on the eastern slopes of the Baldwin Hills that faced the approaching city. Downtown Los Angeles was six miles northeast, Hollywood six miles north, and Venice six miles west.

On the marketing side of the operation, Fritz Burns took advantage of the notoriety surrounding Prince Edward of England and his abdication before coronation as King of England to marry American Wallace Simpson in late 1936. Burns christened the new development "Windsor Hills" to capitalize on the free publicity provided by the breathless press coverage of the scandalized House of Windsor.[18] Furthermore, print advertisements made much of the connection with E.J. "Lucky" Baldwin and his legendary good fortune, and described the area as "the luckiest investment Lucky Baldwin ever made." Burns and Marlow reminded potential investors of Burns' subdivision experience and Marlow's directorship of the local FHA office: "Marketing knowledge and efficiency in merchandising are directly related to homesite costs. It is always good to know that the development of your community is in capable hands."[19] On the engineering side of the development, Fred Marlow finally banished the traditional practice of grading subdivisions with a team of mules, a hand-manipulated soil scraper, and a surveyor with a sharp eye. He replaced them with heavy bulldozers and twelve-ton trucks to grade, fill, and compact the hilly development.[20]

Aside from the existing thoroughfares of Slauson Avenue and Angeles Vista Boulevard, the numerous new winding streets of Windsor Hills required appropriate names to give the development an air of sophistication. Burns had been free to name and rename his streets in Palisades Del Rey without interference. During the Depression, when the irony of his foreclosed seaside home fronting on "Waterloo Street" became too much for him, he had the address changed to "Waterview Street," its name today.[21] With Windsor Hills, however, the results of a clear compromise between Burns and Marlow are visible in many of the development's original street names. For example, a new owner in Windsor Hills could take up residence on "Burnsdale Drive," "Marvale Drive," or "MarBurn Avenue," among others.[22]

Assured that the FHA would safeguard their investment, Burns and Marlow proceeded to install extensive improvements in the Windsor Hills development. Water mains, gas mains, curbs, gutters, sidewalks, electric lines, and streets of crushed rock were all installed before lots were sold, a clear indication of the confidence the two once-burned developers had in the new FHA lending regulations. While Marlow-Burns built the majority of the development's homes, local builders were also invited in to build on undeveloped lots. Buyers who used Marlow-Burns for their construction needs were given eighteen options for their home, all but one designed by Wardell Engineering and Construction.[23] The homes were not low-cost for the time. Prices ranged from $5,150 for a two-bedroom with an unattached garage, with monthly mortgage payments averaging $35, to $6,500 for a three-bedroom, with a monthly payment of $40. The developers aimed at first-time buyers of moderate income, though individual builders offered a wide range of distinct home styles. Many were multiple stories, especially those built on sloped lots. Among the first owners of a "Windsor-built" home in the area was Fred Marlow himself.[24]

Drawing from his experiences in the early 1920s as a young salesman for Dickinson & Gillespie, Burns headed up the sales force at Windsor Hills. To motivate his new workers, Burns resurrected his Palisades Del Rey practice of the morning lecture, and over the course of three years of daily talks prided himself on his ability to impart his hard-won wisdom concerning real estate without ever giving the same talk twice. Burns had inherited a love of literature from his relatives in Minnesota as a child, and he prefaced many lectures with a few lines of verse, a habit he continued throughout his life.

Burns' sales lectures varied from serious to humorously irreverent. The more sober lectures were based on diverse sources, including biblical quotations and professional sports figures. Many were motivational in nature, when he might encourage his salesmen to "turn a fizzle into a sizzle" or become "a whirling dervish of enthusiasm." The bulk of these lectures delved into the psychology of both the prospective buyer and the hopeful salesman. "Life is something like a football game, particularly our sales life," he commented in the final months of sales at the development. "You do something that isn't quite right, you make a little mistake, you don't follow one of the rules, or you get a little loose or lax, which doesn't mean anything fatal happens to you—but you get penalized a little bit. Penalties in a football game very often cost the game. So it is with our business. There are only little things we have to think about. We know the big things."[25]

In three years of sales from its opening in 1938, over 1,500 lots were eventually sold in Windsor Hills. The new FHA loan program proved so lucrative for the developers that Burns produced a number of booklets and pamphlets for prospective buyers on the proper method for selecting a home site and building a home that would meet FHA guidelines.[26] Whereas Palisades Del Rey and the Hollywood Riviera were clearly marketed to the rich and the famous of Los Angeles, and Burns and Marlow would build later developments for the low-cost housing market, they aimed Windsor Hills directly at the new class of moderate-income renters who could afford the new ten percent down payment and were becoming home owners for the first time. The two included advertising slogans such as "Do not be at the mercy of the landlord," "Don't get caught in the rent wringer," and "Rent payers lose a home every ten years," throughout Windsor Hills promotional brochures.[27]

Despite the creation of a whole new class of limited-income buyers as a result of FHA policies, salesmen did not necessarily welcome every prospective buyer in Windsor Hills. Property deeds listed protective restrictions on the use of the property, and included a clause limiting sales to Caucasians only.[28] These restrictive covenants were widely used by real estate developers in Los Angeles for several decades. In 1948, the U.S. Supreme Court declared such covenants unenforceable in *Shelley v. Kraemer*, but not until February 1950 did the FHA prohibit mortgage insurance for real estate developments subject to racial restrictions.[29]

While in many cases such restrictions were advertised to entice white buyers fearful of integrated neighborhoods, the FHA also ranked an area's viability for insured mortgages by various factors that included ethnicity. FHA surveyors inspected neighborhoods and graded them from "A" to "D," with "A" neighborhoods deemed the safest for insured mortgages for the maximum amount. A lower grade, with an accompanying threat of a sudden dearth of insured loans, could be given to a neighborhood which assessors judged to be of mixed ethnicity or populated by a non-white majority. To emphasize the FHA policy, the 1939 FHA Underwriting Manual openly recommended restrictive covenants and warned against mixing different social and racial classes.[30]

Though in his hiring practices and business partnerships Burns displayed a level of religious tolerance unusual for his era, his social attitudes reflected the prevailing outlook of the time. At Windsor Hills and in his later developments, he and Marlow followed the practice of issuing restrictive covenants that specifically banned non-Caucasian residents. "20 Pointers for Selecting Your Home Site," a 1938 brochure put out by Marlow-Burns & Company, also advised against neighborhoods of mixed racial or economic groups. Burns' attitudes toward the latter changed dramatically over the next decade, and by the end of World War Two he rejected economic and social stratification in new neighborhoods as "un-American."[31]

Among those whom Burns first hired for the sales team at Windsor Hills was a recent graduate of Loyola University, William Hannon, who had met Burns in the early 1930s when Loyola University students used the beach near Burns' tent home for volleyball games. Hannon started in 1937 as

one of Burns' home salesmen, and stayed with Burns in varying capacities for more than forty years.[32] Other hires from
those years included Winifred Smith, who came on as a
bookkeeper but took on much larger responsibilities over the
years, and her future husband Fred Pike, an accountant who
worked for Burns as part of a larger practice.[33] These three
individuals were some of the first among many who became
Burns' "lifers," a tightly knit group of friends and employees
who held Burns in high esteem and remained with him in
various real estate projects over the next several decades.

In the course of conducting business at Windsor Hills,
Burns also fell in love with Gladys Carson Scheller, a descendant of one of Los Angeles' founding families, the
Dominguez clan. The Dominguez family traced its lineage
back to Juan Jose Dominguez, who had come as a soldier to
California during Spain's colonization expedition in 1769.
The family received the first large land grant under Spanish
rule, the Rancho San Pedro, over seventy-five thousand acres
of land that covered much of what is today the southern area
of Los Angeles. The sheer size of the Rancho San Pedro and
the influence of its owners on Los Angeles can be seen in the
familiarity of the names of the numerous families descended
from Manuel Dominguez' daughters; Watson, Carson, del
Amo, and Dominguez all live on as names of Southern California cities, streets, parks, and developments.

One of the Dominguez daughters, Victoria, married
George Henry Carson in 1857. Their eldest son, John Manuel
Carson, who was active in the development of the powerful
Dominguez Water Corporation, married Katherine Smythe
and had four children, including Gladys Guadalupe Carson
in 1898. By 1935, descendants of the Dominguez family had
acquired enormous personal wealth from oil pumped from
the rancho's vast land holdings, among other business enterprises including water, livestock, and real estate.[34]

At the time she met Fritz Burns in 1935, Gladys Carson

Scheller was a widow with three young children, Frances, Maria ("Pinkie"), and Edward, who ranged in age from eight to thirteen.[35] Gladys became an investor in Windsor Hills, and Burns courted her over the next five years. "They were really in love—it was so sweet," recalled Frances Morehart, Gladys' daughter, who was a teenager at the time. "He would write cute little poems to her on Valentine's Day, or her birthday."[36] In June of 1940, Burns' associates Winifred Smith and Fred Pike were married in Nevada. Upon Winifred's return, Burns asked her to help him plan a similar trip for himself and Gladys. On November 6, 1940, Gladys Carson Scheller and Fritz Burns were married in St. Joan of Arc Catholic Church in downtown Las Vegas, Nevada, with their four children, Gladys' mother, and close friends present.[37]

Burns' new family also witnessed a rejuvenated, enthusiastic businessman who never let a good idea slip by without writing it down. "He never stopped thinking," said Morehart. "He'd always carry these little notebooks in his pocket to jot things down. He'd write down everything in those little books. He would even stop the car and start writing. He'd do it in church. Wherever he was, he'd get that notebook out and start writing. He even had a Dictaphone next to the bed, and all over the floor he had papers, stacks and stacks of them."[38] Another associate years later recalled visiting the Burns home and seeing a long roll of paper cascading across the bedroom floor that was covered with jottings of Burns' late-night ruminations.[39]

Among Burns' marketing projects at Windsor Hills was a survey of one thousand prospective home buyers. It provided him with valuable information for his next projects, along with design and construction data that would resurface before the end of the decade in his developments at Westside Village and Toluca Wood. The survey revealed that almost 95% of his customers wanted a two-car garage, a clear sign that the automobile was already well-ensconced as the primary mode of travel for Angelenos. Also, more than 93% wanted a stucco house instead of the clapboard or brick abodes more popular in the East. More than half wanted three or more bedrooms. Over 90% wanted a fireplace, and almost 75% wanted a one-story house. Chief complaints were a lack of closet space, inadequate electricity and heating, poor kitchen arrangements, and a lack of sunlight.[40] The typical buyer wanted a bright, airy, single-story stucco home with a big garage, a modern kitchen, and room to raise a family without feeling cramped. In other words, buyers wanted the new suburban dream, a California ranch house.

While building Windsor Hills, Burns made two new investments with an eye towards a booming new market: defense spending on aerospace. In West Los Angeles, he bought a parcel of what was once the Charnock Ranch in 1938, two miles east of Douglas Aircraft in Santa Monica.[41] At the corner of National and Overland boulevards, the subdivision was a ripe testing ground for a new method of homebuilding: mass production. Burns hired a "lumber and nails" man, builder J. Paul Campbell, to handle construction.[42] A standard, FHA-approved home design of 885 square feet, with two bedrooms, one bath, and a two-car garage, was selected and used for every unit. Lot sizes were also standardized between five and six thousand square feet, which left ample room for expansion and improvements by buyers. Open acreage along National Boulevard was used as an outdoor factory, and homes were constructed simultaneously, as if each street were an automobile assembly line. By rotating the position of the garage, altering the appearance of roofs and porches, and leaving to buyers the job of painting their new home, Burns was able to create an impression of diversity on each street. At the same time, Burns saved the extensive waste of time and materials that building individualized units entailed. The development was also finished far in advance of what could have been accomplished with individual builders, with the first units selling in 1939.[43]

A home in Toluca Wood, 1943. Note the star in the window to the right,
denoting a husband or son fighting in World War Two.
The "Dick" Whittington Collection, USC Regional History Center.

By the time the new "Westside Village" was complete, 788
homes had been constructed and sold at extraordinarily low
cost and price. The 1939 model went for $2,990, while the
next year's "1940 Super Models" went for $300 more. Mort-
gage payments were less than $30 a month, with a down pay-
ment of $150 on an FHA mortgage. The development did
not include the sidewalks, streetlights, curbs, and driveways
found in Windsor Hills and later required in all new subdivisions in Los Angeles, but the combination of low cost,
straightforward financing, and proximity to jobs made Westside Village a model for future projects. The subdivision also
marked the first time a lending institution issued a loan for a
housing project larger than forty units.[44]

Fresh from their success at Westside Village, Burns and
Campbell moved on to Burbank, where the combination of

frantic prewar aerospace operations and the entertainment industry's growth gave Burns a perfect chance to hype a development close to plentiful jobs. "Toluca Wood," a project of four hundred homes located on the border of Burbank and North Hollywood off Cahuenga Boulevard, was started in May 1941. Minutes away were Lockheed and Vega Aircraft, Warner Brothers, Disney, Universal, and Columbia Studios, while Barham Boulevard and the Cahuenga Pass allowed Burns to boast the project was only "eight minutes from the heart of Hollywood."[45]

The construction methods employed at Westside Village were duplicated at Toluca Wood. An assembly yard was set up on the property, raw materials were bought in bulk and finished on-site, standard house designs were used in slightly different configurations, and a unified building program "from acreage to occupant" eliminated waste and cost from the final product. Prospective buyers were encouraged to visit the construction site to witness a "mountain of shingles" and huge stockpiles of lumber and other raw materials. The development was completed in little more than a year, and prices ranged from $3,850 to $4,490, with down payments ranging from $95 to $290.[46]

Although similar to Westside Village in its construction methods and appeal to working-class buyers, Toluca Wood broke from its predecessor in several important ways. The earlier development had offered a two-bedroom home of standard size and design, but at Toluca Wood, three-bedroom models were offered in addition to the basic model for $500 more, reflecting a growing consumer demand for more space. Also, buyers could choose from varying designs, such as the featured "Colonial," the "Suburban," and the "New Englander." The extra amenities offered reveal that Burns had put his Windsor Hills research into practice. For example, all the homes in Toluca Wood included extra clothes closets in an interior hall as well as a storage cupboard above the bathroom door. Advertisements for the development heavily emphasized "light, cheerful, airy rooms." For an extra $1,000, buyers could even purchase a home fully furnished by the Barker Brothers department store. Finally, in contrast to the unfinished look of Westside Village, many streets in Toluca Wood featured curbs, driveways, and painted homes that gave the development an overall appearance of gentility and moderate wealth.[47]

Westside Village and Toluca Wood preceded more famous postwar suburban developments by almost a decade, making both subdivisions pioneering examples in the field of large-scale suburban home construction and sales. Including units in Windsor Hills, Burns' housing tally for the years 1938 through 1941 was well over a thousand homes, making him easily one of the largest builders in Los Angeles. By way of contrast, in 1939 fewer than one tenth of one percent of Los Angeles builders completed more than one hundred units *total*.[48] This is without consideration of the cost, material, and effort necessary to grade land and put in improvements and infrastructure, factors in mass housing construction that did not affect small builders. With Toluca Wood and Westside Village, Fritz Burns showed that low-cost, mass-produced housing was a viable commodity, and in doing so prepared the way nationally for the titanic housing developments of the postwar period.

In addition to Windsor Hills, Westside Village, and Toluca Wood, Burns also subdivided and marketed another subdivision in the late 1930s, "Riverside Ranchos" in Burbank. Designed for upscale buyers as a mix between a country house and city living, this development along Riverside Drive was a return to Burns' early Dickinson & Gillespie business model. He subdivided the area, invited in local builders, advertised the area as a "pleasure-land of beauty," and sold the lots at low prices, from $675 to $990. He advertised the subdivision's proximity to Griffith Park as well as

Burbank's movie and television studios.[49] While small in comparison to Burns' other developments of the late 1930s, Riverside Ranchos nevertheless demonstrated that Burns had recovered from the ruinous years of the Depression, and was financially both willing and able to risk using a business model that had brought him nearly to bankruptcy just a few years earlier.

Late 1941 advertisements for Toluca Wood included a four-inch disclaimer in the corner that advised potential buyers that "due to large government defense demands, conditions in the material market may necessitate an increase of prices and terms quoted."[50] What did not need mention was that by the time Burns began construction at Toluca Wood, the country was clearly on a path to war, with unforeseen consequences for the nation as well as the region. In addition to the normal anxieties of Americans unprepared for the possibility of another world war (both Burns and Marlow had draft-age sons at the time), builders and developers such as Burns also had to face potential financial ruin just as they were finally establishing a sound business model and regaining their losses from the Depression. While the country and region's industries were gearing up for a period of maximum production, the home building and real estate industries were facing the possibility of collapse. Private builders faced material shortages in lumber, chicken wire, copper, and cement. Further, the possibility loomed that the federal government would respond to housing shortages in areas with high demand for war workers such as southern California by instituting large-scale public housing projects anathema to the private housing industry. In spite of these concerns, Fritz Burns went into the uneasy pre-war days of 1941 with three large residential projects under his belt, recovered from his earlier losses and prepared for an uncertain future.

CHAPTER FOUR

"The Suicide Troopers of the War Building Industry"

"I do not believe in fairies...I do not believe in 'wishing will make it so.' I do believe that whether you are shooting craps, playing poker, or selling real estate, if you are convinced that something is about to happen, if you feel that you are within striking distance, if you think that this prospect is a potential sale...it does something to you. It adds that extra five percent. A sale has to be hundred percent. Ninety five percent won't do."
Fritz Burns, 1941.[1]

On October 14, 1940, the United States Congress approved the Lanham Act, a measure designed to provide relief to specified industrial areas with an existing or expected future shortfall in adequate housing for workers in crucial defense industries. The Lanham Act was passed in response to widespread acknowledgment in both government and private industry circles that if the United States were to enter the current war in the near future, numerous defense industries would quickly encounter a severe shortfall of skilled workers because of inadequate or nonexistent housing stock in proximity to new defense industries. Mindful of the myriad problems caused by high labor turnover in U.S. defense industries during World War One, Congress authorized the federal government to acquire land and build 700,000 units of public housing in areas with industries devoted to the production of war materials, such as southern California. The Lanham Act, however, also allowed for assistance in gaining priorities and FHA funding for private builders willing to construct low-cost developments in areas with acute short-ages of affordable housing for war workers.[2]

Fritz Burns was immediately affected by the Lanham Act and its nationwide ramifications. From the day the Lanham Act was approved until the day World War Two ended almost five years later, in fact, this legislation affected every business and political decision Burns made. His Toluca Wood and Westside Village developments fell into the category of housing the federal government was requiring from private builders to provide mass housing for war workers. Burns needed only to continue his existing pattern of development in order to reap the benefits of the new program. More ominously for private builders, the Lanham Act had also authorized more than one billion dollars for construction of public housing in the same areas Burns and other low-cost builders were working. As a result, the federal government emerged as a potential rival competitor with a budget far in excess of anything a private builder could finance through the FHA.

Burns had followed a strict policy in earlier years of remaining uninvolved in political causes, mindful of the public relations damage his housing developments would suffer if his name were associated with a controversial political cause. While he identified himself as a Republican, he supported candidates from both parties in Los Angeles political campaigns for many years and kept his political donations discreet.[3] Any political battle over public housing was guaranteed to be both public and heated. Burns stood to gain a great deal both financially and politically by cooperating with the FHA and the requirements of the Lanham Act, but also feared that any large-scale foray into mass housing by the federal government could mean the economic evisceration of the private builder. His solution to this dilemma unfolded over the first half of the 1940s. Forced to choose between fighting the federal government's war housing program or participating in it on behalf of his own developments, Burns chose both.

With sales still pending at Toluca Wood and Westside Village, Burns and Marlow used their profits from those developments and Windsor Hills to purchase over one thousand acres of undeveloped land in 1941 in what was then known as the "West Coast section" of Los Angeles, immediately north of Mines Field in present-day Westchester. Burns was no stranger to the area. Dickinson & Gillespie's Palisades Del Rey development of the 1920s was located three miles west at the terminus of Manchester Avenue, Windsor Hills was to the northeast, and Westside Village was several miles north in what is now Mar Vista. The discovery well from Burns' 1934 oil strike was also immediately to the west, as was Loyola University, on the land grant Burns and Harry Culver had engineered over a decade earlier. The land was spotted with scattered houses, a large hog farm at the corner of Manchester and Sepulveda, and beanfields as far as the eye could see. "You wonder why an area like (Westchester) lies dormant for so many years," Burns noted years later. "The answer is that the distance from one place to another isn't measured in miles, but by the amount of intervening vacant territory. There was plenty between Westchester and downtown in those days, so Westchester was considered a long way out."[4]

Because of the perceived remoteness of the entire area, Burns and Marlow were able to get their acreage at low cost, paying $1,100 an acre in January 1941, "and the bank was glad to see us," as Burns put it.[5] Douglas Aircraft, North American, Northrop, and a number of other aviation firms had commenced operations around Mines Field, and the area fit the model Burns had established with Toluca Wood and Westside Village. The combination of proximity to jobs in a major growth industry of the time, aviation, and a marked lack of affordable housing for the expected workforce in the immediate area made the property what Burns called "a white spot," ripe for development. Burns' practice of constructing his housing developments near expected job centers ran counter to the operative model for Los Angeles real estate developments in earlier decades, when proximity to a trolley line, major boulevard or pre-existing public amenities drove subdivision development instead of proximity to jobs. Developers across the nation, however, followed Burns' lead in the first decade after World War Two. "Burns and Marlow are making very conscious decisions about location at the time," said urban historian Greg Hise. "And location has everything to do with regional patterns of expansion, and proximity to employment is a key element. So every one of their sites in the forties and the fifties is located near the aircraft industries. It's the growth industry of the time. If Burns were developing today, I'm sure he'd be looking to see where all the entertainment and digital media is located, and he'd build there."[6]

For the West Coast district, aviation was indeed the growth industry in the early 1940s. North American Aviation, literally within walking distance of Westchester to the south along Sepulveda Boulevard, employed 4,500 workers and reported an anticipated shortage of 1,500 skilled workers by January 1, 1940. As the federal government placed massive orders for military aircraft in anticipation of being drawn into World War Two, North American held over $27 million in U.S. military contracts in addition to an estimated $30 million in orders from Great Britain and France. At Douglas Aircraft's plants in Santa Monica (near Westside Village) and El Segundo, employee rolls surged from 11,000 in November 1939 to over 17,000 by mid-1940. Douglas built up a backlog of more than $78 million in aircraft orders that same year. "This can't be called a boom bubble that will burst with the end of the war in Europe," company president Don-

The ride board at Marlow-Burns headquarters in Westchester, 1942.
Home sales at Westchester were restricted to defense workers, the vast
majority of whom worked in the aerospace plants adjacent to the airport.
Fred Marlow is at front center.
The "Dick" Whittington Collection, USC Regional History Center.

ald Douglas commented in 1939. "America is going ahead
with its own air armament. Who knows what will be next
after the European nations settle their quarrels? Now that
they are talking in terms of hemisphere defense, 5,500 airplanes (present War Department quota) won't be enough."[7]

In Westchester, Burns and Marlow were not alone in dis-
cerning the potential of the area for housing defense workers.

The Silas Nowell Building Company had already laid out the first streets of a subdivision on the northeast corner of Manchester and Sepulveda Boulevard in 1940. The next year, Charles Crawford, a representative from Security-First National Bank who had negotiated the original purchase with Burns and Marlow, brought the builders into a master-planned community with three other developers, centered on a business district located at the intersection of Manchester and Sepulveda. Crawford also christened the new development "Westchester."[8] In addition to Silas Nowell, who developed the northeast area of the original development under the name "Westport Heights," Bert Farrar built "Farrar Manor" on the southwest parcel and Frank Ayres and Sons erected "Kentwood Homes" on the northwest. Burns and Marlow's initial tract was east of Sepulveda and south of Manchester, bordering La Tijera Boulevard. At the corner of Sepulveda and Manchester, where the four quadrants met, Security-First National Bank planned a central business district anchored by a 10,800 square foot supermarket. Since the population of Westchester was expected eventually to top fifty thousand residents in fifteen thousand single- and multiple-family dwellings, the acreage devoted to the business district was far in excess of the initial demand. All four original developers were made investors in the business district.[9] "I like to think of this as another Westwood," Marlow said in 1942. "It lays [sic] between Los Angeles and the ocean. The property is as good if not better than Westwood. All the conditions that Westwood had, we have, and this is even better planned than Westwood. We are able to plan our business center streets right away…if you remember how Westwood grew, you can visualize it to other people."[10]

Following practices they had standardized at Toluca Wood and Westside Village, Burns and Marlow subdivided their quadrant into 669 home sites on sixty by one hundred foot lots and built their standard two- and three-bedroom models, with J. Paul Campbell again in charge of construction. Financing for all the homes was arranged through FHA Title VI regulations, which allowed Burns and Marlow to borrow ninety percent of the costs of the development in advance of construction or sales in exchange for restricting home sales to defense industry workers and their families.[11]

Three-bedroom models in the Marlow-Burns tract, as well as two-bedroom models with a den, were 1,200 square feet. Two-bedroom homes ran from eight to nine hundred square feet, exclusive of garage and porch. The relatively small size of the two-bedroom model was ameliorated by a construction technique Burns and Campbell had first introduced at Westside Village and put into place in the mass at Westchester. Because the garage was usually attached to the house in any case to minimize material cost and maximize perceived lot size, Burns and Campbell situated the garage on the living room side of the house and built an extra door-frame into the wall separating the living room from the garage. Exterior walls were of wood-frame construction with a plaster overlay on chicken wire, so workers could simply plaster over the extra doorway as if it were two standard support beams. Later, homeowners with growing families could easily turn the garage into an extra bedroom or den opening on the living room by breaking through the plaster and installing a door into the pre-existing frame. Because the houses took up a comparatively small portion of each lot, room for another driveway and garage was available on the other side of the house.[12]

Three similar floor plans were used throughout the Marlow-Burns development, and exterior designs included "Californian," "Cape Cod," "American Farmhouse," "Suburban," "Colonial," and "Modern." Buyers could also choose minor variables if reserving a house before it was built, such as window placement, roof style, and color. As always, Burns and Campbell reversed floor plans and altered the depth of building lines from the street to create the impression of diversity within a unified development. In addition, individual amenities could also be purchased (in cash) if the buyer requested the items before the loan amount was sent to the FHA for approval. These included a double garage for the small two-bedroom homes for $95 extra, a fireplace for $125, and a farmhouse porch for $50. As a cost-saving measure, Burns and Marlow tried to anticipate the demand for these individual items so that they could be installed with the house frame itself. Installing fireplaces and porches in already-completed house frames constituted a waste of both time and materials, eliminating the major advantage of mass construction. "Extras—fireplace, double garage, and farmhouse porches—cannot be added on at will. We have anticipated what the demand will be," Burns noted to his salesmen in January 1942. "Once the house is started, we can't take it through the FHA again [for mortgage approval], but you may be able to find the model they want across the street. In buying a suit of clothes the salesman has enough different suits so that he can usually find a certain material in another model, rather than remodeling a suit. We want to work on that same principle."[13]

Initial prices in Westchester were only slightly higher than their predecessors in Toluca Wood and Westside Village. A two-bedroom home with an attached single garage sold for $3,650 complete. The initial deposit, which doubled as a down payment, was only $95. The larger two-bedroom model with a double garage sold for $3,990, with a down payment of $165. Three-bedroom homes were $1,000 more and required a down payment of $265. Prospective buyers were also given a choice of nine furnished models to visit, ranging from the straightforward "Cape Cod" and "Suburban" to the "Harmony Home" and "Personality Home" to the patriotic "Defender" and "Victory Home," among others. Furniture companies, including Barker Brothers and Sears, Roebuck, and Co., furnished the model houses in exchange for the free publicity generated by home seekers.[14]

While economies were realized wherever possible in the Westchester homes, Burns also began to include improvements that were not strictly called for by FHA regulations or considered necessary to induce buyers. In the Marlow-Burns tract at Westchester, Burns first gave evidence that he saw himself as a builder of a genuine community, responsible for delivering "livable homes for those who love living."[15] The Marlow-Burns homes were already cheaper than their counterparts in Westchester, with both Westport Heights and Kentwood homes selling between $4,800 and $6,000, on average $1,000 more per house than Marlow-Burns homes.[16] For the first time at Westchester, Burns and Marlow also deeded land within their acreage to the Board of Education for a public school, a genuine and pressing need, because the nearest schools in 1942 were several miles to the north in Venice.[17] At the same time, Burns gave new residents of his tract the opportunity to beautify their new homes and neighborhoods by offering trees and shrubs at below cost to soften the stark look of the development in its early days. "We had many a tree and shrub sale," remembered William Hannon, a home salesman for Marlow-Burns at the time. "Burns would buy out a whole nursery. We'd sell you a Magnolia or a Jacaranda or a Brazilian Pepper for twenty-five or fifty cents. Burns wanted people to beautify their property to enhance their value and the appearance of the area."[18]

As the country drew closer to entering World War Two, the implementation of widespread restrictions on building materials by the federal government became imminent. For homebuilders especially, such restrictions could be crippling if exemptions and priorities were not granted for such crucial materials as lumber, cement, chicken wire, and aluminum and steel. Reminding his sales force of the numerous shipbuilding and aircraft factories springing up in the area, Burns

exhorted his sales force to redouble their efforts while building materials were still plentiful. "I would like to ask you fellows to do something," he asked his salesmen. "Like to ask
you to go nuts, stark, raving, screaming mad. This is no time
to withhold your ohs and ahs. Take down your hair and rave,
be rabid, fanatical, a whirling dervish of enthusiasm. This is
no time to become blasé. We have to make the final play. We
have to take these people and make that last run with a main
pass to the division manager, and he makes a touchdown."[19]

In October of 1941, Burns announced to his staff that his
own nephew, Robert Burns, Jr., had been drafted into the
army. Much of his sales force, consisting largely of young
men, knew that they would be called as well in the coming
months. "I don't blame the whole outfit for wanting to know
where we go from here and more about what the future
holds," Burns commented. "I don't know of anybody in any
business that is positive about his future . . . we don't know
what next week holds in store for us. This is the final opportunity for people to do business with us . . . let's use our internal fortitude. Give them courage."[20]

The first foundations for the Marlow-Burns homes in
Westchester were poured in the late fall of 1941. Fred Marlow
recalled years later the shock he received not long after: "I was
standing in my patio in Windsor Hills on December 7, 1941,
and heard the broadcast that the Japanese had bombed Pearl
Harbor. I practically fainted because I had just signed a contract to buy $1,000,000 of land and with war in the Pacific it
appeared that there would be no business in the real estate
market."[21] Burns had not yet heard when Marlow called him
with the news. "Fred called me the next morning and asked
whether I thought we ought to go ahead with the development," Burns said. "I hadn't heard about the bombing of
Pearl Harbor, so I said 'sure, why not?' Then he told me."[22]

The impact of World War Two on the real estate industry
was immediate. With the exception of public and private

construction for war workers in defense industries, housing starts across the United States dropped dramatically in every category. In 1941, builders began construction on over 706,000 non-farm houses across the nation. In 1942, that number was down to 336,000, and by 1944 it was barely over 140,000. By contrast, 1946 saw that number increase eight-fold to over a million.[23] The federal government had already passed restrictions in February 1941 that gave priorities in procuring construction materials to builders of homes selling for less than $6,000. In April of the next year, the War Production Board banned entirely any home construction not deemed essential.[24]

Because of the heavy concentration of defense industries in Los Angeles and specifically near Westchester, in both cases Marlow-Burns qualified for continued priorities. Marlow had feared a collapse of the real estate market, but saw the opposite in Westchester and other areas proximate to defense plants, where the housing demand for war workers remained strong. At the Marlow-Burns tract, they stepped up production to thirty houses a week by February 1942, while Burns complained of having been "severely scolded by representatives of the government for not having proceeded faster."[25] Three separate construction crews worked consecutive eight-hour-shifts when production fell behind schedule, working at night under searchlights.[26] The original Marlow-Burns tract of 669 houses was completed by March 1943, just twenty-two months after the property had been purchased and fifteen months after construction began, for an average of over forty homes a month.

The northernmost boundary of Burns' real estate holdings in the area, along Manchester Avenue, had been left untouched during the frantic construction of the rest of Westchester. Once their initial development was completed, Burns and Marlow began construction on "Manchester Village," a complex of two-family homes centered on the intersection of La Tijera Boulevard and Manchester, two blocks east of Sepulveda Boulevard. Burns began similar projects on land holdings in Torrance and in Burbank, which were also experiencing a tight housing market for war workers.[27] Burns advertised the new two- and three-bedroom attached homes as "double bungalows," perfect for war workers who were also looking for rental income. Landlords not involved in defense work were also allowed to purchase the property, provided they rented both units to war workers or their families. This provision brought Burns and Marlow new customers who were otherwise restricted from purchasing single-family homes. By August 1945, they had built over two hundred of the double units on the Manchester property, which brought their building total for the years 1941—1945 to over one thousand homes in Westchester alone.[28]

Westchester appeared so suddenly out of the beanfields and was so closely tied to World War Two defense production that it soon became for many observers a symbol of both the growth of Southern California and the emergence of a lucrative single-family home market during and after the war. The varied and sometimes contradictory reactions of outsiders to Westchester gave it the air of a "shock city," a term first used to describe Manchester, England in the 1840s, for an urban area so new that it disturbs and confounds visitors and forces them to reconsider their definitions of city life.[29] In an essay in *Harper's Magazine* in 1949, historian Carey McWilliams marveled that "everything in Westchester is new and shiny: its streets, its homes, its growing shopping center, its schools." At the same time, McWilliams offered a surprising criticism of the district: "Never formally planned, the streets of Westchester are a jumble of unrelated numberings and sharp, crisscrossing turns; only the oldest inhabitants can find their way about with ease."[30] McWilliams' analysis stands in direct opposition to the plans and projections of the builders of Westchester in 1941-42, who saw their master-planned community as a "little village" where curved streets, single-family homes, and a central business district were the epitome of sound planning and community building.[31]

Grid layouts and mixed-use development were not the only conventions Westchester overturned in its first few years of existence. Because a majority of residents were homeowners rather than renters, the population of Westchester tended to remain homogeneous and stable in comparison to older urban districts. That population was also made up entirely of war workers and their families, and later, war veterans, which meant the adult population was severely skewed towards the under-34-years age bracket for a decade. As in Levittown, New York, after the war, Westchester's residents also raised an entire generation of children who were remarkably close in age, with the attendant growing pains and logistical difficulties. Despite three grammar schools and four more under construction, as of 1948 Westchester's schools were accommodating only forty-nine percent of the primary school-age population; many students were bussed to schools in Venice.[32] The entire high school-age population had to be bussed out of the area because there were too few teenage residents to justify building a new high school. Religious congregations in Westchester faced similar problems with space, and for several years the local Jewish congregation worshipped in the Baptist church. Existing churches found themselves serving as makeshift community centers and town halls in the absence of local public facilities and civic organizations. There were no fire or police stations in the area, nor emergency medical care. Despite all these encumbrances to community life in Westchester, McWilliams conceded in his analysis that the area was still politically very active and aware. Westchester boasted a fifty-seven-percent voter registration rate in 1949, and McWilliams also credited the community for an "absence of a warring sectarianism" and a certain "ferment of newness."[33]

Even while Westchester was confounding the expectations of pundits who expected a traditional city, at the same time the area differed in fundamental ways from the new residential suburbs that followed it in the 1940s and 1950s in and around Los Angeles. First, despite the preponderance of single-family homes at Westchester, the housing stock was much denser than in the typical suburb. The 669 single-family homes in the Marlow-Burns tract approached a density of five houses an acre, while their two hundred "double bungalows" along Manchester Avenue had a density twice that. Second, because Westchester was constructed with war industries in mind, it completely reversed the model of a remote, wealthy residential area far from industry and accessible only by car. Many residents could walk to work in the nearby defense plants, and while the once-ubiquitous Pacific Electric trolleys no longer served the area, two bus lines passed through Westchester and were heavily advertised as an inducement to potential buyers.[34] Ultimately, the market for which Westchester was built, war workers and veterans with stable but modest incomes, gave the district its unique position as something less than a city and more than a suburb.

After the success of his housing developments in the late 1930s and early 1940s, and his subsequent recognition as a major builder in the Los Angeles area, Fritz Burns was elected president of the Home Builders Association of Los Angeles in 1942.[35] The previous year, he had served as Vice Chairman of the National Committee of Home Builders and Subdividers, one of a number of small real estate lobbies then operating across the nation. Burns had also been a charter member of the Home Builders Institute of America, a group with national aspirations but insignificant lobbying power at the time.[36] The average private builder in the nation in the early 1940s ran a small, independent operation that concentrated on relatively miniscule tracts of land, developing ten and twenty homes at a time. While operations similar to or larger than Marlow-Burns existed, they tended to focus on single markets across the nation. Among many others, San Francisco had David Bohannon, Kansas City had J.C. Nichols, New York had the Levitt family, and Houston had Hugh Potter, all of whom were major builders engaged in large-scale development, but no national organization represented the interests of the entire industry.[37] Passage of the Lanham Act in 1940 spurred an immediate consolidation in these organizations. Recognizing the danger to their markets inherent in any major governmental home construction programs, private builders from throughout the country formed the National Association of Home Builders (NAHB) in 1942.[38]

Burns took advantage of any down time he could find in the accelerated production and sales schedules of his development in Westchester and began a sporadic two-year campaign in 1942 to canvass the nation, bringing individual private builders and regional organizations under the umbrella of the new NAHB. This potentially monumental task was made easier by a proposal made by the War Production Board the year before that recommended private builders be eliminated from the war worker housing market and all housing contracts be given to public housing agencies.[39] Private builders were sufficiently alarmed by this development that by 1943, Burns had effectively unified the country's major builders under the NAHB after traveling "from Maine to California" delivering speeches. He also worked with other major builders such as Bohannon to set up a permanent presence for the NAHB in Washington, D.C, and visited with regional builders and organizations to stress the importance of a unified approach.[40] "I can get along

without HBI," Burns told the Home Builders Institute in
1942. "I can go back to Washington alone, representing individual, unfounded, prejudiced opinions, talking but not
being listened to ... We are in the grasp of government; if we
are not strong enough to make ourselves heard, we are too
weak to exist."[41]

After the merger of the NAHB with the National Home
Builders Association, a parallel organization headed by
Harry Durbin of Detroit with policies as similar as its name,
Burns became president of the NAHB in 1943. It was by then
a powerful lobby that included major builders from throughout the nation, the United States Chamber of Commerce,
the United States Savings and Loan League, and the Mortgage Bankers Association. Its builder members were estimated to be handling over eighty percent of the non-public
war housing constructed in the United States. The organization also established a permanent headquarters in Washington, D.C., with Burns' close friend, Frank Cortwright, as
Executive Secretary of the organization.[42]

Burns developed a national reputation as a speaker in his
new role, and slowly became an outspoken advocate of private home ownership as a remedy for social ills. In September
of 1943 he took the dramatic step of wiring U.S. President
Franklin Roosevelt to plead his case against local "public
housers." The telegram, released to the press, hinted at
socialist influence and alluded to the troublesome labor
turnover in World War One that had been the original reason
for the Lanham Act and the government's entry into large-
scale public housing. "Until private housers fail to deliver the
goods, socialization of the building industry should be
averted in Los Angeles," Burns wrote. "Private builders of the
. metropolitan Los Angeles area are ready, willing, and able to
construct the estimated 30,000 homes needed for war workers in this region, either on a rental or for sale basis. Experience has shown that occupancy turnover in privately built

This 1943 cartoon was intended to convince private builders to join the newly constituted National Association of Home Builders. The "private 'unorganized' builder" gets only an outhouse as his share of the "Juicy Post-War Housing Pie."
The "Dick" Whittington Collection, USC Regional History Center.

homes for war workers is decidedly under public housing projects. Good private housing will attract immigrant workers in this district to a greater extent than temporary public housing."[43]

Burns' spirited defense of private builders was more than just a political move on behalf of the NAHB. In his own market in Los Angeles, public housing projects were not only under construction, but receiving favorable publicity for their innovative approach to housing war workers. A prime example was Channel Heights, built in 1943 with federal funds in a hilly coastal ravine in San Pedro. Overlooking Los Angeles Harbor, Channel Heights was designed to house defense workers employed in the port's shipbuilding industries. The architect of the project, Austrian-born modernist Richard Neutra, had built his reputation on indoor/outdoor homes that took advantage of the Southern California climate "to improve the health and well-being of its inhabitants."[44] Neutra had also built private homes with steel and pumped concrete, demonstrating the potential for low-cost dwellings of steel sash and concrete construction in the future. At Channel Heights, Neutra used redwood, cement and stucco to build six hundred apartment units of one and two stories at a density of 3.6 units per acre, significantly lower than the density of the single-family homes in Westchester, Toluca Wood, or Westside Village. Every unit at Channel Heights faced the ocean, and individual apartments ranged from one to three bedrooms. In addition, the complex included a nursery school, a supermarket, and a community center for the residents.[45]

In 1944, *Architectural Forum* gave the development glowing reviews for its individuality, calling it "instructive" for mass builders.[46] For Burns, a project like Channel Heights exemplified the disadvantages a private builder faced in competition with federal housing. The housing density of Channel Heights more closely approximated a middle- to upper-class suburb in Los Angeles, but acquiring land for private construction of such low-density suburbs required costs that would necessitate home prices far in excess of the government's $6,000 ceiling. Similarly, the excess land and materials needed to construct community centers, schools, and local markets on the Channel Heights scale required the private builder to contribute significant acreage for non-income-producing purposes, a fairly straightforward task for a federal agency unconcerned with profit but an onerous proposition for a builder working to make a single project profitable.

In addition to constant lobbying against public war housing, Burns and the NAHB also pressed the government and the War Production Board for higher priority ratings for access to building materials, streamlined FHA mortgage applications, and the standardization of individual materials in FHA-approved homes to put private builders on an equal footing with government projects. A byzantine system of local building codes across the nation during World War Two made procurement of proper materials difficult for private builders attempting large-scale developments outside their original operating area. For example, builders in Denver were prohibited from using wood-frame construction in their developments, despite the preponderance of this construction method throughout the West. In Tennessee and Arkansas, on the other hand, brick houses were outlawed, and only wood-frame construction was allowed. For private builders to be competitive, Burns and his fellow builders argued, they needed standardized materials and requirements issued by the FHA and applicable across the nation. Only then could they hope to compete with the federal government, its vast resources, and the attendant economies of scale it could achieve in home construction.[47]

Also at issue in Burns' battle against public war housing was the composition of the postwar housing market. The national real estate lobby had successfully pushed through an amendment to the Lanham Act in 1940 that mandated the destruction or sale of all government-produced war housing at the conclusion of hostilities, rather than conversion of millions of units into low-cost housing.[48] This eliminated a major concern of private builders. No longer would they have to fear that the expected boom in low-cost housing upon the return of millions of servicemen would vanish if government housing were plentiful and inexpensive. Nevertheless, it was widely accepted even by NAHB members that government housing projects made more efficient use of crucial building materials than private developments.[49] If the federal government implemented a substantial housing program after the war to house veterans, particularly while quotas and material

shortages still remained in effect, private builders would find
themselves at a serious disadvantage. Burns estimated in 1943
that the postwar housing market might require the building
of millions of units annually, and warned home building
industry leaders that "public housing already is making elaborate plans for a huge postwar building program."[50]

To combat this possibility, NAHB members began to
emphasize the importance of individual home ownership as a
remedy for social ills, a hedge against a postwar depression,
and an essential element in any returning soldier's desire to
fulfill the American Dream. "It is no less important now than
in days gone by for people to have their own 'vine and fig
tree,' their own bit of this earth, where they are at least to
some extent masters of their fate," Burns wrote in a 1943 essay
on individual home ownership with the equally emphatic
title, "To Own—Certainly."[51] Previously, Burns had roman-
ticized the plight of the private builder against the over-
whelming resources of the federal government, calling
himself and his fellow private builders "the suicide troopers
of the war building industry."[52] The next year he denounced
"socialist aspects apparent in overzealous public housing officials" at a meeting of public and private housing officials in
New York. "The government builds a temporary structure
which, I admit, uses less critical building material than private housing in building a more permanent structure," Burns
noted. "But the most critical material now is manpower, and
our experience shows that men living in temporary buildings
are unable to give as much to their job as those living in more
permanent dwellings. This is saving of one material, but
wasting a more valuable one—manpower."[53]

Burns' concerns over the postwar housing market were
temporarily put to rest with the passage of the Serviceman's
Readjustment Act of 1944, the G.I. Bill, which guaranteed
every returning war veteran a free college education and an
interest-free home mortgage. The automatic market those

veterans created for single-family homes all but guaranteed a booming home construction market at the war's close, with or without new government housing construction. Burns, an authority on both low-cost housing developments and government restrictions and regulations on the housing market, was particularly well prepared for the coming peace. As a result of Burns' recruitment efforts, a newly powerful NAHB was also in a position to lobby more effectively for the private building industry's needs and interests after the war. Despite heated political battles over housing and occasionally troubling news for private builders, Burns and his colleagues approached the end of hostilities in World War Two in a financial and political position far more secure than that with which they had had entered the war housing market.

Burns' optimism for the postwar market had led him to create a Housing Research Division in 1943 and charge it with forecasting postwar housing trends and testing the materials expected to be used in the new single-family housing market.[54] In an industry known more for conservatism and incremental change than for aggressive research and experimentation, the Fritz B. Burns Research Division demonstrated that Burns and his colleagues intended to enter the postwar period aggressively seeking new markets, materials, and construction methods. Burns assured prospective homeowners in 1944: "I may say at this point that after the war is won and 'V-Building' begins on a great and widespread scale, I and my associates will be right in the thick of it, with an improved formula and improved materials whereby we shall continue to offer 'the most home for the least money."[55]

CHAPTER FIVE

"The Greatest House-Building Show on Earth"

"'The Ideal Community' is the objective of Kaiser Commu-
nity Homes and the guiding start of its future endeavors...
Its success will be measured by the health and happiness of
its children; the contentment and well-being of its
grownups. It shall be a community designed, created, and
dedicated to the home-loving families of America... for the
fullest enjoyment of the nation's greatest heritage, 'Home
Ownership.'"

Fritz Burns and Henry J. Kaiser, 1945.[1]

The official end of World War Two came on August 14,
1945 with the surrender of Japan, though the conclusion had
slowly become apparent over a year and a half earlier with
Allied invasions in Europe and steady United States
advances across the Pacific. For Fritz Burns, these developments held much more than just professional or patriotic
interest. His son-in-law, Jack Morehart, served in the United
States Army from 1944 until the war's end, and his own son
Patrick served in the United States Navy in the Pacific from
1943 to 1946 and received a Bronze Star.[2] With an end to hostilities in sight by late 1944, Burns could look forward to the
safe return of his family members as well as many salesmen,
employees, and associates from wartime activities to a
promising peace.

Burns' work as president of the National Association of
Home Builders in 1943 had brought him into contact with
the best practices of home builders, industrialists, and real

estate operations throughout the United States, while his new Fritz B. Burns Research Division had been closely watching coming trends in home construction and consumer preferences. As early as 1943, Burns, along with numerous other government and private industry leaders, concluded that peacetime America would face a critical shortage of affordable housing after the war, not only for the approximately sixteen million returning soldiers (over a million of whom had married during the war) but for the vast numbers of workers and families who had moved to industrial and military centers around the nation such as Los Angeles. Families were doubled up, existing homeowners had been encouraged to take in boarders, and over half a million Americans lived in Quonset huts or other temporary housing. In California, over three million new residents moved into the state between 1941 and 1949, over six hundred thousand of them in 1943 alone.[3] "While new war housing is being constructed in shortage areas, the condition of existing houses in those areas is generally declining," commented John Blandford, Jr., administrator of the National Housing Agency, in October 1943. "If surplus supplies of materials and manpower not needed for direct war production should develop prior to the end of the war, and if the war housing program is by then substantially complete, housing construction for civilian use should be one of the first outlets for such supplies."[4]

The sheer number of Americans in need of permanent housing in the 1940s was only one factor contributing to the anticipated postwar housing crisis. Overseas servicemen harbored visions of an America dominated by single-family homes on quiet streets, in contrast to the bombed-out apartment blocks of Europe and the endless temporary shelters they had experienced in the military.[5] With the passage of the Serviceman's Readjustment Act in 1944, these veterans were guaranteed a federally insured, interest-free home mortgage upon their discharge. They would not return will-ingly to the cramped city apartments and attics that housed millions during the Depression and the war. Young, materi-ally ambitious, and, in many cases, possessing skills easily transferable to well-paying jobs in defense plants and other industrial fields, these G.I.s would need anywhere from three to five million new single-family homes.[6] By contrast, the U.S. Department of Commerce had reported only 141,000 housing starts in the United States in 1944.[7] This number included housing for war workers built by private industry. A project similar in scale to Westchester, an unprecedented undertaking for private builders in 1941, would have to be duplicated over a thousand times to meet the estimated demand across the nation for postwar housing.

While the looming housing crisis challenged America's industries, the shortage also presented Burns and his fellow builders with a new market for home construction that was orders of magnitude greater than even the wildest speculative boom. Lurking behind this bright opportunity, however, was a possibility that Burns and his NAHB associates had fought throughout the war: federally built mass housing. "We must face this [possibility of public housing] realistically," Burns noted in 1943, "and be fully prepared to fight for private builders' just share of this postwar market which, it is esti-mated, will require the building of 10,000,000 units annu-ally."[8] Hyperbole aside, the mere possibility of federal participation in the home-building industry beyond its role as guarantor of FHA mortgages was enough to cause Burns and other builders associated with the NAHB to lobby gov-ernment officials extensively for price controls, subsidies on building materials, and federal policies in favor of single-family homes. In 1946, Burns arranged several tours of his developments and production facilities for Wilson Wyatt, Housing Expediter for the National Housing Authority and a proponent of both price controls and government subsidies

to private home builders. Wyatt also made a point of personally consulting home building and industrial leaders before
making official NHA announcements.[9]

To meet the challenge and to exploit the opportunity presented by the postwar housing crisis, Burns began planning
for peace a full year and a half before World War Two came to
a close. At the forefront of his efforts was the Fritz B. Burns
Research Division for Housing, established in 1943. While
internal research divisions were commonplace in other
industries such as aerospace and automobile production,
their use in the private housing field was unprecedented.
Under the leadership of director Joseph Schulte, the staff
studied the efficiency and viability of new materials for home
construction and tried to discern current and future trends in
the housing market. Schulte had caught Burns' attention six
years earlier at Burns and Marlow's development in Windsor
Hills. A private operator building homes for individual owners on already-purchased plots in Windsor Hills, Schulte
earned praise from Burns for a number of homes that Burns
considered to be of excellent design and construction. Burns
contracted with Schulte to build the model homes to display
to prospective buyers in Windsor Hills, and soon after hired
him as a full-time employee.[10]

In addition to studying new techniques for home construction and marketing, the Fritz Burns Research Division
for Housing also served as a resource for new homeowners, of
which there were many in Burns' World War Two developments. Through publications such as a "Fix It Yourself"
brochure printed in 1944, the Research Division sought to
give lifelong apartment dwellers and renters the necessary
expertise in home repairs and improvements to ease the transition from renting to home ownership and maintain the
value of their new homes. New owners were offered advice
from the Research Division on how to repair roofs, how to
mix and use concrete, how to care for hardwood floors, and

other tasks for basic upkeep. Los Angeles-area manufacturers, merchants, and appliance firms sponsored these free booklets in exchange for endorsement in the text, and Burns explained the purpose of the free advice in an introductory note: "The day of 'fix-it-yourself' is here . . . 'Charlie' or 'Joe' or 'Pete,' the fellows who used to run over and do a little job of 'fixin' for us, are just not available any more. They are too busy doing the broader job of 'fixin' up that unholy pair of scoundrels, 'Adolf' and 'Hirohito'."[11]

A more serious task of the Research Division was the creation of what Burns called "a laboratory to try our new products, materials, designs, and methods." Much of the Research Division's study, experimentation, and analysis of the postwar housing market from 1943 to 1945 found its way into what became known as the "Postwar House."[12] Located on a busy intersection at the corner of Wilshire Boulevard and Highland Avenue in Los Angeles, the Postwar House was designed by the locally well-known architectural firm of Wurdeman and Becket. One of the principals of the firm, Welton Becket, was one of the premier American architects of the twentieth century. A close friend of Fritz and Gladys Burns, Becket moved in Hollywood circles and designed homes for movie stars, while Wurdeman and Becket as well as his later architectural firm, Welton Becket & Associates, designed a number of Southern California landmarks. "Becket buildings" in Los Angeles included the famous Capitol Records building at Hollywood and Vine, the now-demolished Pan Pacific Auditorium, and portions of Los Angeles International Airport.[13]

At the Postwar House, J. Paul Campbell again supervised construction, and along with Burns, financed the $175,000 residential showplace. Burns handled marketing efforts himself, and the onetime salesman returned with relish to his favorite pastime. "Feeling as I do about the tremendous postwar building activities that lie ahead, I am already plan-

The backyard of the "Postwar House," 1946. Architect Welton Becket's U-shaped
design reversed the traditional streetward orientation of the private home and
emphasized the enclosed backyard and "indoor/outdoor living."
The "Dick" Whittington Collection, USC Regional History Center.

ning—and am actually building—a Postwar House—now!"
Burns announced in 1944, well in advance of the Postwar
House's completion. "It will not only be an outstanding
example of peace planning in the midst of war—but it will be
a big guide-post—an articulate blueprint—for the ultimate
low-priced house of tomorrow . . . this experimental house
may not be perfect, but at least it will point the way to what—
based upon practical experience in the past—may be
expected in the post-war house."[14]

Over one hundred manufacturers supplied their most
advanced products for the Postwar House, which garnered
nationwide press coverage both for its innovations and its

high cost. New features presented in the Postwar House included the first electric garbage disposal in Los Angeles, the first residential large-screen television, an automatic climate control system, and two-way intercoms between all rooms in the house. Burns' employees displayed the new "washable walls" to visitors with a dramatic gesture, smashing a bottle of ink against a white wall before easily wiping it away. Other innovations included the first touch-activated home electrical system in the nation and the first use of "storage walls," room-length closets with sliding doors that replaced conventional bedroom closets and were a constant in Burns' later housing developments.[15] *House Beautiful* called it "the most thought-provoking house in America" and complimented Burns and Campbell for their "personal contribution toward the end of crystallizing opinions of both the industry and public alike and determining to a degree which of the post-war building innovations are within reach and which as of today can be relegated to the realm of pure fantasy."[16]

The proclivity of reporters and home building industry publicists towards that "realm of pure fantasy" was a personal obsession of Burns' and a primary reason for the existence of the Research Division and the creation of the Postwar House. Generally scornful of fanciful approaches to home construction, Burns remained wary of postwar housing designs that failed to account for the conservative tastes of moderate-income home buyers. "I feel—and so do my associates—that people today and in the near future—prefer the 'home-like' type of house," Burns explained in an advertisement in the *Saturday Evening Post* in January 1944. "In the mass, they like an exterior design which is reasonably familiar to them. That's why we offer familiar styles of American home architecture . . . the 'revolutionary,' the strange and bizarre, is, I believe, disconcerting."[17]

By the late 1940s, over one million visitors had passed

through the Postwar House at a cost of one dollar a head
(later lowered to 35 cents).[18] When that torrent of visitors
eventually slowed to a trickle, Burns again worked with
Becket to turn the Postwar House into an example of the best
of California living, renamed "The Home of Tomorrow." Its
formal reopening in March of 1951 was a fundraiser for St.
Sophia's Greek Orthodox Cathedral and St. Anne's Maternity Home, a home for unwed mothers with which Fritz and
Gladys Burns were closely involved. The evening featured
over four hundred civic, religious, social, and business leaders
from Los Angeles and garnered extensive media attention,
both for the star power generated by the guest list and the
sleek modernist home Burns and Becket unveiled.[19]

Using redwood, fieldstone, and huge glass walls, they constructed the house with an emphasis on an indoor/outdoor
lifestyle specifically well suited to the California climate,
including a central garden and a private terrace for each bedroom. Built on a "U" shape, the house upset traditional
homebuilding techniques by forsaking the traditional for-
ward-facing design for a focus on the backyard, which was
flanked on both sides by the wings of the house and was visible from every bedroom and from the living room. The central terrace also featured radiant heating, a newly popular
home heating method where electrical coils were run
through a concrete slab before it dried and hardened. A large
surface area could then be warmed by heating the electrical
coils, eliminating the need for costly and space-consuming
wall heating units.[20]

While the Postwar House of 1946 and its reincarnation as
the Home of Tomorrow in 1951 represented homes beyond
the financial reach of most buyers of moderate income, Burns
had intended the 2,400-square-foot showplace as an "idea
house" more than a realistic model. Visitors to the Home of
Tomorrow were not the prospective buyers who toured
model homes in Westchester or Windsor Hills with the

intention of making a deposit on a similar house. Burns stressed that the Home of Tomorrow was intended "not to decree what shall constitute the house of tomorrow in design, construction methods or materials, but to bring into the focus of public opinion the very best in post-war thought that architects, builders, and manufacturers have to offer." With an eye towards publicity, Burns also built a helicopter landing pad onto the house. The public's interest was piqued, and once again lines formed outside 4950 Wilshire Avenue to catch a glimpse of the lifestyle of the future.[21]

Fritz Burns' introduction of new design elements and their formal presentation to the public in the Postwar House in 1946 and the Home of Tomorrow in 1951 were not isolated events. In Hempstead, New York, twenty-five miles east of Manhattan, William Levitt had built six thousand single-family homes in 1948 on land that had been potato farms just two years earlier. The seventeen thousand individual homes he eventually built in the development of Island Trees (quickly renamed Levittown by its autocratic builder) featured radiant heating and a backyard-focused floor plan. These homes facilitated an indoor/outdoor lifestyle and included a large picture window in the living room, which itself faced the rear of the house. Levitt also incorporated numerous construction elements that Fritz Burns had employed in Westside Village and Toluca Wood almost ten years earlier, such as the time- and cost-saving production methods of an on-site lumber cutting yard and pre-assembly of wood panels. Like the Postwar House, by 1949 each house in Levittown came with a television set. Even the composite appearance of Levittown was remarkably similar to Burns' developments; every lot was sixty feet wide by one hundred feet deep, featured a two-bedroom home designed to be easily expanded by owners with growing families, and fronted on a curvilinear street.[22]

Many of the similarities between Burns' developments

and Levittown were the inevitable result of builders in similar markets attempting to meet standardized FHA guidelines for house and lot size, bedroom size, and even construction materials. Burns, Levitt, and countless other builders in the postwar period, were building as much to take advantage of FHA and G.I. Bill mortgage guarantees as they were to fill a burgeoning market for moderately-priced homes. That new market undeniably existed in part because of FHA mortgage guarantees. However, the similarities between Burns' homes, Levittown, and the millions of "ranch" homes built throughout the United States between 1940 and 1955 were also due to an unprecedented level of industry-wide cooperation and sharing of best practices between home builders of the postwar period. While a number of smaller organizations, including the Community Builders' Council and the National Association of Manufacturers (NAM), existed to facilitate cooperation and advisory assistance among builders, a major reason for the nationwide dispersal of new methods for mass building was Fritz Burns' two-year crusade of the early war years to create the National Association of Home Builders.[23] Construction innovations—for example, Levitt's widespread use of radiant heating, or Burns' "storage walls" and mass production techniques—quickly appeared in new developments around the country. Builders gained new access to each others' practices and advances through a new national literature and closer contact to similar developments.[24]

Major home builders in the immediate postwar period rarely competed directly with each other, in part because the pent-up demand for single-family housing meant a seemingly limitless market and in part because of geographic dispersal. Los Angeles was a prime example. Despite the city's rapid expansion from 1880 to 1929, huge tracts of undeveloped land remained within Los Angeles city limits through the late 1950s. Fritz Burns and his partners were able to build thousands of homes throughout Los Angeles without coming into direct competition with builders throughout the city embarking on similar projects. Burns was a close friend of Ben Weingart, who built seventeen thousand homes in Lakewood with fellow builders Louis Boyar and Mark Taper from 1949 through 1953. Weingart also developed apartment buildings, shopping centers, and hotels in Southern California, theoretically putting him in direct competition with Burns in four major industries. The two shared a close friendship over four decades, however, and were even joint owners of a parcel of undeveloped land in Los Angeles in the 1950s.[25]

The combination of this geographic dispersal of large builders with the centripetal pull of the NAHB resulted in a surprising level of openness and sharing of practices between organizations. For example, Burns disliked William Levitt for what he perceived as Levitt's "above-the-organization" attitude toward the NAHB; nevertheless, in 1950 Burns undertook an extensive tour of Levitt's developments on Long Island. "I don't want to seem a traitor to California, but the builders are really doing a job on Long Island," Burns commented. "They are not only producing a better house today for less money, but are also setting the pace for the entire house building industry."[26] Like his colleagues around the nation throughout the postwar home construction boom, Burns took advantage of his organizational connections to Levitt to gain valuable insight for his own home building enterprise by studying the famous builder's field operations.

Through his contacts in the NAHB and through Joseph Schulte's work with the Research Division, Fritz Burns had by 1944 established close relationships with builders, realtors, contractors, and industrialists throughout the nation. In March of that year, an informal meeting and tour of his Toluca Wood development with the most famous of those industrialists, Henry J. Kaiser, provided the impetus for a major expansion of Burns' home building career. Their meeting and subsequent partnership within the structure of their new corporation, Kaiser Community Homes, resulted in the construction of over eight thousand homes between 1945 and 1952 throughout Southern California as well as in San Jose, California and Beaverton, Oregon. It also set the stage for another revolution in the home building industry. These two visionaries incorporated widespread prefabrication, factory construction, and assembly-line production into what became a vast operation on thousands of acres of land in what Kaiser proudly called "an assembly line 100 miles long."[27]

By the time Fritz Burns met Henry J. Kaiser in 1944, Kaiser was a national legend for his industrial exploits. During the 1930s, he and various partners built the Hoover Dam across the Colorado River, the Bonneville Dam and the Grand Coulee Dam across the Columbia River, and laid the pilings for the San Francisco-Oakland Bay Bridge. At the same time, Kaiser had assembled a huge cement plant on Permanente Creek in Santa Clara County in California.[28] By the outbreak of World War Two, Kaiser had gained accolades in the construction and contracting industry and admiration from the general public for the sheer size of his projects and the speed and efficiency with which he completed them. Like Burns, Kaiser was noted by his friends and associates for his powerful personal magnetism, which gave him the ability to enter any gathering and change the tenor of the event by sheer force of personality alone.[29]

All Kaiser's earlier accomplishments, however, paled in comparison to his shipbuilding exploits. From April 1941 until Japan's surrender in August 1945, Kaiser built and managed shipyards in Richmond, California, and Portland, Oregon, that produced 1,490 ships for the war effort. The yards were staffed by hundreds of thousands of workers, many of them migrants from the Midwest and South, and Kaiser took advantage of the large size of his shipyards to implement "sub-assembly" techniques previously unseen on such a large scale in shipbuilding, much as Fritz Burns was doing in the housing industry at the same time. Although ships of varying types were built at Richmond and Portland, the efforts of both shipyards were largely devoted to the famous "Liberty Ship," a modified tramp steamer used in World War Two to carry troops and supplies. Over eight hundred were produced at Kaiser's shipyards during the war years, at a rate of over one a day at the peak of production. The successor to the Liberty Ship was the "Victory Ship," of similar design but of larger capacity. Over two hundred of these were produced at Richmond and Portland before the war's end.[30]

Kaiser found his shipbuilding accomplishments printed and reprinted in newspapers and magazines across the nation. He was hailed as "The West's Paul Bunyan," and a *Colliers* cartoon in 1943 depicted a husband lost in concentration over a model ship, while in the background his wife whispered to a friend, "So far he's got Henry Kaiser licked by four hours."[31] His reputation for accomplishment and leadership grew so large that by 1944, rumors circulated that President Franklin Roosevelt intended to drop incumbent Vice President Henry Wallace from his reelection campaign and replace him with Kaiser.[32]

In addition to his shipbuilding successes, Kaiser was also producing steel after 1942 at a mill in Fontana, outside Los Angeles, and his cement operation was joined by new ventures in magnesium and aluminum production at the war's end. His central offices ultimately estimated the total value of Kaiser industrial efforts from 1941 to 1945 to be in excess of five billion dollars, and estimated the net profit for all Kaiser ventures during the war in the vicinity of $40 million.[33] Faced with a serious procurement and production slowdown just as his industrial efforts were reaching their peak performance, Henry Kaiser was by 1944 searching for new industries and markets beyond military ships, steel, and other war materials. He found them that year in a meeting with Fritz Burns.

In March of 1944, Fritz Burns met in Los Angeles with Carl Boester of Purdue University. Boester and Burns had been informal associates for many years. At the time, Boester was heading a housing research project at the Purdue Research Foundation, and came to Los Angeles to confer with Burns and Joseph Schulte after attending a conference on postwar home construction on March 8-10, 1944, at which Henry Kaiser had addressed the National Committee on Housing. Kaiser's speech, "Building the Future," had spoken to the need for mass developments of detached housing for returning soldiers and for the large portion of the working population living in substandard housing. For the private housing industry to accomplish this mammoth task successfully, Kaiser noted, a unified effort by government, private banking, business, and labor unions would be required. At the same time, Kaiser warned that if private builders were unable to provide the millions of homes needed, the federal government would quickly move in the postwar period to build mass housing itself, a prospect he viewed with suspicion despite his own reputation for profiting on huge government contracts. "The extent to which we fail this challenge," Kaiser noted a year later, "will be a direct invitation to the Federal Government to take over the job, which is fundamentally ours."[34]

In Los Angeles, the same subjects occupied Fritz Burns and his associates in the Research Division in 1944. Burns had just concluded two years of travel establishing and organizing the NAHB, which provided him with unparalleled contacts in the national housing industry. Burns also remained wary of the federal government's presence in the home construction market after the war. Burns did not oppose public housing of every kind, suggesting that the federal government "should build housing for people of substandard income who can't pay the lowest rents at which existing decent housing is available." He feared the federal government's vast resources and disregard for profit would bring private builders to financial ruin if forced to compete with government projects in the moderate-income housing market expected after the war.[35]

Schulte was deeply involved in the research, planning, and construction of the Postwar House at the time of Boester's visit, and Boester asked Burns if Schulte could accompany him to Henry Kaiser's offices in Oakland, where Boester had a similar appointment with Kaiser to discuss postwar housing. In Oakland, Schulte and Kaiser talked at length about the Postwar House as well as about Toluca Wood, which Schulte had always admired as Burns' finest project. Intrigued, Kaiser traveled to Los Angeles shortly after and toured Toluca Wood with Burns.[36]

Neither Burns nor Kaiser kept any written record of their joint tour, but continued to meet over the next year to discuss a potential homebuilding partnership. In March 1945, Fritz and Gladys Burns traveled to Kaiser's shipyard in Richmond, California. Gladys Burns had been invited as a sponsor to christen the latest "Victory Ship" to be launched from Kaiser's Richmond shipyard, and on March 21, 1944, she smashed a champagne bottle across the bow of the S.S. Loyola Victory, named in honor of Loyola University of Chicago.[37] The invitation was no casual matter, because the pool of potential ship sponsors was generally limited to women in the public limelight (men were prohibited in accordance with old superstitions of the sea). Previous sponsors of Liberty and Victory Ships had included Eleanor Roosevelt, as well as the wives of United States senators, congressmen, and senior state officials. Kaiser himself, his son Edgar, or a senior Kaiser official normally extended these invitations.[38]

The Richmond shipyard greatly impressed Fritz Burns. Kaiser's approach at Richmond was a familiar one for a large-scale home builder, and the manner in which Kaiser's yards had made the transition from undeveloped land to hectic assembly lines churning out finished products in just a few short years differed only in scope from Burns' approach at all three of his war developments. "He thought a lot of Henry Kaiser after he visited the docks up there," remembered Frances Morehart, Burns' stepdaughter. "He said that Henry could stand there before anything was built, when there was nothing there, and just see the docks built. He just had the biggest vision."[39] Burns' comments were strikingly similar to remarks made by his own coworkers concerning Burns' ability to conjure up a community of homes out of a deserted field.[40]

Over the next few months, Burns and Kaiser sketched out the details of a postwar homebuilding partnership that would combine Burns' expertise in land valuation, marketing, and on-site home construction with Kaiser's strengths in factory management, high-volume industrial production, and materials procurement. In addition to their complementary business strengths, the two men also shared an uncommon willingness to take risks. Kaiser was famous for charging aggressively into new endeavors with little regard for financial minutiae or potential pitfalls, an approach that had paid off with dramatic results in his successful bids for huge construction projects such as the Hoover Dam and Grand Coulee Dam. Burns possessed a similar aggressiveness and breadth of vision in business matters. Though the harrowing lessons of the Great Depression had tempered his natural enthusiasm for financially risky projects, Burns still approached new opportunities with a surety of purpose that amazed his associates. His longtime friend and business associate Joseph Rawlinson, who worked as Burns' business lawyer and accountant over three decades, noted that "in private consultations with me, he was always the utmost optimist. He would have to hide some of that in public, but every time we started a new project he was always one hundred percent optimistic [that] it would be a success."[41]

Not all of Burns' associates shared Burns' admiration for Kaiser or his methods. Fred Marlow, who had been Burns' partner since they subdivided Windsor Hills together in 1937, balked at joining any joint operation with Kaiser. "After having had a few meetings with Kaiser, I grew to dislike him and his methods of harshly bulldozing his partners," Marlow later noted. "This turned out to be a mistake on my part, inasmuch as the various projects which Burns entered into with Henry Kaiser, both in Los Angeles and in Honolulu, were highly successful and most profitable."[42] Although Marlow's name appeared for years on Kaiser Community Homes brochures and internal documents as a director of land development, the title appears to have been largely honorary.

While Burns was clearly Kaiser's superior in his understanding of and experience in home construction, housing had been a lifelong business interest for Kaiser. His legal filings for his first business back in 1914 had included home construction among company aims, which included the more predictable Kaiser fields of paving, production of cement and steel, and development of water and power resources.[43] In addition, near his Richmond shipyard in August 1942, Kaiser and his associates had built six thousand housing units in seven hundred buildings for yard workers using government funding. The first units were complete and ready for occupancy just four months after construction began in the new community of "Vanport." The development was of a substantially lower quality than FHA Title VI war-worker housing developments such as Westchester—one resident called Vanport "a huge collection of crackerbox houses strung together fast and cheap"—but the shipyard had managed to provide housing for over nineteen thousand people in Vanport by May 1943.[44] At his Richmond shipyard, Kaiser also eventually constructed a similar project of ten thousand units, two schools, and a hospital under contract from the U.S. Maritime Commission.[45]

After the March 1944 meeting with Burns, Henry Kaiser's staff worked to ascertain the optimum design and construction methods for a postwar house. Kaiser had already studied the feasibility of building prefabricated steel-frame houses in December 1942, just as his Fontana steel plant began production, and in 1943 Kaiser Industries studied the possibility of producing three-family attached homes.[46] Because Burns had given Kaiser his plans and figures from his construction of Toluca Wood in March of 1944, Kaiser employees could use the costs and materials of homes in that development as a useful comparison for new methods and materials. Other Kaiser plans included homes built of steel and wallboard, aluminum, or even plastic. The plastic house would have been based on the two-bedroom Toluca Wood design, but would have employed a flat roof for efficiency and been entirely prefabricated, a remarkable departure architecturally from contemporary developments.[47]

Kaiser Vice President Howard Lindbergh concluded in an August 9, 1944 memo to Kaiser's Housing Division that Kaiser engineers had found no method to gain substantial savings from the estimated $6,000 cost of a conventionally built home on the Toluca Wood model. They then considered three alternatives. They could build houses for export to China, Russia, England, or South America, areas free of restrictive American building codes and with postwar housing markets relatively free of competition from other mass builders. Another option was to "conduct research until a super-house is developed," and a third alternative was to "advance the art of prefabrication" to become a retailer of individual house construction parts to local retailers. Lindbergh's advice was for the organization to enter a limited partnership with a builder such as Burns to give Kaiser engineers a test case to observe. Kaiser engineers ultimately selected the Toluca Wood house as an "ideal starting point" for large-scale housing developments.[48]

In April 1945, just one month before Burns and Kaiser publicly announced their joint venture, executives for what was then still called "Kaisercraft Homes" met in Oakland to discuss the operating procedure for the crucial first few months of the program. Scaling back earlier plans to convert the Richmond shipyards to mammoth home production facilities, the new company instead resolved to sell homes through already established channels, essentially local builders, and avoid investment in the business of individual builders franchised to construct Kaisercraft Homes. Using two- and three-bedroom homes similar to the Toluca Wood model, Kaiser executives expressed their reasons for selecting Fritz Burns as the builder of choice for the first phase of building in their April report: "Initial operations might begin in the Los Angeles area with the establishment of Marlow-Burns as first franchised builder, due to the fact that this company owns the necessary land for a community of 5,000 homes and has at its command experienced personnel for the project."[49] Markets in which franchises were expected to be sold to local developers eventually included Seattle, Boise, Salt Lake City, San Francisco, Portland, San Diego, and unspecified regions in the eastern United States.[50]

The initial Kaiser-Burns venture in Los Angeles was only a prelude and testing ground for a far larger national system of home production. At the same time, Burns and his organization were considered an essential component of the new venture far beyond initial production in the Los Angeles market, for the same reasons that had initially brought Burns national prominence as a home builder during World War Two. "Fritz B. Burns' organization possesses knowledge of land acquisition and development and knowledge of the design, building, and marketing of homes using mass production methods," Kaiser's staff noted. "It also possesses the advantage of two years of recent extensive research and developmental work devoted entirely to new concepts of

existing units and additional units never used in housing, all
of which will be incorporated into the model home about to
be built."[51] Despite Kaiser's confidence that he could make
the transition from shipbuilder to nationwide home builder,
his staff quickly realized the important contribution needed
from Burns in his capacities as a housing expert, experienced
builder, and a well-connected powerbroker in the housing
industry at the end of the war.

The small size of Fritz Burns' organization both in manpower and financial resources relative to Henry Kaiser's
operations was belied by the substantial role Burns and his
associates took in the organizational structure of Kaiser
Community Homes. Senior officers of the new enterprise
were almost evenly drawn from the two companies. Organization charts from May 1945 announced Burns as President,
with Henry Kaiser's son Edgar and trusted Kaiser associate
Eugene Trefethen as Vice Presidents. Another Kaiser man,
G. G. Sherwood, became Secretary and Treasurer. Henry
Kaiser took the title of Chairman of the Board, with Burns,
Joseph Schulte, and Burns' close confidant Fred Pike joining
Trefethen and Howard Lindbergh on the Board of Directors. Fred Bauersfeld, a real estate broker who had first
worked with Burns at Palisades Del Rey in 1924, was
appointed general manager in charge of residential real estate
sales. Each side also put up fifty percent of the initial financial outlay of $100,000, and Burns matched a Kaiser land
purchase in San Jose, California by contributing sixty-three
undeveloped acres adjacent to his Westside Village development in Los Angeles.[52]

Burns and Kaiser became equal partners in Kaiser Community Homes despite the glaring disparity in the size of
Kaiser's vast industrial operations relative to Burns' compact
organization. The $50,000 initial investment in Kaiser Com-
munity Homes was a far more taxing burden on Burns'
finances than that of a massive industrial conglomerate such

as Kaiser Industries. As World War Two neared its conclusion, however, Burns received news of an unexpected windfall that would augment his financial reserves. On May 1, 1945, a bond issue of $12,500,000 was approved for the westward expansion of Los Angeles Airport (now LAX) to accommodate increased traffic and jet airplanes. A decade earlier, Burns had used oil revenues to purchase land between Pershing Avenue and Sepulveda Boulevard at a tax sale, and his holdings were directly in the path of the airport's westward expansion. The City of Los Angeles had already initiated condemnation proceedings on the 640-acre parcel, known as Section 35, and was obligated to pay Burns an appraised value of $600 an acre for the property within a year. After the bond issue was passed, however, it was discovered the city's option on Section 35 had lapsed and the land would have to be purchased at market value. Burns realized an immediate fivefold increase in the value of his property. Amid charges of "dilatory tactics or skullduggery" by Los Angeles City Councilman Lloyd Davies, Burns was paid $3,000 an acre for the land in 1946, for a total sale of almost two million dollars. Los Angeles International Airport's current passenger terminals stand on Burns' Section 35 property.[53]

On May 22, 1945, less than three weeks after Germany's surrender, Kaiser Community Homes was officially incorporated in California. From the beginning, Burns and Kaiser set high expectations for the company, and announced a long-term goal of one hundred thousand two- and three-bedroom houses a year through partnerships with local builders throughout the United States. By contrast, the total number of houses built and sold by Burns during World War Two had totaled slightly more than two thousand—and Burns was one of the most prolific home builders in the nation at the time. On New Year's Day, 1946, Henry Kaiser gave a speech on ABC radio entitled "Forecast for

1946," which cast the postwar housing crisis as a defining moment in American history. "In war we have just met the greatest crisis in history," Kaiser spoke. "Our ability to deal with the housing problem will test our capacity for peace. Not only national welfare but the American way of life is in the balance...the record of 1946 will be written in terms of work and sacrifice." He announced a short-term goal for 1946 for Kaiser Community Homes that was more modest but still historically unprecedented. "In our organization we are now building a house every day," Kaiser noted. "In California we have set our goal for 1946 in these terms: two houses a day in January—three a day in February—ten a day in March—thirty a day in April, with whatever increase is necessary to complete ten thousand homes by the last day of December."[54]

Such an enormous task required the acquisition of thousands of acres of land, development of unprecedented production facilities, a finished product that would meet buyers' expectations, and a marketing effort to keep the company in the public eye. To address the first and most pressing concern, Burns had worked since May 1945 on a dedicated program of property surveying and land acquisition. Almost all his purchases were in or around Los Angeles, and KCH policy was to restrict itself to developments of two hundred homes or more. Burns created an eleven-page property evaluation form that was sent to sellers of desirable land, after which Burns would visit each parcel. Suitable properties had to be more than just easily subdivided or inexpensive. Burns looked at the land's proximity to existing suburban development and also checked for indications that the local housing market justified construction. An important factor was the presence of local firms building homes nearby. Burns noted, "I do not like to be the only one who thinks the area is worthwhile."[55] Burns and Kaiser also made tentative plans to furnish each Kaiser Community Homes development with a small airstrip in the event planes should supplant automobiles as the future preferred mode of travel.[56]

Over sixteen months, Kaiser Community Homes purchased and graded properties that included 188 acres on the San Jose-Santa Clara border in the San Francisco Bay area; 185 acres in North Hollywood; 118 acres in Monterey Park, a suburb of Los Angeles; 74.5 acres in Ontario, near Henry Kaiser's Fontana steel plant; 63 acres at Westside Terrace, adjacent to Burns' earlier Westside Village development; and ten acres in Compton in southeast Los Angeles County. In addition to Burns' holdings in Westchester and Playa Del Rey, Kaiser Community Homes purchased two more large parcels of land in that district from Burns' fellow Westchester builder Silas Nowell, one of 45.4 acres and another of 61.5.[57] While an output of ten thousand houses within a year was more a marketing slogan than a realistic production goal, by the end of 1946 the combined acreage controlled by KCH, including an affiliate in Portland and property outside Henry Kaiser's Kaiser-Frazer automobile plant in Willow Run, Michigan, totaled 11,500 lots worth over four million dollars. In the Westchester area alone, Burns had assembled 4,407 lots.[58]

Creation of production facilities capable of turning out the necessary finished materials for thousands of homes a year also proved a challenging task. Using some of Burns' industrial-zoned property east of the Marlow-Burns development in Westchester, KCH began construction in March 1946 of a huge production plant at 5555 West Manchester Boulevard. Covering sixteen and a half acres, the $750,000 plant included a building of 104,000 square feet that resembled a Kaiser shipyard production facility. A rail spur terminating in a ten-car siding ran along the east edge of the property to unload precut lumber shipments from mills in the Pacific Northwest. Outdoor facilities included storage yards for lumber, plumbing parts, and plywood, as well as a plumbing assembly area where the plumbing for an entire house was pre-assembled into a single "tree." Roof panels and porches were assembled immediately outside the factory using a combination of pre-cut lumber and rough lumber that was "remanufactured" by teams of men with planing equipment. A nearby access road allowed trucks to pull directly up to the production area before loading and shipping out to field operations; another exit bordered the plumbing production area, and a third was built into the factory building itself. Inside the factory, prefabrication of wall, floor, ceiling and partition panels took place on six horizontal conveyor lines. Even doors and windows were installed into exterior wall panels at the factory rather than in the field.[59]

At the terminus of the six conveyor lines, completed panels were hooked to a moving overhead rail that took them to the storage area, which could hold enough finished panels to build thirty houses. At the opposite end of the KCH factory, workers assembled cabinets and "storage walls," the huge wall-length closets Burns had introduced in his Postwar House. All items were pre-painted in the factory before a final finish coat was applied in the field. Once all the materials were trucked from the factory to KCH's various housing tracts under construction, Kaiser Community Homes achieved Henry Kaiser's boast of "an assembly line 100 miles long."[60]

While the Manchester production facility earned Kaiser Community Homes extensive publicity, including a March 1947 feature in *Architectural Forum* calling it "The Greatest House-Building Show on Earth," most construction work on KCH projects still took place in the field. Because Henry Kaiser entrusted on-site production details almost entirely to the more experienced Burns, field operations closely resembled the methods Burns had perfected when building Toluca Wood and Westside Village. Even with the Manchester plant operating at full efficiency, fifty-five percent of construction had to take place on-site because of the nature of home construction. Preassembled plumbing trees still had to be installed, walls and roofing panels had to be attached to house frames, foundations had to be poured, and the Kaiser-produced "mechanical core" for the kitchen and bathroom had to be hooked to plumbing and sewage systems. In addition, each house also required roof shingling, interior carpeting, linoleum installation, and the application of an exterior "skin," a process whereby outside walls were covered with a combination of felt paper, chicken wire, and stucco.[61]

Kaiser Community Homes also included traditional "improvements" in their developments, such as curbs, electric lines, sewage pipes, and roads. As a result, each development already required a steady on-site flow of workers during construction that lessened the value of factory construction of parts. In addition, labor troubles entered the picture in 1947. Ken Skinner, a longtime associate of Burns and Executive Vice President of the Fritz B. Burns Foundation, met Burns when he began at Kaiser Community Homes as a junior bookkeeper in April of 1947. He remembered a serious problem with the plumbers' union. "The prefabs didn't work out because the unions became involved. We were assembling rough plumbing at the plant, then shipping it out to the field for them to lay it. [The plumbers' union] said no, that it all had to be done out in the field. Then the labor costs started getting out of line."[62] Although Burns' opposition to public housing and professional association with the National Association of Home Builders often put him at odds with labor unions, both he and Kaiser generally enjoyed a strong rapport with unions in their respective industries. In order to comply with the plumbers' regulation, Kaiser Community Homes began to ship plumbing parts directly to the housing developments for assembly and bypassed the Manchester plant.[63]

In outlying developments, such as Orchard Park in San

Jose and Monterey Park in Los Angeles, factory prefabrication was eliminated entirely. Though the homes in these developments were constructed with the same materials as those in the Manchester Boulevard facility, everything from wall panels to cabinets to porches and roofs was assembled at a storage yard located within the development itself. The difference in cost was minimal, and in the different approaches one can see the personalities of KCH's partners. Burns had built thousands of homes in Los Angeles using on-site assembly with great success in previous years and disliked the notion of prefabrication. He insisted that the home building method used in the Manchester plant not be called "prefabrication," but instead a "perfect blend between site fabrication and factory fabrication."[64] Kaiser, experienced in the assembly-line production methods for ships and cars, hoped for added efficiency and more operational control through a centralized production facility. He also sought to align KCH's efforts with government policies in order to guarantee both a steady stream of materials and, eventually, contracts from the government for guaranteed purchase of prefabricated homes as part of the May 1946 Veterans Emergency Housing Program.[65] Before the Manchester plant had even opened, Burns and Kaiser had calculated both the costs and the profits to be gained through the production of as many as 150,000 low-cost homes in response to the FHA's policy of granting priorities in materials and potential guaranteed contracts for homes "constructed with 'prefabricated' materials."[66]

By May 1947, the federal government was easing restrictions on a number of scarce construction materials as the nation began to return to a less regulated peacetime economy. This decreased the pressure on builders such as KCH to qualify for prized government priorities by building homes using prefabricated materials. Burns continued to campaign for field production of houses, and by the end of that year

Kaiser Community Homes began to phase out their factory-assembly operations. The Manchester plant was eventually leased to Restwell, a furniture manufacturer, then sold in 1949.[67]

Aside from production matters, the sheer size of the Kaiser Community Homes developments also required a standardized house layout and construction method. By far the greatest advantages a large builder such as KCH had over countless smaller builders were economies of scale in everything from purchasing materials to production of parts to subdividing of property. These economies were only realized if use of materials, production methods, and property specifications were all standardized. As a result, Kaiser Community Homes began with only two house designs, a three-bedroom rectangle of 956 square feet and a slightly smaller two-bedroom model. They were sold in five styles, "Colonial," "Cape Cod," "Ranch House," "Californian," and "Contemporary."[68] To avoid the appearance of cookie-cutter conformity, Burns continued and expanded his wartime practice of using "fundamental variables," a pre-selected number of elements in each house that could be altered to provide diversity within each development. The most prominent variable was the garage, which could be placed in six different configurations, including complete detachment from the house. Roofs also came in different styles, shapes, and colors, as did exterior wall appearances, porches, and paint schemes. Houses were also placed in various locations on individual lots to open up sight lines. KCH officials claimed that over 5,184 different exterior appearances were possible, though only 28 were used. Streets were also laid out in the "curvilinear" pattern and tight corners were given extended street widths, what KCH publicists called an "arthritis bend," to decrease corner accidents and to extend sight lines and lot frontages.[69]

In each Kaiser Community Homes development, the company also offered shrubs and trees at less than wholesale cost. New residents could buy everything from Chinese Elms to Acacias for one dollar and rose bushes for a quarter, providing each new community with instant shade, variety, and a way to eliminate the stark appearance of the tracts upon their sale. Every new KCH owner was also given a Kaiser Home Service Manual entitled "Keeping Up With The Joneses." A twenty-five-page brochure clearly derived from the Burns Research Division's "Fix It Yourself" handout of the war years, "Keeping Up With The Joneses" offered new home-owners tips on how to fix a leaky faucet, change a fuse, build a fence, and numerous other household improvement tips. Both the brochure and the shrubbery sales were designed to give new owners what Burns called "a psychological equity," a stake in their home far beyond the mortgage and property value, which would encourage the upkeep and improvement of their property and thus raise property values throughout each development.[70]

Burns and Schulte's work on the Postwar House had convinced Burns that the market for single-family homes was a generally conservative one in terms of taste as well as openness to housing innovations. This was particularly true with mass-produced housing such as that produced by Kaiser Community Homes, because in developments aimed at war veterans the vast majority of buyers would be purchasing their first home. Oftentimes the buyers' primary measure of value would be an appearance and structure consistent with that of other homes the buyer had seen and visited. To please a cautious buyer, a builder had to walk a careful line between outmoded production methods and alienation of one's market by overly radical innovations. To reassure their nervous buyers, Kaiser Community Homes consistently depicted their finished product in brochures and press releases as a compromise between radical innovations and the tedious, inefficient methods of the past. A March 1947 article in *Architectural Forum* exemplified this careful strategy. Empha-

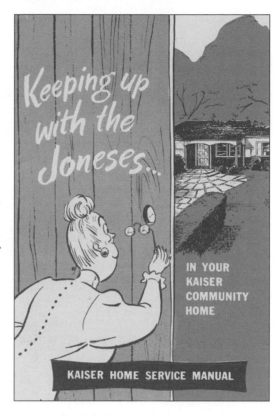

"Keeping Up With The Joneses" was distributed for free to every Kaiser Community Homes buyer. The brochure offered new homeowners tips on a variety of household maintenance tasks, from building fences to turning off a water heater.
Fritz B. Burns Collection, Loyola Marymount University.

sizing the company's "admittedly cautious estimate of public taste" and "houses of conventional appearance," the feature finished with an assurance that "with one foot to the left, the other to the right of house-building's center line, KCH stands ready to give extremists on either side a real run for their money."[71]

A classic Burns marketing strategy at the time demonstrates the company's understanding of the cautious nature of its new market. Kaiser engineers had determined that the company could save time and money by using plywood in panels for ceilings, partitions, and walls. Once a design and size had been selected, the panels were relatively easy to prefabricate because they were lightweight (the heaviest panel in the house was 450 pounds), could be made to standard size, and could be shipped out from the Manchester factory in bulk. To convince prospective buyers of the strength and viability of the new wall panels, Burns and his marketing team employed a merchandising strategy that was explained in KCH brochures as "Showmanship bolsters the self-selling design." A plywood partition panel from the Manchester plant was laid across two sawhorses, and an elephant was brought out to stand on it. The resulting image reinforced the notion that KCH homes were as sturdy as houses of conventional construction. As a further reassurance to first-time buyers, Burns also expanded on his model home strategy. Each KCH development featured several completed, fully furnished model homes that buyers could study to visualize their own completed homes. With Kaiser Community Homes, however, Burns also left several homes unfinished during the selling process so that anxious buyers could study electrical systems, plumbing, and construction methods.[72]

On September 16, 1946, Fritz Burns and Henry Kaiser walked up to a new home on Stewart Avenue in Westchester before a large crowd of photographers and curious onlookers. At the front door, they welcomed the owner of the first house built by Kaiser Community Homes' "sub-assembly method" as Henry Kaiser inserted a gold key into the door. Clyde C. Henley, a 34-year-old Army veteran and native of Lafayette, Indiana, had with him his wife, Lois, and their two children. Since his discharge from the Army, Clyde and his family had been living with friends in Los Angeles, one of the many veterans "doubling up" because of the housing crisis. At a press conference preceding the ceremony, Burns and Kaiser explained in detail their housing program, then restricted by the federal government to veterans purchasing homes under the G.I. Bill. The two partners jointly declared Clyde Henley's receipt of his new home to be "America's answer to the

so-called accomplishments of Communists and Fascists."
Five months later the cameras and reporters were back, this
time on Reading Avenue to witness a simultaneous move-in
by forty families of veterans into forty new KCH houses.
These forty homes were the first steps of a remarkable transformation of wide swaths of farmland into Kaiser Community Homes developments. Over the next five years, Kaiser
and Burns would produce over eight thousand homes in a
half dozen communities throughout Southern California.[73]

For veterans and non-veterans alike, the most powerful
inducement to purchase a KCH home was the price. By
March 1947, over 3,500 applicants had added their name to
the registration list for a new Kaiser Community Home.
Prices averaged slightly more than $9,000; the vast majority
(83 percent) was purchased by veterans under the Veterans
Emergency Housing Program, with payments between $40
and $60 a month. Even the $290 down payment could be
borrowed from the government. From September 1, 1946 to
September 1, 1948, 5,319 homes built by the partnership of
Fritz Burns and Henry Kaiser were constructed, sold, and
occupied.[74] This included 1,410 in San Jose; 1,295 in Westchester; 562 in Monterey Park; 471 in Ontario; 430 in Compton;
and 300 at Westside Terrace in West Los Angeles.[75] In those
two years, more than twenty thousand California residents
moved into houses built by Kaiser Community Homes.
Among those twenty thousand were Burns' and Kaiser's own
family members: Fritz Burns' stepdaughter, Frances Morehart, who lived with her husband Jack and their young family
in a three-bedroom Westchester home, and Henry Kaiser's
son, Edgar, who lived just a block away.[76]

Around the nation, the return to a peacetime economy in
combination with a severe housing crisis and generous government funding had led builders in every major city to
embark on ambitious single-family housing construction
programs. Housing starts for single-family homes leaped

from 114,000 in 1944 to 937,000 in 1946 to 1,183,000 in 1948.[77] Burns and Kaiser, however, had set out to do more than build homes for twenty thousand people when they began Kaiser Community Homes. A second goal had been the creation of what Burns called the "Total Community," which in addition to homes would include shopping centers, industrial work-places, schools, churches, libraries, and recreational facilities. After building thousands of homes and working for almost thirty years in real estate, Burns still had not entirely achieved that goal, best described in a 1947 Kaiser Community Homes brochure: "It shall be comprised of attractive, well-kept dwellings in a setting of pleasant environment. It shall abound with spiritual, cultural, healthful, recreational, and commercial opportunity. It shall be a complete and balanced Community of work, of worship, of learning and of play."[78]

In April of that same year, 1947, Fritz Burns purchased on behalf of Kaiser Community Homes four hundred acres of the Panorama Ranch in the San Fernando Valley for devel-opment into a residential community.[79] Fourteen months later, he and Kaiser began work on what would turn out to be the culmination of their home building efforts together, a "City Within A City" that would allow Burns a chance to create his total community. With Kaiser Community Homes, Burns was about to embark upon his largest, most famous, and most successful housing development of all, Panorama City.

A Fritz B. Burns Photo Essay

Fritz Burns (right) at age ten, with his brother Robert, age six, and their dog, "Brownie," in Minneapolis in 1909.
Courtesy of Sarane Van Dyke.

An eighteen-year-old Fritz Burns in his "doughboy" uniform as a lieutenant in the U.S. Army, September 1918.
Fritz B. Burns Collection, Loyola Marymount University.

Fritz Burns leading the Dickinson & Gillespie salesmen in daily morning
calisthenics exercises on the beach at Palisades Del Rey, circa 1925.
Fritz B. Burns Collection, Loyola Marymount University.

A Dickinson & Gillespie brochure
for "Edison Square," a subdivision
in what is now the El Sereno
neighborhood of Los Angeles.
Note the emphasis on the subdivision's proximity to industrial sites,
major thoroughfares, and trolley
lines.
*Fritz B. Burns Collection,
Loyola Marymount University.*

Fritz Burns in his roadster in Los Angeles, circa 1923.
Fritz B. Burns Collection, Loyola Marymount University.

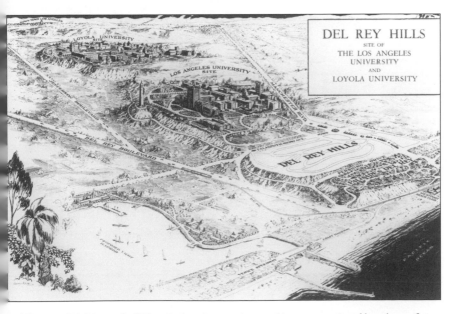

This 1928 Dickinson & Gillespie drawing was inserted into promotional brochures for
Palisades Del Rey and Del Rey Hills. Note the Pacific Electric streetcar running along
Del Rey Boulevard and the "proposed yacht harbor" in the foreground.
Fritz B. Burns Collection, Loyola Marymount University.

Fritz Burns with a promotional
poster for Windsor Hills, 1938.
Windsor Hills was Burns' first real
estate venture since the devastating
losses of the Depression, and also
marked his entry into home construction.
Fritz B. Burns Collection,
Loyola Marymount University.

A showman at heart, Fritz Burns never missed a chance to market the attractiveness of his developments. Here, "starlets" do some yard work at Fritz Burns' sales
office at Riverside Ranchos in Burbank, 1939.
Fritz B. Burns Collection, Loyola Marymount University.

Fritz Burns distributed "Fix It Yourself" to home buyers in Westchester during World War Two. The brochure offered advice on simple home repairs and encouraged new owners to improve the value of their new property.
Fritz B. Burns Collection, Loyola Marymount University.

"Unit #2" under construction at Toluca Wood in Burbank, 1941. Note the progression from simple foundations, far right, to completed homes, left-center. Fritz Burns has marked the locations of Warner Brothers and Columbia Studios, as well as his own subdivision, Riverside Ranchos. Barham Boulevard, top right, allowed quick access to Hollywood and Los Angeles.
Fritz B. Burns Collection, Loyola Marymount University.

Fritz Burns (left) and Fred Marlow (right) celebrate the completion of their five hundredth home at Westchester, 1943. Held in Fritz and Gladys Burns' home on June Street in Hancock Park, the party also featured Marlow–Burns investors. Gladys Burns is visible behind Marlow. Note the special guest at top left: Burns is apparently unable to get the monkey off his back.

Courtesy of Lynne Marlow.

Board of Directors meeting of the National Association of Home Builders, 1943. Burns (at far right), was president of the organization in 1943 and a driving force behind its creation. Many of the nation's well-known war builders are present, including Franklin Burns (sitting at far left), George Nixon (standing, third from left), Hugh Potter (hidden, sitting at table on left), Robert P. Gerholz (sitting, fifth from left), and Joseph Merrion (sitting, seventh from left). Next to Fritz Burns is Frank Cortwright, Executive Secretary of the organization.

Fritz B. Burns Collection, Loyola Marymount University.

Workmen roofing an entire street of homes in Westchester, 1943. J. Paul Campbell, the building contractor whose name appears on the truck, worked with
Burns for almost thirty years on his projects in California and Hawaii.

The "Dick" Whittington Collection, USC Regional History Center

Interior of the Kaiser Community Homes housing factory in Westchester, 1946.
Once assembled, these wall panels were hooked to an overhead monorail for
painting in another area of the factory. Note the completed panels ready to be
moved to the field in the shipping bay at top right.

From the "Dick" Whittington Collection,
courtesy of the Huntington Library, San Marino, California.

Gladys Burns christens the S.S. Loyola Victory, March 21, 1945, at Henry J. Kaiser's Permanente Metals Corporation shipyard in Richmond, California. Fritz Burns is behind Gladys, partially obscured by a ribbon. Two months later, Burns and Kaiser became partners in Kaiser Community Homes.

Courtesy of Frances Morehart.

Visitors line up for a tour of a model home at the Kaiser Community Homes development in North Hollywood, 1947. Burns arranged for local department stores such as Barker Brothers to furnish these models; for an extra fee, home buyers could have their new house furnished before occupancy.

*From the "Dick" Whittington Collection,
courtesy of the Huntington Library, San Marino, California.*

The "Home of Tomorrow," a remodeled version of the "Postwar House," garnered tremendous publicity when it opened in March 1951. Used by Burns to test and demonstrate housing innovations, the "Postwar House" and "Home of Tomorrow" attracted more than a million visitors.
Los Angeles Herald-Express, March 16, 1951, in the Hearst Collection, USC Regional History Center.

Fritz and Gladys Burns with Vice President Richard Nixon and his wife Pat at an Eisenhower reelection rally in Panorama City, 1956. Fritz Burns arranged for the rally to be held in the parking lot of the Panorama City Shopping Center. Note Burns' "I Like Ike" handkerchief.
Fritz B. Burns Collection, Loyola Marymount University.

Fritz Burns, Henry Kaiser, and architect Ed Bauer study plans for the Hawaiian Village Hotel, 1955. From seventy small cottages in the summer of 1955, the complex had grown by 1977 to over 1,800 rooms.
Fritz B. Burns Collection, Loyola Marymount University.

Henry Kaiser, bandleader Spike Jones, and Fritz Burns laugh at Kaiser's modest catch while fishing at Kaiser's Lake Tahoe home, circa 1955. Jones was one of many famous entertainers Burns and Kaiser hired to perform at the Hawaiian Village Hotel in its early years.
Fritz B. Burns Collection, Loyola Marymount University.

Fritz Burns and Conrad Hilton at the Hilton Hawaiian Village, 1963, two years after the creation of Hilton-Burns Hotels. Burns remained close friends with Conrad and, later, Barron Hilton for the rest of his life. He became Vice Chairman of Hilton Hotels in 1964.

Fritz B. Burns Collection, Loyola Marymount University.

F. Patrick Burns, Gladys Burns, and Fritz Burns with Jackie Akeo and Muriel Tani, performers, at the Hawaiian Village Hotel in 1957. Pat oversaw furnishings and décor for the hotel, and supervised his father's operations while Fritz and Gladys split their time between their homes in Kahala and Los Angeles.

Fritz B. Burns Collection, Loyola Marymount University.

The Wilshire Chamber of Commerce honored Fritz Burns & Associates in 1975. Pictured from left to right are N.S. "Bill" Ridgeway, Charles Getchell, two representatives of the Chamber, F. Patrick Burns, Fritz Burns, another Chamber representative, Carl Herziger, and Ken Skinner.
Courtesy of Ken Skinner.

Directors of the Fritz B. Burns Foundation with Fr. Thomas O'Malley, S.J., President of Loyola Marymount University, at Loyola Marymount in 1994. From left to right: J. Robert Vaughan, W.K. "Ken" Skinner, Fr. Thomas P. O'Malley, S.J., Richard Dunn, William H. Hannon, Edward F. Slattery, Joseph E. Rawlinson, and Donald Freeberg.
Courtesy of Ken Skinner.

CHAPTER SIX

Panorama City,
"Jewel Of The Valley"

"You might say I have three hobbies. Work, swimming, and
reindeer."   *Fritz Burns, 1965.*[1]

Occupying a thousand acres in the heart of the San Fernando Valley, the Panorama Ranch in 1947 was one of the
largest dairy farms in Southern California. The acreage had
been under almost continuous cultivation since the construction of the San Fernando Mission to the north by Spanish
missionaries a century and a half earlier. Like much of the
Valley, its fertile, loamy soil and arid climate were well-suited
to growing barley, corn, and alfalfa, especially after William
Mulholland completed the Los Angeles Aqueduct at
Owensmouth in 1913 and provided the Valley with a plentiful
water supply. Sheep and cattle were also raised on the land for
many years. Despite its location only fifteen miles from Hollywood, the Panorama Ranch was separated from developed
Los Angeles by both psychological and physical barriers.

The former existed due to a perception Burns had encoun-
tered years before at Westchester, that "the distance from one
place to another isn't measured in miles, but by the amount of
intervening vacant territory."[2] Aerial photos of the Panorama
Ranch in 1947 show the undeveloped nature of the surrounding land, and a bank appraisal of the property that same year
noted the Panorama Ranch's neighbors consisted largely of
scattered home sites and farms.[3] The various mini-cities and
communities to the east and west of the area were a patch-

work of isolated residential developments and agricultural operations often linked by nothing more than rutted dirt or gravel roads. A notable exception to the rule was Burbank, where the economic impact of Lockheed and associated industries had produced a residential boom and build-up before and during World War Two. The six-mile distance from the Panorama Ranch to Burbank, however, would appear much longer to any potential buyer who noticed that the major local traffic arteries, Van Nuys Boulevard and Woodman Avenue, were a dusty two-lane road and an unpaved ditch respectively. R.E. Driscoll, a Burns publicity aide who became a real estate broker in Panorama City, remembered eight years later that passersby in the early days of the development would lean out car windows and scoff, "Who's going to live in this deserted pasture?"[4]

The physical barrier separating the ranch and the San Fernando Valley from Los Angeles was more immediately obvious: the imposing bulwark of the Santa Monica mountains. Running the length of the southern border of the Valley, the mountain range prevented immediate access to Los Angeles except by a limited series of winding roads through steep, narrow canyons that were susceptible to mudslides and were hardly viable as automobile commuter routes. Easy automobile and streetcar access could be found only at the far east end of the Valley. "My first trip [to Panorama City] was on January 11, 1949, and I'll never forget it," remembered Ken Skinner, Burns' longtime associate and an accountant for Kaiser Community Homes during the construction of Panorama City. "It had snowed the night before, and there was a foot and a half of snow on the floor of the San Fernando Valley! My first attempt was to drive over Sepulveda Boulevard, but I was turned away because of ice. I then attempted Coldwater Canyon, Laurel Canyon, and all the other canyons, but was turned back. Eventually, I was successful when I attempted to drive over the Cahuenga Pass."[5]

The snowfall was an anomaly, but the relative inaccessibility of the area at the time made it an unattractive location for a commuter suburb and a likely financial quagmire for the brave developer who undertook such a project. The first sign of change was General Motors' announcement in 1945 that it had bought a hundred-acre cornfield to the south of Roscoe Boulevard for its new Chevrolet and Fisher body assembly plant. The plant, which would not open until February 1948, would be one million square feet at completion and would offer 1,500 new jobs. Two national brewing companies, Schlitz and Anheuser-Busch, soon followed with huge nearby facilities that employed over a thousand workers apiece.[6] The area began to take on the appearance of one of Burns' "white spots," ripe for residential development. Burns had been interested in the property even before he joined with Henry J. Kaiser to form Kaiser Community Homes, and had been meeting with the owners of the Panorama Ranch since August of 1944.[7] In the spring of 1946, Burns and Kaiser Community Homes began negotiating in earnest with the land's owners, the Pellissier family, to purchase a 411-acre parcel of the original Panorama Ranch. Frank Pellissier was still operating a dairy on the property, and was represented during negotiations by his nephew, Henri de Roulet, a land developer himself.[8]

A Bank of America appraisal of the property for Kaiser Community Homes in April of 1946 listed the assets of the Panorama Ranch to be its proximity to major highways and employment, its suburban atmosphere, and its potential for a "self-contained residential community," in language strikingly similar to that of KCH promotional materials for its contemporary developments. The appraisers also listed as liabilities inadequate public transportation and the area's sparse residential districts and farm sites. They appraised the value of the Panorama Ranch land at $2,240 an acre, almost $700 an acre below the Pellissiers' asking price. Burns authorized the purchase on the Pellissiers' terms, stressing his belief that the Panorama Ranch land was the best available for development at the time. He also realized the economic implications of the nearby General Motors plant under construction, as well as the attractive force of a huge new residential development itself on the surrounding area.[9]

In addition to the housing Kaiser Community Homes constructed in its own developments, mass housing projects of the KCH type also attracted independent developers who built on property adjacent to or nearby the initial work site. The reasons for this were numerous and readily apparent. A small, independent developer could take advantage of the marketing efforts, publicity, and customer recruitment programs paid for by a larger developer without the substantial investment required to draw interest to a new area. Even more appealing to the independent builder was the immediate establishment of value that necessarily accompanied a mass housing development. If Kaiser Community Homes announced it would be selling four hundred homes in a specific area for $9,000 apiece, for example, a local builder could safely assume a new development of twenty similar homes nearby could draw the same price per house. The reverse was also true, and Burns used it to his advantage. At the Kaiser Community Homes development in Ontario, California, a portion of the land was sold to private builders in advance of construction in order to determine what prices the local housing market would bear.[10]

The economic draw of a huge residential development proximate to a large number of well-paying, semi-skilled jobs was strong enough for Burns to gamble that other developers and industries would follow his company's advance in Panorama City. A letter from Burns' financial advisor and confidant Fred Pike to the Bank of America in 1952 demonstrated that Burns' gamble paid off almost immediately. The value of land surrounding the parcels that the Bank of America had appraised at $2,250 in 1946 had "skyrocketed," in Pike's words, to more than $5,000 per acre by 1952.[11]

In addition to their requested purchase price, the Pellissier family also received a 21.5 percent interest in both the residential and commercial development of Panorama City, with Kaiser Community Homes controlling the remaining 78.5 percent. The initial boundaries of the Panorama City development were Osborne Street to the north, Woodman Avenue to the east, Roscoe Boulevard to the south, and Van Nuys Boulevard and Vesper Avenue on the west. The commercial district comprised 75 acres along Van Nuys Boulevard terminating at Roscoe Boulevard. A second and far smaller commercial center was laid out on the Woodman Avenue side of the development as a neighborhood shopping center. The residential areas, which included both single-family homes as well as duplex units containing identical two-bedroom homes on larger streets, comprised the remainder of the original acreage. Kaiser Community Homes added to the initial 411-acre property in 1950 by purchasing 400 more acres south of Roscoe Boulevard for further residential development, with other private developers building on the surrounding raw acreage to fill out the geographic area now known as Panorama City, which is considerably larger than KCH's original development.[12]

At Panorama City, Burns was able to institute elements of his imagined "total community" to a degree not seen in his previous housing efforts. Reasons for this included the remote location of Panorama City, the freedom of its planners to design the development free of preexisting structures, and the relatively large size of the holding in comparison to other KCH developments. Eleven acres at the center of the residential development were deeded to the City of Los Angeles for a playground and elementary school, while other parcels were sold at cost to churches and private schools. Burns recognized that he was neither required nor expected to donate the public school property, but considered it a fundamental element in a successful planned community. In a later speech on private housing, Burns framed such donations as a personal concern: "We give a school site now and then...that's something every [developer] must decide for himself."[13]

The Community Church of Brethren, Panorama Presbyterian Church, Panorama Baptist Church, Calvary Lutheran Church, and St. Genevieve Catholic Church were among a dozen churches to take advantage of the low cost of land in the new community, and the latter three all also built schools adjacent to their houses of worship.[14] Civic groups also received donations of commercially-zoned land. Single-acre plots bordering on all major avenues and the commercial area were designated as "greenbelts" to isolate the commercial center's noise and car traffic from residential areas. These properties were initially used as chicken ranches for the first few years of the development. As the value of the land increased, the greenbelt areas were eventually used to build higher-density apartments.[15]

Burns also took an active interest in the affairs of the community and retained close ties with many of its business owners and residents after completion of construction. A Kaiser Community Homes sales office was donated to the nascent Chamber of Commerce, and the company offered a ten percent discount for Kaiser Community Homes employees who purchased houses in Panorama City. The popularity of the latter program meant that a significant portion of the new residents had played a part in building the community, including salesmen, construction workers, and office personnel. Many became leading figures in Panorama City civic life. Several KCH salesmen and commercial leasing agents headed the Panorama City Chamber of Commerce and a local coordinating council for civic groups for a number of years after the development was completed.[16]

Burns himself sponsored a local "Pee Wee" baseball team, the "Panorama City Shoppers," which competed against teams from around the nation and even played a match in the Los Angeles Coliseum.[17] He also sponsored local YMCA fundraising drives and maintained a visible presence at Panorama City's business establishments. With friends and family, Burns frequented "Phil Ahn's Moongate," a Chinese restaurant that became a "see-and-be-seen" social spot for area residents.[18] During Dwight Eisenhower's 1956 reelection campaign, Fritz and Gladys Burns arranged a Republican rally for Vice President Richard Nixon and his wife Pat in the Panorama City Shopping Center parking lot. Burns became a recognizable face to the area's early residents, and press clippings listed him as the "Dean of Panorama City."[19]

In 1948, Fritz and Gladys Burns purchased the nearby Griffith Ranch in the northern San Fernando Valley for use as a weekend retreat. Later, Burns turned the ranch, the one-time locale for D.W. Griffith's 1915 film *Birth Of A Nation*, into a free picnic and recreation spot for area residents. It became a popular leisure spot in the San Fernando Valley, hosting community fairs, charity benefits, and political gatherings for a number of years.

When his stepson Ed Scheller expressed interest in drag racing, Burns also converted land he owned near the Ranch, adjacent to the San Fernando Airport, into a free public racing strip. The strip soon drew more than five thousand racing enthusiasts on Sunday afternoons to cheer on over three hundred drivers who competed in time trials. Both the picnic area at the Griffith Ranch and the drag racing strip soon became San Fernando Valley institutions for families moving into the dozens of suburban developments that were soon built around Panorama City. Because so many baby-boom children became teenagers simultaneously in the Valley (and in other large suburban developments), teenage delinquency was a constant and oft-mentioned local concern. Burns' drag strip earned him accolades from the press for providing Valley youngsters with alternatives to juvenile crime.[20]

The task of marketing Panorama City to prospective buyers offered Fritz Burns the chance for the most dramatic promotion of his career. He was a close friend of Art Linkletter, a famous radio personality and the host of the popular show, "People Are Funny." In cooperation with officials at the radio show, Lockheed Aircraft, the Committee for American Remittances (CARE), and Henry Kaiser's auto plant in Willow Run, Michigan, Kaiser Community Homes offered a new home in Panorama City, a new 1948 Kaiser-Frazer sedan, and a good job at Lockheed's Burbank plant to the winner of a letter-writing campaign to "want-ridden Europeans" on the benefits of democracy. The final winner was selected from weekly contestants who were brought to the "People Are Funny" studio in Hollywood to solve a cryptic on-air riddle for millions of listeners.

The genius of the "People Are Funny" promotion lay in the details. The featured employer, Lockheed, was sure to be a major source of work for the residents of Panorama City's initial two thousand homes, and the company's participation in the contest reminded listeners that the promised new community would have plentiful jobs for homeowners nearby. The Kaiser-Frazer sedan advertised Henry Kaiser's own automotive efforts, which challenged Detroit's production and solid market share. The car also suggested a suburban lifestyle as yet unseen by millions of veterans who had been fed images of a postwar America of prosperous suburban homeowners. Finally, the patriotic tone of the promotion itself contrasted "want-ridden" Europe with the advantages of being a good American and living in a suburban development. Burns had long stressed the relationship between home ownership and responsible citizenship, and the contest offered a chance to sell the point to an audience of millions. Over half a million listeners around the nation entered, unaware that Burns and Kaiser had not built a single home in Panorama City when the contest was launched.

To participate, contestants were required to submit ten cents and a hundred-word letter on the benefits of a democracy. Writers of exemplary letters were chosen to appear on the weekly program, while the letters and the relief aid purchased with the CARE money were sent to Italy by the State Department for election propaganda against communist candidates in that country. At the show's Hollywood studio, Art Linkletter asked each contestant to solve the following riddle, offering as the only clue that the answer was a place-name:

> Big Chief Windbag, gloomy and gay,
> I'm one over many that lie in decay.
> Where may I be found?
> Upon low ground . . .
> That's all, that's all I will say.

Thirty weeks passed before Vivienne George, a 31-year old from Lebanon, Oregon, solved the riddle. George and her husband Ward, a disabled war veteran who was training to be a nurseryman, had been living on his disability pension and various odd jobs she picked up in the small town. Vivienne was trying to break into journalism, which she had studied at Oregon State College. Like any good journalist, she was trained to end her articles with "30," a notation to signify to editors that a story was complete. Recognizing that the last line of the riddle, "that's all, that's all I will say" could be rephrased as "30, 30," she checked maps and found that Cairo, Egypt lay near the intersection of thirty degrees longitude and thirty degrees latitude. Furthermore, the word "Cairo" contained "air," making it a "windbag" of sorts, and the city lay on ancient ruins at a relatively low elevation.

George's on-air triumph was followed several days later by a visit to her prize, complete with a helicopter ride with Burns over the area so she could get a sense of how the completed neighborhood would look. As with the first completed KCH home and with the move-in of forty families in Westchester, Burns alerted the media and general public to the event, and a curious crowd saw Burns and Art Linkletter hand Vivienne George the keys to her new three-bedroom home with a two-car garage. Burns then took her on a tour of her house, and the Kaiser Community Homes press release reported Mrs. George's happy response: "I'll be eternally grateful for Cairo, Egypt." Her husband came down several days later and posed for more pictures with their new house and car, and Kaiser Community Homes officials erected a large sign for curious passersby identifying the home as "the house won by Mrs. George."[21]

Ward and Vivienne George lived in their new house for less than a year before they sold it to one of Burns' salesmen, but they exemplified the type of customer Burns was trying to reach at Panorama City. The development was aimed to attract war veterans (and their families) of moderate income who were seeking a tranquil, suburban lifestyle near enough to jobs to be convenient but removed from the congestion of America's urban centers. Promotional materials for Panorama City used carefully crafted language and pictures to reach this market. Panorama City was simultaneously "rustic" but "scientifically planned," "traditional" but "modern." The area was described as "surrounded by majestic mountain ranges and the verdant and colorful gardens of the Valley," while brochures noted that "over one hundred new precision, aircraft and industrial plants, in addition to five major motion picture studios, are within a fifteen minute radius of Panorama City."[22]

Marketing materials also stressed Henry Kaiser's national reputation for record-breaking construction, and declared "Henry J. Kaiser achievements have always been identified with large-scale operations." Over two thousand Kaiser Community Homes workers were building eighteen miles of sewers, twenty-five miles of sidewalks, twenty-two miles of curbs, and over two million square feet of paving in the new community. Burns repeatedly stressed that Panorama City was to be an entirely new community for a new generation of first-time homeowners.

Despite the severe postwar housing shortage in urban areas, Burns' salesmen initially had trouble selling homes in Panorama City. Once the initial excitement surrounding Mrs. George's prize home died down, the lines of customers on Van Nuys Boulevard grew shorter and shorter. On the winding streets behind the anxious salesmen, Kaiser Community Homes personnel were constructing two thousand homes that were suddenly in danger of going unsold. "We went a little bit fast," Burns told a reporter years later. "At one point we had eight hundred unsold homes on our hands."[23] In addition to the problems caused by Panorama City's relative isolation, the stream of war veterans purchasing homes began to dry up as the nation experienced an economic downturn in 1949. Inflation had also caused home prices to rise. By the time Panorama City officially opened in 1948, homes in the development were selling from $9,195 for a two-bedroom home to $10,150 to $10,850 for a three-bedroom home. Duplexes, featuring identical twin two-bedroom units, were selling for $15,950. These higher prices meant that war veterans who were able to purchase a home with a $290 down payment one year earlier needed $500 plus loan costs in December 1948.

The entry of the United States into the Korean War eventually boosted the sagging housing market at Panorama City, when local manufacturers and military industries increased production and the demand for worker housing increased. For the first few months after the development opened, however, the salesmen had to work without the long waiting lists and eager prospects that had characterized other Kaiser Community Homes projects. Burns asked his sales manager, William

Hannon, to reestablish the morning sales lecture that had been the hallmark of Burns' sales operations earlier in his career. Once a week, Burns arrived to deliver the morning pitch himself. Herb Lightfoot, a World War Two veteran, had visited Panorama City looking for a house in 1949 and had instead been hired by Hannon as a salesman. "It was all but a Depression there in 1949, and selling slowed down considerably," Lightfoot remembered. "We had to do whatever we could to get a commitment from people. We didn't need the down payment right away, only a deposit to hold the house. We would take anything for that deposit—pink slips on cars, pink slips on boats, you name it. I remember there were plenty of times you would get someone who didn't have the money for a deposit but qualified for the G.I. loan, and you'd just lend him the $35 commission you'd get for securing the sale, and you'd get paid back later."[24]

Herb Lightfoot set the individual record for Kaiser Community Homes salesmen at Panorama City by selling 23 homes on a single Sunday. His efforts and those of the zealous sales force were buttressed by further marketing and showmanship on the company's part. Large floodlights blazed until late at night at the work site and allowed prospects to "let the supper dishes go" to visit the development in the evening if work prevented a day trip. Fifteen separate model homes were open at one point in Panorama City, five of them fully furnished and two more left deliberately unfinished with plumbing, framing, and electrical systems visible.[25]

As in other Fritz Burns and Kaiser Community Homes developments, building economies were realized by making every house at Panorama City almost identical, though three-bedroom units incorporated a slightly larger floorplan. All construction was done in the field, with the isolated nature of the development during early construction facilitating on-site storage and fabrication of parts. Burns again employed the "fundamental variables" used in his other developments to give each house an individual look within its block. Below-cost shrubbery sales and his "Keeping Up With The Joneses" brochures encouraged new owners to give each house an individual character.[26] Kaiser Community Homes also rebuffed concerns that developments such as Panorama City sacrificed architectural taste and complexity for a less expensive but plainer, "cookie-cutter" approach, suggesting that the predetermined nature of such communities held architectural benefits for new residents. "A common criticism of established neighborhoods in American cities is that they exhibit too much variety in style and actually are a patchwork of clashing designs," claimed a Kaiser Community Homes press release. "The principles used by Kaiser Community Homes might be termed a system of 'controlled variations' under which expert architects assure that the variety is tasteful and definitely an enhancement to the community. It is as if the individual buyer of a low-cost Kaiser home had the benefit of an architectural commission such as passes on house plans in high-cost residential areas."[27]

Those who did purchase homes at Panorama City were from the exact demographic group Burns and bank appraisers had predicted. Almost all were veterans, and many worked at the General Motors plant a quarter of a mile down Van Nuys Boulevard, or at Lockheed's vast operations in Burbank. Other large-scale employers in the area included the Schlitz and Anheuser-Busch breweries, a Carnation laboratory and production facility, and the Rocketdyne division of North American Aviation.[28] Unexpectedly, entertainment industry stars enjoyed the community's proximity to Burbank and Hollywood. Residents saw their share of movie stars in the late 1940s and early 1950s, and Herb Lightfoot remembered seeing stars such as Clark Gable driving past the salesmen every day on their way to the studios.[29] Liberace and his mother shared a Panorama City home for a time, and

Jane Russell also was a resident for several years. The entertainment industry also provided moderate-income jobs for
many more homeowners in Panorama City.

Young couples were the predominant demographic, with
the result that Panorama City's homes remained perpetually
under construction. Growing households required new bedrooms, larger living spaces, patios, and other improvements
to the basic two- and three-bedroom homes. These improvements could sometimes lead to unexpected discoveries, as
when contractors dug holes for swimming pools. "There had
been a terrible epidemic of hoof-and-mouth disease at the
Panorama Dairy a few years previous," Lightfoot remembered, "and the herd had been decimated. The carcasses had
just been buried a few feet under the ground, and there were
certain areas that, wherever you dug, you'd eventually come
across a big pile of bones."[30] Despite such surprises, records
for the first years of Panorama City showed that between
thirty and sixty improvement permits were issued every
month, as new owners expanded their basic homes to fit their
growing needs.[31]

Despite his primary focus on home construction, Burns
also held ambitious plans for commercial development in
Panorama City. He envisioned the seventy-five acres of commercial property on Van Nuys Boulevard as a mix between a
neighborhood shopping center and a regional catchment
area for the spending power of his own homes as well as the
as-yet-undeveloped areas around Panorama City. By 1956, it
was clear that the Panorama City Shopping Center would
vastly exceed those early expectations. In its heyday, the district was the economic heart of the San Fernando Valley and
a commercial dynamo that supported over eighty retail stores
and some of Los Angeles' first major department stores.
Because of its central location in the Valley as well as the
sheer volume of sales and stores, shopping at the Panorama
City Shopping Center became by the late 1950s and 1960s a

shared experience of San Fernando Valley residents, who made it their virtual downtown.

Stimulus for the commercial center's development was provided by the million-dollar Panorama Market, which opened in May 1950 under the guidance of Carl Herziger, a longtime Burns associate who served as owner's representative for Kaiser Community Homes developments. Designed by architect Arthur Froelich, the 63,000-square-foot building was of a colossal size for a neighborhood convenience store and served as a clear indication that Burns, Fred Bauersfeld, and leasing agent Bill Ridgeway had ambitious plans for the commercial center. The Market was also one of the only early properties that were not owned outright by Kaiser Community Homes. In most cases the company created a unified marketing effort and financial structure for the center by leasing buildings constructed by the company itself. "Panorama City Market becomes a monumental attraction for consumers of goods of all lines, as it creates a constant traffic flow—the lifeline of successful retail business," Burns commented at the Market's grand opening. "To neighboring business establishments, the Market brings assurances of fulfilled expectations."[32]

Burns' prediction proved accurate within three years, when a Bank of America branch, a Thrifty drug store, Security-First National Bank, and dozens of other smaller businesses moved into Panorama City. In October 1955, a Broadway Valley department store fully four times the size of the Panorama Market served as the centerpiece for an elaborate staged event in which seven new stores simultaneously opened their doors.[33] That year marked the first time retail sales in the San Fernando Valley surpassed those of the downtown commercial district.[34] The huge new Broadway store, a forerunner of "anchor" stores in malls, was followed over the next six years by major department stores for J.W. Robinson, Ohrbach's, and Montgomery Ward, as well as San

Fernando Valley headquarters for Western Airlines and Coast Federal Savings. In 1961, the first phase of a $20 million office building development opened on the corner of Van Nuys Boulevard and Titus Street, and included two thirteen-story buildings flanking a twenty-story tower.[35]

As freeways pushed into the Valley after 1955, the commercial district benefited further from its central location. Roscoe Boulevard was an exit for both the Golden State Freeway (5) and Hollywood Freeway (170) to the east and the San Diego Freeway (405) to the west, while Van Nuys Boulevard connected via off-ramps to the Ventura Freeway (101) to the south and the Golden State Freeway to the north. In addition, Parthenia Street brought southbound traffic from Sepulveda Boulevard directly to the shopping center.[36] From the beginning, Burns had set aside considerable acreage for parking, a much-advertised feature designed to distinguish Panorama City from its commercial counterparts throughout the area. By 1965, the Center could provide on-site parking for more than five thousand cars. The acreage devoted to parking is a testament to the size of the market Panorama City was serving, far larger than the 65,000 population of the immediate surrounding area.[37]

One of the Panorama City Shopping Center's biggest success stories, Ed Hogan's Pleasant Hawaiian Holidays, came to the community a few years after the commercial center was largely completed. Hogan brought a small travel agency from Point Pleasant, New Jersey, to Panorama City in 1962. He gave Fritz Burns and members of Burns' organizations much of the credit for his early success, calling him "a guiding light" who helped him make the company a multi-million dollar operation. In 1962, Burns arranged for Hogan to rent the former Panorama City Chamber of Commerce building in the commercial center for his business. The building was perfect for a travel agency, Burns noted, "because it has great conspicuosity [sic]."[38]

After introducing Hogan to members of the local Rotary Club and Chamber of Commerce, Burns offered him a deal. In exchange for Hogan's periodic advice and feedback on the tourist industry and economic conditions in Hawaii when Burns needed it, Burns would rent him the building for $250 a month. This business strategy also involved expenses for Burns that Hogan didn't discover until years later. "He would call me and ask me how things were doing in Hawaii, what was happening, and I would give him reports," Hogan remembered. "It was sort of my consulting job for my low rent. But I later learned that he put about $7,500 into fixing the [new office] up... he had the Heath Company come out and put a Tiki god up on the top of it, and I told him 'I really like everything about it, but I think what I'd rather have up there is a post that shows the mileage to Hawaii, to France, to everywhere, because I'll be selling trips all over.' And he said 'Well, all right, that seems like a good idea,' and he paid for the whole thing."[39]

Hogan eventually expanded his Panorama City operations to other Burns properties as a tenant, and his connections with the Panorama City Chamber of Commerce led to booming sales for his Hawaii and Europe travel packages. The company grew rapidly over the next two decades and became one of the world's most successful travel companies, with over $400 million in yearly sales in 1999.

While Burns' assistance to business owners such as Hogan helped them on an individual level, the Panorama City commercial center as a whole struggled financially during its first year of operation. To draw customers from a larger area and increase publicity for the center, Burns conceived a now-famous marketing ploy which not only gave an economic boost to his business tenants, but became an annual ritual for thousands of families in the San Fernando Valley: visiting Santa and his reindeer at the Panorama City Shopping Center's Christmas celebration. Burns first established his yuletide extravaganza in Panorama City in 1953. In a meeting with the merchants' association, Burns discovered that among the many decorations at the shopping center would be reindeer—but they would be artificial. Cardboard reindeer hardly befitted a man of his reputation for elaborate marketing schemes, and Burns took matters into his own hands. He purchased six white fallow deer from a herd kept at the San Simeon estate of deceased publishing mogul William Randolph Hearst, and set up a seven-acre compound at his Griffith Ranch in San Fernando for their upkeep until the holiday season. The animals, each no larger than a goat, were remarkably similar to the flying, sleigh-pulling reindeer of myth on account of their large antlers and white fur.[40]

A select number of the deer were brought yearly to the Panorama City Shopping Center and placed on display in cages that allowed children close access to the tame animals. Adding mountains of fake snow, thousands of lights, giant white fir trees, an actor playing Santa Claus, and a red nose for the lead reindeer, "Rudolph," Burns found himself the creator of a genuine suburban tradition. Families from throughout the San Fernando Valley made the yearly trip to shop at Panorama City, and a visit to see Fritz Burns' reindeer became a Christmastime ritual. Soon Burns was also sending reindeer to shopping centers throughout the Los Angeles area. The reindeer even showed up at the corner of Wilshire and Highland atop the Home of Tomorrow, which Burns converted into his business offices after 1956. When Gladys Burns was named a delegate to the 1964 Republican convention, she and Fritz organized a rally and picnic for Barry Goldwater's campaign for President at the Griffith Ranch, offering supporters the chance to "put in a good word for Christmas with Rudolph."[41]

Unbeknownst to Burns at the time, the docile creatures

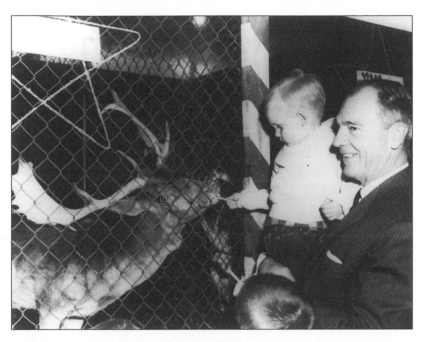

Fritz Burns and an unidentified youngster feed "Rudolph" a candy cane at Panorama City's yuletide celebration, 1959. Visiting the annual display of reindeer became a San Fernando Valley tradition for many families.
Fritz B. Burns Collection, Loyola Marymount University.

approached reproduction with the same fervor with which they pulled Santa's sleigh. The original six reindeer soon numbered more than a hundred, then two hundred, then four hundred by 1965. In addition to becoming a burdensome expense, the reindeer were overflowing their enclosure at the Griffith Ranch. After the Sylmar earthquake in February, 1971 caused portions of the five-foot retaining wall around the Griffith Ranch to collapse, a large number of the animals momentarily escaped into the surrounding streets and hills. Adding to the problem was a battle with the Internal Revenue Service over whether the reindeer constituted a legitimate business or a hobby. Burns advertised around the nation, seeking charities willing to take the reindeer off his hands. "They went all over the United States," Burns' associate Joe Rawlinson remembered, but even that wasn't depleting the herd fast enough. "The Mayor of Nagoya, Japan, came over and the Mayor of Los Angeles donated them in Burns' name. Some went to Ferdinand Marcos, then president of the Philippines, for use in their park."[42] Not until the late 1970s was Burns finally able to dispose of the last of the reindeer by giving them to zoos throughout the nation.[43]

By 1952, Kaiser Community Homes had completed its residential building program. Despite its nervous first few months, Panorama City had eventually proved to be a financial success, with Kaiser Community Homes realizing a profit of over $1,000 a house in residential sales. Due to onerous federal tax laws on excess profit and the steep cost of acquiring more land for residential development in the Panorama City area, Kaiser Community Homes concentrated all its efforts on the commercial center after completing residential building in 1952. A year earlier, Henry J. Kaiser and Eugene Trefethen had decided to suspend further land acquisitions or home construction operations.[44] The homes of Panorama City were the last of over eight thousand built under the aegis of Kaiser Community Homes and the end of Kaiser's venture into the mass housing field, though Kaiser and Burns would remain partners in commercial ventures for many years. Upon the completion of the Woodman Avenue tract of Panorama City in 1952, Burns absorbed the majority of the construction and administrative personnel of Kaiser Community Homes into his ongoing building operations in Los Angeles, and all company profits were plowed back into the increasingly successful Panorama City Shopping Center.[45]

In addition to its financial success, Panorama City also

gained widespread accolades from building and civic groups around the nation as a model for planned communities. As the importance of Panorama City to the development of the San Fernando Valley became more apparent in the years after its completion, Burns found himself the recipient of numerous honors. *Life Magazine* ran a feature on Panorama City in 1949 and again eight years later, and the National Association of Real Estate Boards named Panorama City the winner of its "Best Neighborhood Development" competition for 1949.[46]

After his success with Panorama City, Burns was also honored in 1953 by the Los Angeles chapter of the Building Contractors Association as "Builder of the Year." The award ceremony at the Biltmore Hotel drew over six hundred guests, including the Director of the Federal Housing Administration, the loan guarantee officer of the Veteran's Administration, a number of Los Angeles City Council members and County Supervisors, and high-ranking officials from the savings and loan, construction, and real estate industries. This honor was followed two years later by a "Man of Achievement" in 1955 from the Los Angeles Chamber of Commerce.[47] The awards Burns received in this period recognized a lifetime of achievement in the home building field, both as a developer and a national representative for the home building industry. These notices also praised Panorama City as the epitome of sound planning and community building.

Burns' partner, Henry J. Kaiser, added his own tribute when he congratulated Burns in a 1955 advertisement in the *Los Angeles Examiner*: "We are happy to take this opportunity to pay tribute to the man whose vision, civic awareness, and building integrity has helped to create this 'city within a city'." The ultimate accolade came in the form of a three-part series in the *Los Angeles Mirror* in 1952 on Burns' career and accomplishments. Surveying the three decades in Los Angeles real estate that led to such a widely recognized triumph as Panorama City, the paper bestowed upon Burns a title that reflected his newly prominent role as one of the nation's top community builders, "Mr. Housing, U.S.A."[48]

CHAPTER SEVEN

The Los Angeles Housing Debate

"The trend in this country towards socialized housing is appalling, and must be combated with every resource we can possibly command."   *Fritz Burns, 1952.*[1]

Long before the construction and sale of Panorama City was complete, Fritz Burns began planning larger operations in housing construction, as well as embracing a newfound political activism. Starting in 1949, he expanded his home-building operations for future mass housing developments in North Hollywood and in "West Westchester," on land he owned west of Lincoln Boulevard in Westchester. Neither were Kaiser Community Homes projects, though many of the personnel were former KCH employees, and Burns again used a variation of the home designs from Kaiser Community Homes. In addition, the extraordinary success of Panorama City's commercial center had convinced Burns to build or expand shopping centers in San Jose, Pasadena, and Westchester. Overshadowing all these enterprises, however, was Burns' leading role in the controversy over the future of public housing, both in Los Angeles and throughout the nation. Burns' fight against public housing occupied much of his focus for half a decade, a time in which he traveled, debated, and lobbied extensively on behalf of the private housing industry nationwide.

Despite a Republican majority in both the Senate and the House of Representatives after 1946 and a Cold War political

climate increasingly hostile towards large government programs, United States President Harry Truman made an
extension of the New Deal a hallmark of his first term and a
feature of his reelection campaign in 1948. Truman saw an
amelioration of the postwar housing shortage as a top priority for war veterans and a popular issue around the nation.
His administration had enacted the Veteran's Emergency
Housing Program (VEHP) in 1946, regulating rents, home
prices, and the allocation of scarce building materials, and
authorizing loans to builders of prefabricated housing (such
as Kaiser Community Homes) in order to meet the nation's
housing needs. For builders such as Fritz Burns, the VEHP
offered a mixed bag of inducements and restrictions on business. On the one hand, the program had provided a crucial
flow of restricted building materials and government financing to mass builders in the postwar period, and facilitated the
operations of Kaiser Community Homes. On the other
hand, rent controls and a strict ceiling of $10,000 on home
prices created a cap on the booming market for single-family
homes and apartments.[2]

From 1946 until the election of 1948, the Truman Administration struggled to pass a comprehensive housing program that would please the plethora of constituencies
holding an important stake in the nation's housing policy.
The Republican majority in Congress as well as real estate
and building groups such as Burns' National Association of
Home Builders (NAHB) sought increased government
funds for mortgage guarantees. They also strongly opposed
any comprehensive public housing program for the middle-
class workers who had proved such a large and lucrative
market for postwar mass housing developments. Arrayed
against them and favoring a large new public housing program by the federal government were the majority of the
nation's unions, social reformers, big-city mayors, and a
majority of veterans' groups.[3]

Truman made the housing crisis a prominent issue in his reelection campaign and put the onus on the Republican party for hindering efforts to build new housing and to eradicate slums in America's urban areas. Scholars have suggested that public housing may have been the issue that brought Truman victory in the closely contested election over Thomas Dewey and allowed the Democrats to recapture both houses of Congress in 1948.[4] Those opposing public housing moderated their position, and a compromise housing bill sponsored by Republican Robert A. Taft and Democrats Robert Wagner and Allan Ellender was signed into law as the National Housing Act of 1949.[5]

The Act represented a compromise not only between conflicting economic interests, but also between widely disparate philosophies on the role the federal government should play in solving the nation's postwar housing crisis and rebuilding America's slums. Private builders received a liberalization of FHA mortgage terms as well as guaranteed minimum profits for large apartment complexes that met FHA regulations, an affirmation of their role in the implementation of national housing policy. Over a billion dollars was also allocated for slum clearance and urban redevelopment programs, an issue that had received bipartisan support. The Act, however, also authorized subsidies to local housing authorities to fund the construction of over 800,000 units of public housing, an amount in excess of the 700,000 wartime units approved by the Lanham Act against which Burns had campaigned so heavily.[6]

Private builders and realty organizations, including the National Association of Home Builders, the National Association of Real Estate Boards (NAREB), and the United States Savings and Loan League, allied with politically conservative politicians and trade groups after the passage of the National Housing Act. Shifting focus to the local level, these groups fought for the elimination or marginalization of new

public housing projects in favor of additional assistance for
private builders. In addition to a liberalization of FHA lending policies that had allowed builders such as Kaiser Community Homes to fund large-scale single-family housing
developments with federally guaranteed mortgages, they also
sought to preserve the large veteran housing market for private builders.[7]

As founder and former president of the NAHB, an influential voice in NAREB, and a member of trade groups such
as the National Association of Manufacturers (NAM), Fritz
Burns assumed a major role in the battle for private housers'
interests in the politically charged national housing debate
after 1949. His efforts on behalf of the industry were an
extension of Burns' wartime campaign against federally constructed war worker housing. In the early 1950s, however,
Burns made a marked departure from the tactics of his earlier
campaign, which had focused on national organization and
governmental lobbying efforts. After 1949 he added a new
focus and donned the mantle of Los Angeles' most outspoken opponent to the specific local housing construction programs authorized by the National Housing Act.

Though Gladys Burns was a member of the conservative
John Birch Society, Fritz Burns had continued to avoid close
ties to any political movements because of his concern over
the impact on housing sales if he alienated large segments of
the purchasing public. His public opposition to Los Angeles'
public housing programs demonstrated a clear break from
this policy. Any perception that he was hampering efforts to
eliminate the local housing shortage risked alienating war
veterans, the primary customers for middle-class homes.
Despite a conservative attitude toward issues with the potential taint of socialism in the early years of the Cold War, the
veterans' lobby nonetheless had embraced public housing as
the most effective solution to America's housing crisis by
1949. As a result, his outspoken criticism of a program

designed in part to provide housing for veterans carried professional and political risks for Burns.[8]

Events in Burns' personal life also played a role in his decision to devote so much time to the public housing struggle. Fred Pike, his close friend and financial advisor, was growing increasingly sick from cancer in the early 1950s and died in September 1952. Pike had worked in close concert on all Burns' projects since Windsor Hills in 1937, based on one- and five-year business plans they created for the future of their building operations. Pike was also one of a number of Burns' employees who had become senior directors in the hierarchy of Kaiser Community Homes. Pike's widow, Winifred Cockey, was also a longtime employee and returned to work for Burns after her husband's death. She remembered the powerful effect Pike's death had on Burns: "The loss of Fred meant a great deal to Mr. Burns, both from a personal standpoint and a business one. He was sort of at loose ends, and when I went back to work for him, he admitted that he would like to take a year or two off and get collected before he embarked on any future [housing] projects."[9]

Burns' observations of housing conditions in postwar Europe also contributed to his decision to campaign against public housing programs. "I continue to think of public housing," he wrote to Cockey from a realtors' convention in Paris in June of 1954. "In England there is no longer any hope. It has been accepted as a way of life. The only issue at election time revolves around which candidate favors more liberal subsidies . . . I wish every congressman and senator could see London and Paris. Then at least they could go home and vote honestly as to whether or not they want socialized housing as a national institution for everyone."[10]

On the local level, Burns was joined in the fight against public housing by the National Apartment Owners Association, the local chapter of the Home Builders' Association, the Small Property Owners League, and the Los Angeles

Chamber of Commerce. Prominent Southern California businessmen, including Burns and lawyer Frederick Dockweiler, organized this coalition under the aegis of "The Committee Against Socialist Housing (CASH)." Other allies in Los Angeles included the two local newspapers controlled by the Chandler family, the *Los Angeles Mirror* and *Los Angeles Times*, and the two Hearst papers, the *Herald and Express* and *Examiner*. The *Times* especially enjoyed a degree of political influence in Los Angeles unprecedented for a metropolitan daily, due in large part to the political connections and economic involvement of the Chandler family in Los Angeles. The anti-public housing forces also counted as eventual allies eight Los Angeles City Council members out of a total of fifteen.[11]

Local proponents of public housing in Los Angeles included all of the city's major unions, veterans' organizations, the League of Women Voters, the NAACP, and the Los Angeles Urban League. Their most visible representatives remained Los Angeles Mayor Fletcher Bowron, Howard Holtzendorff and Frank Wilkinson of the City Housing Authority, and, in the early stages, the Los Angeles City Council.[12] A number of church and civic groups also publicly campaigned for public housing, such as the Citizen's Housing Council, directed by Monsignor Thomas J. O'Dwyer, then the director of hospitals and health for the Archdiocese of Los Angeles. Adding another twist to an already complicated picture, Fritz Burns and Monsignor O'Dwyer served together at the time on the board of St. Anne's Maternity Hospital, a home for pregnant single women with which Fritz and Gladys Burns were heavily involved. O'Dwyer and Holtzendorff had also both worked with Burns on a 1945 report for the State of California on postwar housing needs.[13]

Immediately after the passage of the National Housing Act, Mayor Bowron and a unanimous Los Angeles City Council sought authorization in October 1950 for ten thousand rental units to be built over a period of four years in Los Angeles at a total cost of over $110 million. Los Angeles was the first city in the nation to take advantage of the new legislation. Bowron advertised the allocation as a serendipitous "something for nothing" windfall for the city. Frank Wilkinson and the City Housing Authority were charged with finding sites for the new units throughout Los Angeles. The centerpiece of the program was to be Elysian Park Heights, an expansive development in Chavez Ravine to house 17,000 people in a total of 3,364 units.[14]

Chavez Ravine became the focus of the public housing program for a number of reasons, chief among them being its 230-acre size, its central location (a mile from the Civic Center) and the poor housing conditions of the existing population. A vibrant community of Mexican and Chinese residents occupied Chavez Ravine at the time, though city planners and private builders alike condemned the area as a slum for its substandard housing, inadequate plumbing, and high incidence of vermin and disease.[15] The City Housing Authority condemned the property and cleared the houses in Chavez Ravine by the end of 1951, though some residents refused the condemnation appraisals and continued to live on the property for a number of years.[16]

Architects Robert Alexander and Richard Neutra designed the Elysian Park Heights project, which would have accounted for fully a third of the ten thousand units planned for Los Angeles upon completion. Fritz Burns was familiar with both: Neutra was a leading modernist architect who had designed the highly praised Channel Heights public housing development in San Pedro during World War Two, and Alexander had distinguished himself as a young architect with the design of a private development, Baldwin Hills Village, in 1937. Baldwin Hills Village was built on the very site of the 1932 Olympic Village from which a nearly bankrupt Burns had purchased cottages almost two decades earlier.[17]

Like many architects of public housing in the 1950s and 1960s, Alexander and Neutra both drew inspiration from the Radiant City "tower in the park" architectural theories of French architect Le Corbusier. They proposed a total of twenty-four thirteen-story towers situated throughout Elysian Park Heights, with an additional 163 two-story structures placed at their base as garden apartments. Individual apartments featured a wide range in size from 481 one-bedroom apartments to 18 five-bedroom units. Neutra also included elements of community planning in the project and set aside property for three schools, three churches, an outdoor auditorium, community facilities and meeting rooms, and a small commercial section. In response to criticism that the towers would introduce a population density far in excess of Los Angeles' historical housing patterns, Neutra commented, "the area cannot be redeveloped with suburban bungalows."[18]

The City Council approved the Chavez Ravine project along with ten other sites in Los Angeles in November 1950 by a vote of 12-1. Within a year, a number of Council members had switched sides, complaining that some of the projects were to be built on open land instead of replacing existing slums, and that Neutra's thirteen-story towers for Chavez Ravine had been later inserted into the plans without their knowledge.[19] By September of 1951, *Los Angeles Times* headlines warned against the menace of "creeping socialism" and asked, "Where's the housing shortage?"[20] A public hearing on December 26, 1951, on the future of the program drew a large public audience that overflowed Council chambers. By a vote of 8-7, the Council voted to cancel the program. Councilman Ed Davenport provided the decisive vote to halt the program, despite his previous consistent support of public housing. This sudden change of heart later prompted suspicions of bribery, particularly after his wife described $50,000 found in his wall safe upon Davenport's death as "gifts" from the real estate lobby.[21]

After the vote to cancel the housing program, Council member Charles Navarro proposed a citywide referendum on the issue, to be held on June 3, 1952. While the California State Supreme Court decided that the housing contracts were binding and the referendum would have no legal impact, both sides nevertheless campaigned heavily for votes. Fritz Burns stressed the unacceptably high cost of the program, which he estimated as $11,000 per unit, in comparison to such developments as Panorama City, where he had sold two- and three-bedroom homes for less than $10,000 per house: "It would be cheaper to buy, on the open market, already existing homes, selling for less than eight thousand dollars, than to go ahead with this public housing project."[22]

Burns was increasingly recognized as the leading spokesperson against public housing, and made a series of television and radio appearances leading up to the referendum in which he debated Frank Wilkinson and Robert Alexander. The debates were often heated. According to Frank Wilkinson, in one debate that spring Burns used Los Angeles Police Department figures that falsely showed a higher rate of juvenile delinquency in new public housing than in slums. The statistics Chief of Police William Parker had given Burns pertained to property that had already been cleared for development.[23]

Los Angeles voters on "Proposition B" on June 3 decided against the public housing program, 378,000 to 258,000. The death knell for the program sounded three months later. Felix McGinnis, a lawyer representing property owners fighting condemnation proceedings in Chavez Ravine, asked Frank Wilkinson to reveal "the names of all organizations, political or otherwise, of which you have been a member, commencing with the dates of your schooling at UCLA from 1932 to 1936." Wilkinson refused to reveal his political affiliations, citing personal conscience. Three days later, Wilkinson refused to answer if he had ever been a member of the Com-

WHY NOT *GIVE* THEM FREE HOUSES? *IT'S CHEAPER!*

A public housing unit costs the government $17,000. It supports it for 40 years. It could build neat houses and give them away for only $8,000. Does this make any sense? Say *NO* on public housing.

This cartoon, distributed by the Committee Against Socialist Housing (CASH), was included in many Los Angeles mailers during the bitter public relations campaign leading up to the June 3, 1952 referendum on public housing. *Dockweiler Family Collection, Loyola Marymount University.*

munist party. He was immediately suspended from his job at the City Housing Authority.[24]

The City Council voted 10-0 to ask the House Un-American Activities Committee (HUAC) to investigate the City Housing Authority for communist infiltrators. Council member Ed Davenport introduced a resolution naming Mayor Fletcher Bowron as a collaborator with the CHA. Bowron later came to blows with a demonstrator outside Council chambers who had accused him of being a "representative of Stalin." Within two weeks, California Attorney General Edmund G. "Pat" Brown arrived to investigate communist influence in the City Housing Authority. The public housing program in Los Angeles was effectively dead as its supporters fled the taint of communism.[25]

When Fletcher Bowron announced he would run for

reelection in 1953, a group of local businessmen approached Fritz Burns and urged him to run against Bowron as the Republican candidate. Burns told his colleagues the office was not worth the inevitable revisiting of his personal life and his past by the press and his political enemies.[26] Norris Poulson, hand-picked by the Chandler family, defeated Bowron in a mayoral race marked by continued accusations of communist influence in Bowron's administration. Frank Wilkinson had been fired in October 1952 for refusing to answer the questions of the California State Un-American Activities Committee, known as "Little HUAC," and his previous employment at the CHA doomed Bowron's chances for reelection. While Poulson fulfilled the City's obligation to purchase the land for the public housing program, none was ever constructed in Chavez Ravine.[27]

The primary political weapons for Fritz Burns in the debate over public housing were his own apartment buildings then under construction. Although he had made his reputation as a builder of detached single-family housing, Burns also built duplexes along the major traffic arteries in Panorama City and Westchester, and constructed large apartment complexes during World War Two in both Torrance and Burbank. In the latter case, Burns had ironically found himself embroiled in a public battle with city authorities and local citizens' groups who preferred detached housing to higher-density rental projects.[28] Burns returned to apartment building after 1950, constructing large complexes on Fulton Avenue in North Hollywood and along Manchester Avenue in Westchester on empty land zoned for higher-density dwellings than his standard two- or three-bedroom houses. Burns used his new apartments for more than an income stream. They were also valuable public relations tools.

After a heated political battle in 1950, the real estate lobby in Los Angeles had persuaded the City Council to eliminate rent controls that had been in force since World War Two. Historians have noted the rent control debate prefigured the later public housing struggle. The real estate lobby received support from the National Apartment Owners Association, NAREB, the NAHB, the Los Angeles Chamber of Commerce, and the same four daily papers controlled by the Chandler and Hearst families that would later campaign against public housing. Supporters of continued rent controls were the most prominent figures later in support of public housing, including Los Angeles' major unions, veterans' organizations, and the NAACP and the Los Angeles Urban League. The victory of the real estate lobby in the rent control battle demonstrated the strength of the industry and its political allies against a well-organized, influential opposition, and the end of rent control set the stage for the subsequent confrontation over public housing. It also made apartment construction a far more lucrative market for home builders such as Burns.[29]

In North Hollywood, Burns built large apartment complexes at Victory Boulevard and Fulton Avenue, and at Vanowen Street and Fulton Avenue. Ultimately totaling over one hundred units, the two sites became centerpieces of Burns' efforts to show that private builders could solve any housing shortage in Los Angeles. The apartments also became newsmakers because Burns financed their construction with private funds. Rather than seeking FHA financing, he paid for almost half the construction himself, with Occidental Life Insurance providing a loan for the remainder. The loan was repaid over fifteen years, half the length of a traditional mortgage.[30]

While the political connotations of forsaking FHA loans had public relations value, in actuality Burns sought alternate financing because abiding by the FHA requirements for apartment dwellings would have made their construction too costly. He built the apartments with a number of innovations designed to take advantage of the mild Los Angeles climate, including single-loading hallways, termed "Monterey balconies," which ran along the exterior of each building rather than internally. A combination ceiling/floor divided lower apartments from upstairs units instead of the traditional crawlspace used for insulation against intemperate weather. By installing individual wall gas furnaces in every unit, allocating space for uncovered parking spaces, and giving each unit a "storage closet," Burns also eliminated the need for basements or garages. These cost-saving measures, which quickly became standard features in Los Angeles apartment construction, enabled Burns to offer the apartments at an initial rate of $45 per month. A profile in *Business Week* noted that "two years ago, that advertisement in a Los Angeles newspaper would have caused a stampede—or a cynical sniff."[31]

The local press went further. In a glowing feature in the *Valley Times*, real estate editor Joe King pronounced the first completed complex "the answer to the low rent housing problem, government rent control, slum clearance, government-constructed housing, and part of the answer, at least, to the various attacks made periodically upon the so-called real estate lobby." Excoriating both the FHA for its stringent rules on apartment financing and the Los Angeles City Housing Authority, King explicitly linked the new project to the ongoing effort to build public housing in Los Angeles. "How can any member of this government agency imagine themselves sufficiently qualified to constitute themselves the sole judge and jury in the matter of withholding dwellings such as these from the low-salaried workers of this city," King asked, "while the socialist-minded do-gooders continue to try to foist upon the population . . . government-constructed housing, the design of which the office of the FHA will have nothing to say, while the cost to taxpayers for constructing such dwellings will be several times that of the same buildings built by private contractors on a competitive basis?"[32]

One of many vitriolic broadsides fired by both sides in the newspapers over public housing, King's attack conveyed Burns' essential point: private builders could construct and sell low-cost, high-density housing at a profit without government assistance of any sort. "It was his way of combating public housing," noted Ken Skinner, who worked for Burns as an accountant at the time. "[The apartments] were built by private enterprise and operated by private enterprise. He wanted to show that would be the best route to go, rather than public housing. And they're all still standing today."[33]

Both camps in the public housing debate of the early 1950s were in agreement on at least one issue: the need for slum clearance to rehabilitate the nation's urban areas. The issue held pride of place in Title I of the Housing Act of 1949, which obliged the federal government to pay two-thirds of the cost of slum clearance for residential redevelopment. While designed in part to assist developers, Title I also found favor among urban politicians who sought increased tax revenues, social engineers and city planners searching for methods to condemn privately-owned slum properties, and even some business groups, which anticipated increased property values in urban America's increasingly dilapidated downtowns.[34]

For Fritz Burns, the programs initiated by Title I of the Housing Act of 1949 represented a double-edged sword. Any federal assistance for private builders to rehabilitate slum areas, especially on such generous terms as those offered in Title I, was a welcome departure from what he saw as an aggressive attempt by public housing advocates to supplant private builders entirely. On the other hand, the political implications of Title I were clear. With the exception of both world wars, the nation's housing stock in major urban areas had been built over the previous century by private developers, local builders, and realtors without large-scale intervention by the federal government. A sudden infusion of federal money and programs that promised to eradicate slums placed the onus for the creation and growth of the slums squarely on private builders and realtors.

To combat any perception that private real estate and building groups were either responsible for slums or opposed to their eradication, Burns worked with the major trade groups of those industries to create parallel slum clearance and home improvement programs. Beginning in 1952, Burns served as co-chairman, then chairman of the "Build America Better" campaign, which members of the National Association of Real Estate Boards described as "a resurgence against the erroneous but popular notion that they are personally responsible for the existence of slums."[35] Noting that private home builders gained little or no economic advantage from rehabilitation of existing properties, Burns characterized the campaign as both a humanitarian effort to rid the nation of slums as well as an appropriate alternative to public housing for providing shelter to those in the lowest income brackets. "Rehabilitation of old buildings is like half-soling a pair of shoes," he said in 1953. "There is no glamour in it; it is just good common sense."[36]

Burns also acknowledged the alarming decline of Los Angeles' urban center in an open letter in the *California Savings and Loan League Journal* in December 1953, exhorting bankers to liberalize lending rules for property improvements. "We have a lot of people crying about their downtown center going to pot," Burns wrote. "They talk about decentralization. It is ruining their downtown business center. People are going out into the outlying districts to do their shopping. The nature of my business makes me interested in some of those outlying business centers, but not to the extent that I could possibly overlook the fact that the real downtown center, the core of the city, is the essential thing which must be preserved."[37]

Burns focused on five major initiatives in the "Build America Better" campaign: rehabilitation of existing proper-

ties by enforcement of existing city ordinances; the creation
of neighborhood associations to supervise rehabilitation or
clearance of slum property; rezoning of land no longer
appropriate for residential use; improvement of such amenities as parking and public transportation routes; and tax
breaks for developers in areas being redeveloped. Because the
first two initiatives required private funding and voluntary
compliance in most cases, Burns initiated a major national
public relations campaign to encourage participation in
"Build America Better." As the public face of the campaign,
he spent over half his time between 1953 and 1954 traveling
the country to speak to local chambers of commerce, business
associations, civic groups, and property owners. His close
friend and business partner Winifred Cockey estimated he
made over two hundred appearances each year, and NAREB
press releases listed Burns' travel at over 100,000 miles annu-
ally in 1953 and 1954. Burns' associates, including Cockey, also
made a number of presentations and speeches on behalf of
the campaign.[38]

Concurrent with Burns and NAREB's efforts in 1953 and
1954 was a political shift away from public housing around
the nation. Dwight D. Eisenhower had defeated Robert
Taft, one of the architects of the Housing Act of 1949, for the
Republican nomination for president, before beating Demo-
crat Adlai Stevenson in the general election. Eisenhower's
election was a triumph for the real estate and building trades,
particularly on the issue of public housing. Eisenhower asked
Congress for an allocation of only 35,000 units of new public
housing in his first term; in the second, he asked for none at
all. He also refused to execute contracts for housing that had
already been approved as part of the Housing Act. While a
total of almost 600,000 units of public housing was eventually constructed in the decade, the Eisenhower administration's preferred method for solving the nation's housing
shortage closely resembled the approach Fritz Burns was

encouraging around the nation: rehabilitation of existing property and subsidies for private builders of new homes.[39]

By the beginning of 1954, Fritz Burns and NAREB had brought the "Build America Better" campaign to over 220 cities, 173 of which had actively increased enforcement of local building ordinances to varying degrees. NAREB reported 69,000 properties had been rehabilitated at the owner's expense as a result of the campaign, and another eight thousand had been demolished.[40] The campaign was soon followed by the "Operation Home Improvement" program, sponsored by the United States Chamber of Commerce and the National Association of Home Builders, and the American Council to Improve Our Neighborhoods (ACTION), which received the personal endorsement of President Eisenhower. Along with *Life* publisher Andrew Heiskell, Burns played a major role in the formation of the latter group and served as Vice Chairman of the campaign. Supported through contributions, ACTION included the expected prominent members of the banking and manufacturing industries, but also included representatives from labor and religious groups. Both "Operation Home Improvement" and ACTION were similar in mission to the "Build America Better" campaign.[41]

To provide an example of the potential market in rehabilitated housing, Burns purchased several Victorian mansions in the historic Bunker Hill neighborhood of Los Angeles. The once-posh neighborhood had long since declined, with most of the expansive mansions converted into substandard apartments with illegal lean-to additions and below-code electricity and plumbing systems. Burns' selection of Bunker Hill for a rehabilitation project was not coincidental, as the blighted area had long been targeted by public housing supporters as a prime candidate for slum clearance and relocation of residents into newly constructed housing. Rehabilitation efforts required replacing all plumbing and wiring, installing new heating systems in place of gas heaters, lowering fourteen-foot ceilings, and reconstructing stairways to bring them up to modern building code requirements.[42]

With his son, Patrick, supervising renovation efforts, Burns gave $11,000 for overhauling and remodeling on top of the initial $7,000 needed to purchase each property. Each house was converted into two or three units, one of which Patrick Burns occupied himself, and the Burns duo eventually rehabilitated a total of eleven apartments. Proximity to downtown, modern conveniences, and the cachet of the external Victorian architecture resulted in a rental price of up to $165 a month. Patrick Burns stressed that the end result was actually more than just an expensive showplace, because a two-apartment house could provide a yearly income of almost $4,000. An investor could expect to recoup the initial $18,000 for rehabilitation within five years. "It isn't an insurmountable task, nor a thankless one," he told *Practical Builder* in 1955. "The profits we are taking out of our eleven remodeled apartments are more than worth the time and effort. You can cut yourself in on the same source of new business, and it will be good for a long time to come."[43]

The fierce battle over public housing in Los Angeles in the 1950s had a curious postscript. Under the terms of its 1949 contract with the federal government, the City of Los Angeles purchased most of the land the federal government had acquired for public housing after Norris Poulson was elected mayor in 1953.[44] The prize parcel was still Chavez Ravine, coveted by developers and city officials alike for its proximity to downtown Los Angeles and its location between two major freeways. In addition to the 230 acres of land cleared by the government in 1950, there were a few individual parcels extant, including the homes of the Arechiga clan, an extended Mexican-American family which had long lived in Chavez Ravine and refused to vacate the land after their property was condemned. Fritz Burns and developer Ben

Weingart also owned an eighteen-acre parcel of land in Chavez Ravine that they had purchased in 1944 and never developed.[45]

On October 8, 1957, Walter F. O'Malley announced his intention to bring his Brooklyn Dodgers baseball team to Los Angeles. Speculation over the move had been rampant for months, as O'Malley was unhappy with his stadium arrangement in Brooklyn, and Los Angeles offered a huge new market for major league baseball. In May, the *Los Angeles Times* announced, "Bums Coming! Only Question is When?"[46] The new home team played its first official game in Los Angeles on April 18, 1958, before over 78,000 fans in the Los Angeles Coliseum, though the venerable stadium's oval shape was better suited to football. O'Malley had made no secret of his preference for a privately-built stadium in Chavez Ravine. In October 1957, a divided Los Angeles City Council authorized a deal, 10-5, in which O'Malley was given the Chavez Ravine land with improvements in exchange for a minor league baseball stadium, Wrigley Field, which O'Malley previously owned. According to Ken Skinner, Fritz Burns strongly opposed the deal, though he was socially friendly with the O'Malleys. Burns thought private builders such as himself should have been allowed to build homes in Chavez Ravine, and that the city was giving up prized real estate in exchange for a small return.

A public referendum in June 1958 approved the transaction by a scant margin, but further trouble lay ahead. The federal government had stipulated the land be used for a public purpose when it sold it at a loss of almost four million to the City of Los Angeles, and several lawsuits attempted to void the contract with the Dodgers on the grounds that a private baseball stadium was hardly a public use. The Dodgers did not overcome all these legal obstacles until January 1959. In the meantime, both the team and the city had been excoriated for forced evictions of the Arechiga family from their homes in Chavez Ravine. The Arechiga family's property had been condemned in 1953, but the family had refused the financial settlement and remained in their homes. Six years later, at the dawn of the age of television, Angelenos were shocked by images of elderly women carried screaming from their homes moments before the wrecking ball.[47]

The elders of the Arechiga family moved into a donated trailer at Chavez Ravine, new Council hearings were called on the eviction, and the family threatened to sue. The controversy quickly died down when it was discovered that the patriarch of the Arechiga family owned eleven houses in Los Angeles, many of them in good condition. Public support for their cause evaporated, and clearance of Chavez Ravine continued. Fritz Burns and fellow developer Ben Weingart received $120,000 from the city for their jointly-owned eighteen acres. Construction began in September 1959 on a 56,000-seat, privately built and owned baseball stadium. On April 10, 1962, Walter O'Malley officially opened Dodger Stadium in Chavez Ravine. Fritz Burns joked in later years that his condemned property lay underneath home plate.[48]

CHAPTER EIGHT

"How Long Can The Poor Haoles Last?"

Let the Royal be the Dowager,
So stately and aged and prim.
We will be the fun place
With air-conditioning, bikinis, and vim.
                                    Fritz Burns, 1954.[1]

When Fritz Burns received a surprise phone call from Henry Kaiser in early 1954, both men had moved on to new ventures despite remaining technical partners in Kaiser Community Homes. Burns was engrossed in the national public housing debate while overseeing the development of numerous shopping centers in California and continuing his building operations in West Westchester and North Hollywood. Henry Kaiser's involvement in the operations of Kaiser Community Homes had decreased considerably after an initial flurry of activity from 1946 through 1948. He had concentrated on numerous other industrial ventures, including his Kaiser-Frazer automobile company and his aluminum, steel, and associated operations, as well as a rapidly expanding Kaiser Permanente hospital program. By 1954, Kaiser and his wife Alyce had purchased a home in the Kahala area of Oahu and sold much of their holdings in California. Kaiser continued to make frequent trips to the mainland for meetings and pleasure trips to his Tahoe estate, but made Hawaii the focus of his social and business life until his death.[2] He called his move to Hawaii a "semi-retirement," while Burns had joked that semi-retirement for the seventy-one year old industrialist meant "an eighteen hour day instead of twenty four."[3]

Kaiser's phone call concerned a large parcel of land the Salvation Army had offered to Kaiser for sale in Kaimuki, east of Waikiki on the outskirts of Honolulu. He convinced Burns to fly immediately to Hawaii to tour the property and judge its fitness for a large home-building project. The property was a good distance from downtown Honolulu and was alternately rocky and swampy, but Kaiser compared the parcel to land in Florida and Palm Springs, California, that both men had seen become the focus of frenzied land speculation in previous decades. The two businessmen ultimately declined to purchase the property, though the visit laid the groundwork for their future collaborations in Hawaii. When Burns returned to Los Angeles, Kaiser continued to survey various other properties.[4]

Fritz Burns was himself no stranger to Hawaii, having visited the Islands in both 1951 and 1952. At the time, tourism was negligible in comparison to the multibillion-dollar economic industry it would become. The majority of visitors to the Islands at the time arrived during the late summer and winter months by ship. "[Fritz and Gladys] went over on a boat in 1951," Frances Morehart remembered. "My sister and I had gone over ahead of them, so we went out to meet them, and we looked up to the deck and there was my mother and her sister . . . and we said 'Where's Pop? Where's Pop?' They said 'Pop's in the infirmary.' He was very sick—just green, the worst I've ever seen him in my life. They rushed him off the ship, and put him in the emergency room at St. Francis Hospital in Hawaii. He stayed there three weeks. He never got out of the hospital and never saw Hawaii. A year later, they went back, and that's when he saw all the possibilities."[5]

At the time of Burns' visits to Hawaii, the island chain was still a territory of the United States. The Japanese attack on

Pearl Harbor on December 7, 1941 and Hawaii's subsequent central role in American military strategy in the Pacific bolstered the significance of Hawaii as a military and economic outpost. The gradual introduction of regular air travel and growing trade in the postwar period cemented ties between the "mainland" and Hawaii, though not until August 1959 did Hawaii become the fiftieth state.[6]

When Fritz Burns and Henry Kaiser began contemplating development possibilities in the islands in the 1950s, Hawaii's political and social elite were largely whites of European descent ("haoles"), the most famous of whom was Walter Francis Dillingham, a prominent businessman and powerbroker known as "Mr. Hawaii" and "Uncle Walter." The territory's economic activity had been controlled since annexation by an exclusive group of business conglomerates, known as "The Big Five," who held sway over almost every aspect of the Hawaiian economy. Though mainland investment leaped from $17 million in 1948 to $180 million a decade later, the economy remained dependent in large part on sugar, pineapple, sandalwood, and military activity. Tourism, aside from a handful of venerable hotels along the Waikiki waterfront, was a negligible component of the islands' financial infrastructure. The arrival of Kaiser and Burns, followed by the major American hotel chains in the following decade, would result in a radical transformation of the Hawaiian economy, physical environment, and culture.[7]

Kaiser made another phone call to Burns in March 1954, this time concerning twenty acres of beachfront property at the far "ewa" (west) end of Waikiki in Oahu. The property included five hundred feet of beach frontage but was too far from the major hotels of Waikiki—the Moana, the Surfrider, and the Royal Hawaiian—to attract investment. The land and that around it included a mixture of small shacks, dilapidated beach cottages, and the Niumalu Hotel, a venerable Hawaiian institution that had fallen into disrepair over years

of neglect. "[Kaiser] asked Fritz why he didn't come over to
Honolulu," remembered Winifred Cockey, Burns' longtime
business associate who worked with him on a number of projects in Hawaii. Burns later told her Kaiser's sales pitch: "'I
understand you are running around the country making
speeches about slums.' After I admitted to that he told me he
had some for me to clean up and asked if I'd come over."[8]
Burns traveled again to Hawaii to meet with Kaiser. "When
he came back on Monday morning, he said 'Winifred, we're
going to be in the hotel business'," Cockey remembered. "I
said to him, 'But Fritz, we don't know anything about the
hotel business!' And he said, 'Well, we're going to learn.' And
learn we did."[9]

Why hotels? At the time they purchased the Waikiki land,
neither Burns nor Kaiser had any experience in building or
running a hotel. Furthermore, in 1954 the advent of large-
scale passenger travel by air was still several years away. Pan
American Airways had initiated air service to the Islands
with its "China Clipper" flying boat in 1935, but the trip took
an exhausting twenty-one hours.[10] Only when the DC-7C
came into service on Pacific routes in 1956 did the length of a
trip to Hawaii become a manageable eight hours. The arrival
of passenger jets three years later would provide the catalyst
for Hawaii's tourist industry. Local hotels in 1954 were almost
entirely dependent on ship-borne tourists to fill their rooms.
Henry Kaiser claimed in later years that the decision to built
a hotel instead of homes or apartments came from direct
observation of conditions along the Waikiki beach, where he
saw tourists turned away in droves from established hotels.
Kaiser himself had been unable to secure a reservation at the
Royal Hawaiian Hotel on several occasions. Sensing an
untapped market, he and Burns resolved to develop it as soon
as possible.[11]

Burns and Kaiser remained discreet about their new plans.
Addressing growing speculation about what the two famous

builders had in mind for Hawaii, Burns publicly announced in April 1954 that their activity in Honolulu was of a piece with his national program for slum renewal. "Many areas in Honolulu are long overdue for development and rehabilitation," he noted in a Kaiser Services press release. "Our object will be to do just that without losing, but rather enhancing the true atmosphere of the Islands. Our plans are only in a formative stage. Details will be announced later."[12]

After paying $750,000 for the initial property, the pair employed blind trusts to secure surrounding land, because even a whisper of their names in connection with any local land sale would drive up land values for miles around. The painstaking process of purchasing the numerous surrounding plots took almost a year. Finally, in April 1955, the purchase of the Niumalu site for over a million dollars gave Burns and Kaiser the unified parcel they had been seeking. In the interval, they had hired Burns' longtime friend and renowned Los Angeles architect Welton Becket to collaborate with a prominent local architect, Edwin Bauer, to design a hotel complex, to be called the Hawaiian Village Hotel. Burns named his son Pat the general manager, while Kaiser's longtime associate, Lambreth "Handy" Hancock, Jr., was placed in charge of construction. In truth, both Burns and Kaiser supervised almost every detail themselves when in Hawaii, and the younger Burns and Hancock directed operations when business called the two partners back to the mainland.[13]

No one in the new Kaiser-Burns hotel venture held any illusions about usurping the established hotels further east on the Waikiki waterfront. The grand dame of Waikiki destinations was the Royal Hawaiian Hotel, a venerable pink edifice built in 1927 in a Moorish architectural style and known locally as "The Pink Palace." For many years, the Royal Hawaiian Hotel and its neighbors had served the great majority of tourist traffic to Waikiki. To be successful, Burns

and Kaiser needed to fill a different niche or attract an entire
new class of tourists to Hawaii.

Imperative to the success of the hotel was the creation of
an attractive beach. Not only did the new site lie adjacent to
the Ala Moana yacht basin, the shoreline immediately in
front of the hotel site was a barely navigable maze of coral
and rock with little sand. Burns and Kaiser planned extensive
excavation and landscaping to add several hundred feet of
white-sand beach as well as an artificial lagoon adjacent to
the property, complete with a miniature island topped by
palm trees. After dredging a channel through the coral,
Burns and Kaiser agreed to make the shoreline a public beach
in exchange for title to several hundred feet of sand that had
accrued in front of the hotel property as a result of tide patterns at Waikiki. Because Hawaii would not achieve state-
hood until 1959, approval for the land transfer required that
the United States Congress pass a bill authorizing the beachfront reclamation project. Though helped along by Burns
and Kaiser's extensive political contacts, the process was still
tedious and time consuming, and interfered with the accelerated construction timetable Kaiser demanded.[14]

Initial plans for the hotel property itself were modest.
After fumigation to remove a serious termite problem, the
seventy pre-existing beach cottages were renovated and
reshuffled into clusters around three oval swimming pools
and an expanded "Tapa Room" nightclub, the social center of
the Village. Burns and Kaiser first disagreed about the property adjacent to the Tapa Room. Burns, a lifelong swimming
enthusiast, insisted on a pool for the guests' use. Kaiser was
equally adamant that the area be used for a dance floor, given
the Tapa Room's main purpose as an evening entertainment
venue. They eventually reached a creative compromise. The
swimming pool was built, but with rails running along either
side. At night, a motor under the Tapa Room rolled a large
dance floor made of laminated two-by-fours onto the rails

The site of the Hawaiian Village Hotel before construction in 1954, looking east towards Diamond Head. Fort DeRussy is inland from the property. The Ala Moana yacht harbor is in the foreground.
Courtesy of Ken Skinner.

for evening entertainment. Though a large dance crowd could create an uneasy sensation of springiness in the wooden spans, the combination dance floor/swimming pool became a valuable selling point for the hotel in later years.[15]

In order to give the hotel a more "Hawaiian" look, Patrick Burns used lava rock, bamboo trimmings, and palm trees throughout the complex. For the renovated beach cottages, he wanted peaked thatch roofs woven in the traditional Hawaiian style. No native artisans could be found who still possessed the requisite skill, and the younger Burns eventually had to hire a number of Samoan artisans from the Oahu village of Laie to weave the palm fronds. The weavers worked on their own "tropic time" schedule, arriving at six in the morning and leaving at three to fish for food in the evening.[16] Hancock remembered a constant debate with the weavers over the supply of palm fronds. "At first they were free. Then we were paying five cents a frond. Then it was ten cents a frond. Pretty soon we had created a growing cottage industry."[17]

In addition to the cottages, numerous frame-construction studios and two-story modern hotel buildings flanked the central Village, the refurbished Niumalu swimming pool, and the lagoon. A three-story facility housing the hotel lobby, the front desk, and more hotel rooms was situated behind the beach cottages, and the bottom floor was designed for a number of specialty shops supervised by Pat Burns. An unexpected publicity boon arose from a contractor's error in decorating the new lobby building. The leather upholstery for the lobby, purchased unseen as "coral," was discovered upon delivery to be a shocking shade of pink. Time constraints forced Pat Burns to use the brightly colored furnishings, which ultimately drew enthusiastic reviews from visitors.[18]

Henry Kaiser seized on the opportunity to make pink his signature color. Catamarans, bulldozers, jeeps, and Kaiser-Burns equipment of every kind were painted a brilliant shade of pink, and Kaiser himself took to wearing pink suits and shirts, both in Hawaii and in California. Burns' associate, William Hannon, later remembered touring the construction operations at Hawaii Kai and marveling about "equipment painted pink all over the place."[19] Kaiser's new favorite color was also, of course, a sly mockery of the Royal Hawaiian Hotel's famed pink exterior.[20]

All around the Village site in the summer of 1955, contractors and Kaiser-Burns employees rushed to complete as much work as possible before the target opening date of Labor Day weekend, 1955. The lobby building was still under construction even after the Village itself was open for business. The acclerated construction schedule meant that the hotel lost a fair portion of its paying guests in its first few months because they were awakened by the noise of construction workers and bulldozers beginning work every morning at seven.[21]

Though Burns and Kaiser's public relations teams painted the opening of the Hawaiian Village Hotel as a success, the first months at the hotel were a trying time that everyone in the Kaiser-Burns operation would long remember. In truth, the ultimate survival and rapid expansion of the Hawaiian Village Hotel in the latter half of the decade required a level of showmanship, creativity, and marketing finesse far beyond the capabilities of the average developer. Burns recollected those trying early days in 1956:

> KAISER AND BURNS IN THE ISLANDS
>
> So son, you've come to the Islands
> Heard all that you had to do
> Was build a hotel
> And you knew
> Damn well
> The dollars would roll on to you.
>
> They told you at the HVB
> You got all your statistics straight,
> But there's two guys that's wiser
> That's Burns and Kaiser.
>
> So listen what it did
> To those two kids
> Before you decide
> Your fate.
>
> You buy your land
> For a million grand
> By the square foot
> Not by the acre
> The "tourist boom"
> Is at eight bucks a room.
> For deluxe suites
> There's hardly a taker.

> The Bankers are nice,
> But cold as ice
> Credit's a thing
> Of the past.
> And the common expression
> At Pacific Club sessions
> Is, "How long can the poor haoles last?"
>
> You open with a great big bang.
> The newspapers are filled with the story;
> Then your occupancy gets less and less,
> Where are all those expected guests?
> And your life becomes grim—
> There's no more glory.[22]

No one in the Kaiser-Burns organization foresaw this tale of woe in the weeks leading up to the hotel's grand opening. Searching for entertainment for the new venture, Kaiser achieved a marketing coup by hiring Alfred Apaka away from the nightclub of Waikiki personality Don The Beachcomber. Apaka, a handsome 37-year old baritone who had been singing on the Honolulu nightclub circuit and on Hawaiian radio since high school, was something of a local Elvis Presley. His "Hawaii Calls" radio show was wildly popular, and his presence atop a bill of entertainment could be expected to draw large crowds. Both Fritz and Gladys Burns and the Kaisers would become friends of Apaka, whom they later honored with a statue in the Hilton Hawaiian Village.[23]

Burns and Kaiser also paid for an expansive array of food and drink for the opening festivities, and invited hundreds of local dignitaries, businessmen, and socialites. With the entire staff of the Kaiser-Burns operation on hand, a three-day extravaganza began two weeks after Labor Day in September 1955. Burns and Kaiser formally opened the hotel by cutting an elaborate lei draped across the main entrance, after which the Governor of the Territory of Hawaii and his wife became the first guests in the new hotel. The ceremony was followed by a long night and following day of celebration, including an open bar and several free shows by Apaka. The third morning, Fritz and Gladys Burns and the Kaisers opened the doors of the Hawaiian Village Hotel for official business.[24]

"Mr. Kaiser was there. Mr. Burns was there. Their wives. All the parties involved from both sides," Lambreth Hancock remembered years later. "We threw the doors open and got out of the way of the rush. No one. Not a soul. Not one paying guest checked in. Just the invited people. We hired Alfred Apaka away from Don The Beachcomber as the lead entertainer. No one showed up for his show."[25]

Fritz Burns and Henry Kaiser cut an oversized lei to open the Hawaiian Village Hotel in Waikiki, Hawaii. The ceremony kicked off an overly optimistic three-day extravaganza in September 1955.
Fritz B. Burns Collection, Loyola Marymount University.

Fritz Burns and Henry Kaiser had seriously misjudged tourist trends in Hawaii. Room prices at the Hawaiian Village Hotel were not the problem, as they were on a par or slightly less than those of competing hotels. A beach cottage in 1955 could be rented for as low as six dollars a day, while rooms at the high end of the spectrum were advertised at twenty-four dollars a day. As late as 1958, the top price at the Village was thirty-eight dollars a day.[26] Burns and Kaiser had erred in the timing of their grand opening. Mid-winter and summer were the peak periods for tourism, and off-season visitors tended to be devotees of the established Waikiki hotels. In the three months after the grand opening, occupancy barely surpassed ten percent of capacity in the Hawaiian Village Hotel. A significant number of those visitors were complimentary guests of Burns or Kaiser from their California operations. Guests were even lost on their ride to the Village, as some local hotels gave taxi drivers a bounty for every guest stolen away from a competitor. The hotel's finances were in the red. In December of 1955, Burns warned Kaiser in a letter that the hotel venture was "essentially out of money."[27]

Burns and Kaiser spent the next year utilizing their considerable marketing and promotional abilities to save the Hawaiian Village Hotel. The two engaged in a friendly competition to see who could book the most exotic and attention-grabbing talent for the Tapa Room, including the Martin Denny combo and Lawrence Welk.[28] Armed with a huge collection of slides showcasing the Village, they also stumped across the mainland to drum up business from travel agencies and business associations in various cities.[29] Recognizing that the Village was still relatively isolated from Waikiki's signature hotels and restaurants, Kaiser commissioned a squadron of pink jeeps to foil crooked taxi drivers and to shuttle Village guests to and from the nightspots of Waikiki.[30]

To attract large groups of convention guests from the mainland, Kaiser and Burns planned an auditorium/convention center for the hotel complex in 1957. At the same time, famed designer R. Buckminster Fuller was promoting his new geodesic dome for a variety of uses, including sports arenas, meeting halls, and even homes. Fuller's dome concept required no internal structural columns for support, but needed a cheap, lightweight material for the hundreds of individual panels that would make up the structure's beveled surface. Burns and Kaiser had the perfect solution in aluminum, which the Kaiser companies produced in enormous quantities at his Permanente plant in northern California. Prefabricated panels were shipped to Hawaii, and Hancock supervised their assembly in just twenty hours. The finished product was a fifty-foot dome covering over sixteen thousand square feet but so lightweight it had to be anchored to the ground to prevent inclement weather from blowing it away. This new "Kaiser Aluminum Dome" could seat more than two thousand guests at a time. It drew national attention after Elizabeth Taylor and her then-husband Michael Todd used its spacious confines to screen Todd's Academy Award-winning movie "Around The World in 80 Days" in November 1957.[31]

Attracting mainlanders was an important goal of Kaiser and Burns' marketing efforts, but it was also important to establish the hotel's reputation within Hawaii. This time, it was Kaiser who trumped Burns on the best way to market their new operation. In 1957, Kaiser invested in a radio station, KHVH, and a television station, KHVH-TV, both named for the Hawaiian Village Hotel. His goal was simple: "Kaiser's thoughts were that every hotel room had a television and people rented cars that had radios," Hancock later remembered.[32] Every guest, in a competing hotel or not, became a potential audience member, as on-air programs were introduced with a promotional mention of the Village. Kaiser found a partner for the stations in popular local disc jockey Hal Lewis, better known on the airwaves as "J. Akuhead Pupule," Hawaiian for "Crazy Fish Head." "Hal was very, very popular," remembered Ed Hogan, who worked for Kaiser and Burns at the time promoting the Hawaiian Village in the United States. "It was reported that he was the second-highest-paid disc jockey in America. He started his radio station and his television station—the first color television station in Hawaii."[33]

Fierce opposition from existing Hawaiian radio stations, low ratings, and an exorbitant programming budget gave both stations a precarious existence for their first year on the air, but Fritz Burns eventually became a partner when the marketing potential of the stations became clear. Kaiser bought out Hal Lewis as a partner, though Lewis remained as a station disc jockey, and after several years the stations themselves became profitable. By 1960, the television station was capturing fully half of Hawaii's viewers, in large part by focusing on local news and events.[34] Less tangible but far more valuable were the countless on-air promotional spots advertising each new program as sponsored by "Henry J. Kaiser's fabulous Hawaiian Village Hotel."[35]

By March of 1956, occupancy rates in the Hawaiian Village Hotel had grown to fifty percent; within a year, the hotel was making a profit for the first time. Over the next four years, Kaiser and Burns aggressively expanded the size of the hotel to meet the suddenly booming tourist demand. The original 1955 hotel property was dwarfed by 1961 by twin seventeen-story towers, as well as thirteen- and fourteen-story towers holding over a thousand rooms. A major national hotel management chain, Western Hotels, had been contracted to operate the expanded complex. From an isolated upstart hotel consisting of quaint lanais and cottages grouped around an entertainment hall in 1955, the Hawaiian Village Hotel had by 1960 become a bona fide major competitor in the suddenly booming Hawaii tourist trade, and represented almost ten percent of total hotel capacity in Honolulu.[36]

Throughout Hawaii, similar growth was underway. In 1955, *Fortune* had predicted that over 170,000 tourists would spend $88 million a year in Hawaii by 1959. Less than eight years later, those numbers had soared past a million visitors a year spending over five hundred million dollars.[37] Year by year, the hotel industry grew visibly larger; more than ten thousand hotel rooms were renting in Honolulu by 1960, an increase of more than three thousand from the year before.[38] A common complaint of island hoteliers, the scarcity of airline flights from the mainland, disappeared in the late 1950s when major carriers, including Pan American and United, recognized the potential of the tourist market and dramatically expanded the number of weekly flights to Hawaii. The introduction of jet travel and $100 "tourist fares" made vacationing even more attractive in what had become, in August 1959, the fiftieth member of the United States.[39]

The Hawaiian Village Hotel was not Fritz Burns' only concern in Hawaii. After the opening of the Village, he and Gladys purchased a house in the Kahala neighborhood of Honolulu, though business and social commitments required both to shuttle back and forth between their Hawaii home and Los Angeles much of the time. Despite their status as relative newcomers to the Islands, both Fritz and Gladys also soon found their way into the upper echelon of Hawaiian social life. They merited constant mention in society columns and spent their weekends at high-society charity events and cocktail parties. Fritz and Gladys hosted numerous luaus, and their home in Hawaii became a social center for new friends as well as associates from the Kaiser and Burns management teams. Gladys Burns shared a close friendship with Princess Conchita Sepulveda Pignatelli, a descendant of a Spanish land-grant family in Los Angeles and the society columnist for the *Los Angeles Examiner*. Parties at the Burns home in Hawaii soon were featured in Los Angeles as well as Honolulu press outlets.[40]

One frequent guest of Fritz and Gladys Burns at their Hawaii home was Monsignor Benjamin Hawkes, a Roman Catholic priest who oversaw the finances of the Archdiocese of Los Angeles during the decades of rapid expansion from the 1950s to the 1980s. Hawkes, who once described himself as "in charge of everything with a dollar sign in front of it," was close with Los Angeles' most influential kingmakers. He knew Fritz and Gladys Burns both through their charity work and through their relationship with Cardinal James Francis McIntyre, Archbishop of Los Angeles from 1947 to 1970. In the later years of Burns' life, Hawkes' relationship with him was almost that of a personal chaplain. Beginning in 1959, Hawkes used the Burns home in Hawaii every year as a summer vacation home. "I've had some fabulous friends," Hawkes later noted, "and [Fritz and Gladys Burns] have been very good friends."[41]

The marriage of Gladys Burns' daughter, Maria De Los Reyes Scheller, to George Hartman in June 1958 provided a glimpse of Fritz and Gladys Burns' growing social stature on Oahu. The ceremony was held in historic St. Augustine's Roman Catholic Church in Waikiki, with the reception at the Burns' home on Kahala Road. Guests included Hawaii Governor William Quinn, Olympic swimmer and surfing legend Duke Kahanamoku, and social and business associates from Los Angeles and Honolulu. The *Honolulu Star-Bulletin*, *Honolulu Advertiser*, and *Los Angeles Times* all covered the ceremony, while the *Los Angeles Examiner* termed the wedding ceremony "one of the most magnificent ever seen on this island." Henry and Alyce Kaiser arrived just in time for the ceremony, having flown in from Tokyo. Fritz Burns and his son Pat engaged in a poetic joust at the toast, with Fritz noting, "On occasions less ostentatious, I usually wax less loquacious."[42]

In addition to social life and the business of the Hawaiian Village, both Henry Kaiser and Fritz Burns had other plans for the Islands. Kaiser was overseeing an extensive cement operation in the Islands, as well as a new Kaiser Permanente Hospital in Waikiki. Burns had joined with Robert Munro, a contractor who had built many of Burns' commercial properties in Southern California, in a construction venture that built commercial and hotel properties in Hawaii as well as Los Angeles. Burns also joined with his longtime associate from Los Angeles, J. Paul Campbell, to purchase a lumber mill that held a favorable contract with the territorial government of Hawaii to harvest eucalyptus and koa. While many of the two industrialists' ventures were treated as a part of their hotel business for accounting purposes, in reality both men were running numerous side projects along with the Hawaiian Village Hotel.[43]

Henry Kaiser had even more ambitious plans. In 1959, at the age of 80, he began planning a huge new subdivision on six thousand acres beyond Diamond Head, to be named Hawaii Kai. He invited Fritz Burns to join him in what had the potential to be another profitable home-building enterprise, but Burns recognized a familiar devil in the details. His firm was a private enterprise, reliant on a small, devoted core of employees who invested their own money in each venture. A typical Burns company was jointly owned by himself and a small core of investors, usually his son Pat and his employees and partners, Charles Getchell, William Hannon, Winifred Cockey, Carl Herziger, Robert Munro, Joseph Rawlinson, and Ken Skinner. Gregory Dillon, Vice Chairman of the Hilton Hotels Corporation and an associate of Fritz Burns in Hilton-Burns Hotels, remembered Burns' corporate strategy: "He was very hands-on in his management. He was almost—and I don't say this in criticism—almost too hands-on as we were getting into the era of big corporate companies."[44]

Henry Kaiser, on the other hand, headed a mammoth, publicly traded company, and had the vast resources of his many enterprises to offset initial outlays and potential losses on any new project. Nervous about the financial outlay Hawaii Kai would require, Burns turned down Kaiser's invitation to join his as a partner in the development. David Slipher, a onetime Burns employee who joined Kaiser in building Hawaii Kai after working for many years in Kaiser Community Homes, later remembered the seemingly endless resources Kaiser sank into the project: "Fritz foresaw the great costs involved in getting Hawaii Kai going far better than [Kaiser] did from his past development experience. He knew it was going to take twice as long as forecast and cost three times as much in dollars…at one time we had over thirty-five million in Kaiser's after-tax dollars in the ground for streets and utilities, and less than thirty five houses sold."[45]

Less than two years later, Kaiser sold his interest in the Hawaiian Village Hotel and ended his final partnership with Burns. The complicated financial transaction actually entailed both Burns and Kaiser selling the entire Village complex in January 1961, to the Hilton Hotels Corporation. Fritz Burns then formed a new partnership with the company, the Hilton-Burns Hotels Corporation, to become a half-owner of the renamed Hilton Hawaiian Village. He and Kaiser parted on friendly terms.[46] The more conservative Burns had spent fifteen years trying to temper Kaiser's grandiose plans, while Kaiser had continually pushed Burns to expand the scope of their joint economic enterprises.[47] Henry Kaiser continued to supervise work at Hawaii Kai almost until his death, at the age of 85 at his Kahala estate on August 24, 1964.[48]

At the time Burns formed a partnership with Hilton Hotels, construction at the Hawaiian Village Hotel was judged to be largely complete, with over a thousand rooms and extensive convention, shopping, and entertainment facilities. Kaiser biographers even attributed their split to

The Hilton Hawaiian Village in 1980, shortly after completion of the Tapa Tower. Diamond Head and the hotels of Waikiki are visible behind the Village, which lies adjacent to the lagoon.

Courtesy of Ken Skinner.

Kaiser's desire to be "a builder, not a manager," whereas Burns "worked with a finished product."[49] Over the next decade, however, Burns and Hilton aggressively expanded the company's hotel-building operations, both on the site of the Village and throughout the Hawaiian islands.

Between November 1961 and September 1966, Hilton broke ground on three new hotels elsewhere in the islands, including the Kahala Hilton on Oahu, the Hilton Kale Kaanapali in Maui, and the Kona Hilton on the "big island" of Hawaii.[50] At the same time, they continued to expand the Hilton Hawaiian Village property. In 1965, Burns announced a new building program at the Village that included an eight-

hundred-room hotel on the site of the Village's original two-
story lagoon apartments, to be known as the "Rainbow
Tower." At architect Welton Becket's suggestion, the tower
featured a multi-colored beachfront façade clearly visible to
every ship passing Waikiki. It could also be seen from every
plane landing at Honolulu International Airport, so that the
signature rainbow was one of the first impressions of Hawaii
for many tourists. Also under construction was a 234-unit
apartment hotel.[51] They were followed two years later by the
"Lagoon Tower" and expanded shopping and entertainment
facilities on the Village property. These additions dramatically altered the appearance of the area. The tiny cottages and
studios of the original hotel vanished under the foundations
of huge new hotel towers and shops, and the Village became
a premier tourist mecca far beyond the scope imagined by
Kaiser and Burns only ten years before.[52]

Fritz Burns discovered himself in a unique position in his
partnership with Hilton. For the first time since he was in his
twenties as an employee of Dickinson & Gillespie, he was
not the principal executive of his own company. Even in his
ventures with Henry J. Kaiser, Burns had served as president
while allowing Kaiser's name to take top billing in nomencla-
ture and marketing. The two had always worked more or less
as partners in a relatively unstructured corporate environment. Hilton, however, was a well-established corporation
with an executive structure already in place, and Burns had to
adapt to an environment where it was no longer feasible to
analyze every invoice, direct every meeting, and personally
oversee every new structure built. The transition was eased by
Burns' friendship with company founder Conrad N. Hilton.
With the ascension of Hilton's son, Barron, to the positions
of president and chief executive officer of Hilton Hotels in
1966, he and Burns also shared a close relationship.[53]

Burns' extensive social contacts throughout Hawaii
proved a valuable business asset during his partnership with

Hilton. Greg Dillon remembered a social event he attended with Burns in Hawaii while the company was having trouble getting financing from Hawaiian banks for a new hotel. "We were having a cocktail party before a deal which would take place shortly thereafter," Dillon remembered. "Fritz said to me at one point, 'We need to get everyone together [for the bank financing].' I said facetiously, 'They're all here. All the directors of the bank are here at the cocktail party!' So Fritz said 'Well, let's get them over into the corner and tell them we have to have a meeting.' So we got them all into the corner, Fritz closed up the deal, and the next morning the directors held a meeting and ratified it. That's the kind of man he was."[54]

Burns' success in the Hilton corporate environment can be deduced from his rapid acceptance into the upper echelons of Hilton management. Only a year after his local partnership with Hilton at the Hawaiian Village, Burns was made a director of Hilton Hotels in 1962. Two years later, he became Vice Chairman. That the Hilton Corporation, which owned and operated hotels and other business ventures throughout the world, would promote Burns so quickly is a testament to his performance. He remained a Director until 1977, and added to his extensive travel schedule the numerous Hilton executive meetings held around the globe.[55]

When Fritz Burns' health began to decline in the late 1970s and he reevaluated his investments, he judged the Hilton-Burns venture in Hawaii to be too large a financial undertaking for himself and his partners. "Fritz brought us all together and told us 'the hotel business is a young man's game'," remembered Ken Skinner. "We had gotten out of that situation everything Fritz had expected and a whole lot more. We asked Hilton for permission to find an outside buyer."[56]

Burns and his associates found a willing buyer in Prudential Insurance, which had already collaborated with Hilton Hotels on other ventures throughout the world. In 1977, Prudential agreed to purchase the entire Burns stake in the Hilton Hawaiian Village, a massive complex of over 1,800 rooms. After complicated negotiations to divide shared properties and investments, the deal was finalized in December of 1977.[57] A sale price was never made public, though the combined assets of Burns' stake in Hilton-Burns were valued at over fifty million dollars. Burns still held construction and lumber interests in Hawaii, as well as a wide circle of friends and associates, and he remained involved in social and business circles in the Islands. He also continued to visit his Kahala home on Oahu until his death, but his adventures as a Hawaii hotelier were complete. Of his original Hawaiian Village Hotel, by 2000 there remained only a number of the original palm trees planted by him and Henry Kaiser in 1955. For miles in both directions, however, stood the hotel towers of a multibillion-dollar tourist industry which began in earnest the day Burns and Kaiser threw open the doors of the Hawaiian Village Hotel.

CHAPTER NINE

No Rest For The Busy

"Fritz Burns and his associates had the morality that is missing in a lot of companies today, and they inspired that morality in me. You don't have to cheat to make it, and it takes some hard work and discipline, and you can't have immediate gratification. It takes some time. That's what I learned from Fritz B. Burns and his associates."

Ed Hogan, 2000.[1]

Fritz Burns reached the traditional retirement age of 65 years on October 9, 1964. It was a Friday, a work day, and so it came and went with little fanfare. As always, he began his morning with a swim in the backyard pool of his home on South Hudson Avenue in Hancock Park, a fashionable neighborhood located near downtown Los Angeles. As his fortunes had improved since the Depression years when he lived on the beach, Burns had forsaken the chilly waves of the Pacific for a heated pool, but his morning swim was nevertheless a daily ritual. Next, he gathered into two heavy briefcases the various work materials he had carried home. There were office papers, a cascading roll of accounting tape kept at his bedside to scribble down any late-night thoughts, and last, a tiny pocket notebook in which he kept his daily schedule as well as the inspirational phrases and ideas which might come to him at his desk, in his car, or even in church.[2]

He arrived at the office, located in his "Home of Tomorrow" at the corner of Wilshire and Highland boulevards, at precisely ten in the morning, an hour after his staff. They were all his closest confidants; his son Pat, Joseph Rawlinson, Ken Skinner, Charlie Getchell, Dick Schulte, Fran Thomas, and Bill Ridgeway. After a morning greeting, Burns sat down with his secretary, Jackie Sanborn, to go over tasks for the day. Fridays were easier than Mondays, because Burns often organized and evaluated his paperwork on Sundays at home. "He always said that he didn't consider it work, that it was a hobby, that it was his good time," Sanborn commented. "He used to bring in a foot-high stack of papers he'd have worked on at home. He'd put it on my desk, and we'd go through everything he had done. I would be sitting there listening as he turned over page after page after page. There would be tapes and tapes of dictation, too. Then there were his notebooks. They were hardly legible—it would just be all scribbles, to the point where the next day he'd be looking at it and couldn't figure out what he had said."[3]

Lunch would generally be a business affair, with the associates in the office joined by Bill Hannon, who kept a separate office in Playa Del Rey. In the afternoons, Burns could sometimes be persuaded to turn on the wall-mounted television, a holdover from the Home of Tomorrow, if a World Series game or other sporting event was on the air, but otherwise he worked straight through until six in the evening.[4] Much of that time was spent on the telephone to monitor the operations of his own companies in Hawaii and throughout northern and southern California and to fulfill his duties as a director of Hilton Hotels. His quitting time might have been much later had it not been for Gladys Burns' phone calls for her tardy husband. "Pop used to like to have a drink with Mom before dinner," Burns' stepdaughter, Frances Morehart, remembered. "Mom would have to call him at the office and tell him, 'If you don't come home from that office right now you're not getting your drink.'"[5]

In addition to work, Fritz and Gladys Burns' high social visibility and charity work involved them in a busy calendar of social obligations in the evenings and on weekends. Both were friends of Los Angeles' most prominent political, business, and religious leaders, and Burns remained close with a number of his fellow developers, the most prominent of whom was Ben Weingart. Weingart's career path had paralleled Burns', and he had enjoyed considerable success in building suburban housing, shopping centers, apartments, and hotels in the Los Angeles area after World War Two. Like Burns, Weingart left the bulk of his fortune at his death to a foundation that bore his name and focused on social services and education. Fundraisers for charity and the social circuit frequented by members of society all demanded much of Fritz and Gladys' time. In addition, Gladys was closely involved with conservative political causes. Family obligations were also not neglected. All three of Gladys' children were married with families, and Fritz and Gladys had twelve grandchildren. The number and scope of these multiple commitments might have merited retirement from a business routine, but Fritz Burns nevertheless arrived for work at the corner of Wilshire and Highland boulevards every day at ten in the morning, six days a week, until he was 75 years old. His focus had changed slightly over the years from house and community building to include industrial parks, shopping centers and hotels, but in work ethic and method his "retirement" years featured no dramatic difference from his earlier career.

Since the days of Marlow-Burns and the development of Westchester during World War Two, Burns had retained extensive land holdings in the Westchester and Playa Del Rey area. He had developed much of the land for single-family housing under the aegis of Kaiser Community Homes from 1946 to 1948, and 640 acres had been condemned in 1946 for expansion of Los Angeles International Airport. The bulk of the remaining property lay south of Manchester Avenue and to the west of Lincoln Boulevard. Los Angeles International Airport marked the southern boundary of the property, and to the east was the wartime development of Westchester. When Kaiser Community Homes scaled down its home construction operations in the early 1950s, Fritz Burns & Associates had undertaken another large community building program in this area, "West Westchester."[6] Along Manchester Avenue, Burns set aside land for civic groups as well as for churches of numerous denominations, all of which were allowed to purchase the land at cost. He also deeded a substantial parcel of land abutting Manchester Avenue in Playa Del Rey to the City of Los Angeles for the construction of Westchester High School. On the majority of the acreage south of Manchester, Burns and his associates built over a thousand single-family homes, using the house plans, construction methods, and even many of the same employees as Burns' earlier Kaiser Community Homes operations.[7]

Undeveloped acreage between West Westchester and Pershing Boulevard, near the coast, was sold piecemeal to private developers for apartment complexes and condominiums, although Burns built two large apartment developments in the area himself.[8] He also set aside further land on Manchester for a small community shopping center to be built and managed by his commercial leasing company, Lincoln-Manchester Properties. Burns did not have far to travel in order to find the planning and subdivision maps for the area; he and his associates in Dickinson & Gillespie had drawn them up originally over three decades earlier.[9] "West Westchester" was built entirely within the original boundaries of Burns' ambitious Del Rey Hills luxury subdivision from the Dickinson & Gillespie days before the Depression. Immediately behind the shopping center was the site of his oil strike in 1934, while on the bluffs less than a mile to the west sat his onetime home on the renamed Waterview Street, and the beach where he had pitched his lonely tent during the Depression. While developing the westernmost parcels of West Westchester, Burns commented to friends and family that he was possessed of an eerie sense of *déjà vu*, for in many cases he was selling land for which he had made the original sales pitch thirty years earlier.[10]

As the population of the area expanded, Burns began working with Cardinal James Francis McIntyre, the Roman Catholic Archbishop of Los Angeles, and his archdiocesan chancellor, Monsignor Benjamin Hawkes, on plans for a Catholic high school in the area. Burns had been close friends with both McIntyre and Hawkes since the early 1950s, and in 1961 the Cardinal named Burns a "Knight of Malta," a prestigious honor for a lay person in the Catholic Church. After surveying various locations for the school, the three decided on a large undeveloped parcel Burns owned in West Westchester south of Manchester Avenue. He arranged the land transfer in a manner that would benefit not only his church, but also one of his favorite philanthropic beneficiaries, Loyola Law School. Dividing the property in half, Burns donated half to the Archdiocese and half to the law school for the Archdiocese to purchase at cost in February 1963. All parties benefited. Burns received a tax write-off for both donations, the Archdiocese acquired the necessary acreage for its high school at a fraction of the value of the whole parcel, and Loyola Law School gained $100,000 in funding for a new building on its downtown campus.[11]

When construction began, Cardinal McIntyre offered to name the new school after Burns to honor his donation and contributions to the Archdiocese. Burns had spent a lifetime in business deferring to partners in the naming of his ventures; only in Fritz B. Burns & Associates did his name have pride of place. He thought the notion of a "Fritz B. Burns Roman Catholic High School" unseemly, particularly because he was still living. He reached a compromise with the Cardinal by transferring the honor to his grandfather and namesake, Bernard, and the institution became St. Bernard Roman Catholic High School after St. Bernard of Clairvaux.[12]

Fritz Burns with Cardinal James Francis McIntyre, head of the Roman Catholic Archdiocese of Los Angeles from 1948 to 1970 and a close friend of Fritz and Gladys Burns, at the opening ceremonies of the Airport-Marina Hotel, January 1962. Burns' jacket pin identifies him as a member of the Knights of Malta, an honor bestowed upon him by McIntyre a year earlier. *Fritz B. Burns Collection, Loyola Marymount University.*

Because the area was still without adequate sewers and storm drains at the time, Burns was required to build a drainage ditch near the high school to gather runoff and rainwater in order to gain building permits for the surrounding plots. Once completed, the "pond" proved an irresistible draw to the nearby students. William Hannon remembered Fritz Burns' reaction to the potential danger. "Burns came out and took a look at [the pond]. He said 'Bill, we'd better put a fence around it' . . . so we put the fence around it. Then he came out again, and he thought about it and then he said, 'You better hire some of the kids to watch this.'" The job was a choice one for a high school student, and for years afterward, graduates of St. Bernard approached Hannon at social events to thank him for giving them jobs as "pond sitters."[13]

At the northeastern boundary of West Westchester, Burns still held a valuable piece of undeveloped property on the corner of Manchester Avenue and Lincoln Boulevard, a mile north of Los Angeles International Airport and a mile south of the new yacht harbor, Marina Del Rey. Although the land was well suited for a shopping center because of its central location for the area population and its frontage on two major traffic arteries, Burns had the success of the Hawaiian Village Hotel fresh in his mind. He envisioned a hotel complex attached to a shopping center. It would offer lodging to tourists and business travelers from the airport and simultaneously exploit the large retail market created by the rapidly growing population of West Westchester and Playa Del Rey.

In January 1958, Burns announced he had hired Welton Becket to design the 250-room Airport Marina Hotel on the corner of Lincoln and Manchester. Construction was handled by Jackson Brothers, which Burns and Robert Munro later owned under the title of Munro-Burns & Jackson Brothers. Pat Burns was placed in charge of furnishings and decorations for the entire complex. Adjacent to the hotel, Burns built a shopping center with a full-service supermarket, bowling alley, a number of small shops, a branch of Security-First National Bank, and a multi-level parking garage.[14] In addition, Ed Hogan opened a branch of his travel agency in the lobby of the hotel.[15]

Los Angeles' hotel industry was heavily concentrated in the downtown area at the time, and rival hotel operators reacted with scorn to Burns' hotel "way out there in the boondocks."[16] Burns was gambling that the arrival of the jet age would mean an enormous increase in the amount of air travel, and those passengers would be loath to take a taxi all the way downtown when a comparable hotel existed just a mile from the airport. The gamble paid off. Within several years of opening in January 1962, the Airport Marina Hotel was boasting the highest occupancy rates of any hotel in Los Angeles. "As fast as we could build those doggone rooms, we would fill up the hotel," Ken Skinner remembered. "And the occupancy was astounding. We would tell people we were operating at a 92% occupancy, anywhere from 92% to 95%, and they just couldn't believe it."[17] Through several expansions, including a twelve-story tower visible from the airport, Burns eventually increased the hotel's capacity to 760 rooms. He later signed a long-term lease with the AmFac Corporation to operate the hotel, but held ownership of the complex until his death.[18]

In the shopping centers at the Airport Marina and in Panorama City, Fritz Burns made the transition from builder to landlord. Instead of realizing a single large profit from the sale of commercial structures, he and his partners gained steady revenue streams from retail and office space rentals while retaining ownership of the property. He replicated this financial model in the following years with shopping centers in Fremont and Pasadena. On the east side of the San Francisco Bay, Fritz Burns and Henry Kaiser had initially planned a large residential development at Fremont as part of Kaiser Community Homes.[19] Kaiser had purchased the land for use as a quarry, and the high cost of grading the land for housing development in the 1940s led the two men to seek other home building sites. While much of the land was eventually sold or condemned for public use, Burns built a shopping center in anticipation of residential population growth in the surrounding area. Because the area population grew more slowly than expected, the center struggled for years and never achieved the success of Burns' other retail centers. Fremont was also physically removed from Burns' Los Angeles base of operations, which hindered the micro-management style Burns had always used with such success to revive other struggling projects.[20]

In Pasadena, Burns joined a syndicate including local business magnate Edwin Pauley, Fred Marlow, and Harrison Baker, among others, to develop the Foothill-Rosemead Shopping Center. Burns had previously been a partner in the residential development of Hastings Ranch, on 1,100 acres bordering Sierra Madre that Marlow and Baker had subdivided in the early 1950s, though they left home construction to small local builders.[21] Recognizing the substantial retail market created by Hastings Ranch as well as the rapidly growing population of Pasadena and Arcadia, Burns and his partners built a new shopping center at the junction of Foothill Boulevard and Rosemead Boulevard, at the foot of the Sierra Madre Mountains. The Foothill-Rosemead Shopping Center, now known as Hastings Ranch, grew to become a highly profitable complex including movie theaters, supermarkets, and a wide array of restaurants in addition to its retail base. Burns later commented that he and his partners had gone from "collecting a crop-sharing rental on alfalfa to collecting a percentage rental on everything from benzedrine to kiddy rides."[22]

In addition to new retail ventures, Burns and his associates also leased and operated various industrial parks, a venture uniquely suited to Burns' numerous land holdings adjacent to airports. He had long planned for future residential developments near airports and aerospace operations, recognizing the growth potential of the aerospace industry both during and after World War Two. As a result, after Kaiser Community Homes completed its homebuilding operations in 1952, Burns still held valuable land near growing airports in Los Angeles, San Fernando, and San Jose.

At San Jose, Burns purchased over ninety acres of land adjacent to the local airport, a minor facility in 1946, but rapidly on its way to becoming a major economic transfer point by the 1960s. The property had been condemned and cleared by the airport years before for a planned expansion that was never implemented. Beginning in 1962, Burns put the property to a different use and developed it as the Santa Clara–San Jose Industrial Park.[23] The majority of new tenants, freight and aerospace companies seeking a financial advantage in proximity to the airport, built their own facilities while leasing the property. The Park was an immediate success, with over eighty percent of the available acreage rented in the first year of business.[24]

In San Fernando, north of Panorama City and adjacent to Burns' Griffith Ranch in the San Fernando Valley, this success story was repeated with the San Fernando Airport Industrial Park. Much like the growth of Panorama City's shopping center had been spurred by freeways pushing into the Valley, the industrial park profited from a peerless location, within a mile of the intersections of five major freeways at the north end of the San Fernando Valley. Burns also captured a significant market for aircraft hangers, because the adjacent airport was in constant use by flight training companies and numerous private plane owners. Warehouses, aircraft hangars, and shipping companies soon occupied the land where Burns' stepson, Ed Scheller, and thousands of others had once raced hot rods.[25]

Just as it appeared Fritz Burns might finally be out of new land development opportunities in the 1970s, he looked toward the desert east of Los Angeles. Years before, he and Henry Kaiser had lamented their failure to foresee the Palm Springs real estate and tourism craze that had made overnight millionaires out of developers and speculators alike. Kaiser had used that missed opportunity to convince Fritz Burns to join him in Hawaii. Two decades later, Burns saw new opportunities in the desert, both as a hotelier and as a home builder. With these tasks in mind, he began two new enterprises after 1965, a planned residential community in La Quinta and the Erawan Garden Hotel in nearby Indian Wells.

Located thirteen miles south of Palm Springs, La Quinta was a hot, dusty desert town when it first piqued Fritz Burns' interest in 1964. Burns visited the area to negotiate a potential deal for the La Quinta Hotel and Country Club. One of his top salesmen from Westchester, Al Kerwin, had built a successful real estate practice in the area after leaving Marlow-Burns in 1941.[26] Unable to make a deal with the hotel operators, Burns went for an exploratory drive with Kerwin to survey the surrounding land. The physical condition of the area reminded him of the San Fernando Valley in the 1920s, isolated but ripe for housing development once utilities and proper transportation routes were built. The town had already been subdivided for residences by a hopeful real estate speculator in the 1930s, but never developed. The remoteness of the area did not bother Burns; the same had been true of Westchester, of Panorama City, and of the Hawaiian Village Hotel, and all were proof that vision and proper marketing could triumph over physical distance. In March of 1965, Burns partnered with Al Kerwin in the Desert Siesta Company and began acquiring land in La Quinta.[27]

Kerwin was charged with purchasing lots to avoid a speculative bubble if Burns' involvement in the enterprise became public. One of their first purchases, a La Quinta ranch once owned by the influential Rosecrans family of Los Angeles, became a vacation home for Pat Burns.[28] Kerwin assembled over 1,600 individual lots and a number of large ranches, but only seven houses were built before Fritz Burns' health began to fail in 1977. Burns and Kerwin agreed to suspend home construction and to sell the lots individually to builders. There was a touch of irony to the decision. In one of the final business ventures of his life, Fritz Burns had returned to the business model with which he had begun his career fifty years earlier, by reselling undeveloped home sites to hopeful speculators and private builders.[29]

In nearby Indian Wells, Burns returned to the hotel industry in 1968. The operators of a local 125-room resort, the Erawan Garden Hotel, had filed for bankruptcy. The Transamerica Corporation had foreclosed on the loan and was looking for a buyer. Burns recognized a situation similar to one he had confronted years earlier with the Hawaiian Village Hotel. Indian Wells and Palm Springs had a limited tourist season, from January to April. In order to survive, the hotel needed to attract corporations and business groups for annual meetings and conventions. The hotel lacked convention facilities, however, and 125 rooms were inadequate for large groups. Burns purchased the property from Transamerica on favorable financing terms and began an expansion program. Over the next three years, he added another 125 rooms and a two-story annex for conventions and large meetings. Pat Burns also oversaw a complete renovation of the hotel to bring it up to par with similar operations in nearby Palm Springs. "It was a fine little property that really carried itself," commented Ken Skinner. "We closed down during the summers, but the group business we booked in the fall and then the tourists kept it [profitable]."[30] As the Erawan Garden Hotel became financially successful in the 1970s, it was eventually joined by a number of other resort hotels built by national hotel chains in La Quinta and Indian Wells.

As he approached his seventy-sixth birthday in 1975, Fritz Burns began preparations for the maintenance of his business assets, philanthropic endeavors, and personal legacy beyond his death. The structure of Fritz Burns & Associates had already begun to reflect Burns' recognition of his advancing age. For a number of years his contemporary, Charles Getchell, had held the title of President of the company, while Burns served as Chairman. In June of 1975, Burns elevated Ken Skinner to the position of President, with Getchell becoming Vice Chairman. Bill Ridgeway had been established for a number of years as the sales and leasing manager of the Panorama City and Pasadena shopping centers, with William Hannon in charge of the Westchester and Playa Del Rey commercial and residential properties. In addition, over the years Burns' inner circle of associates and employees, including Charles Getchell, William Hannon, Bill Ridgeway, Joseph Rawlinson, Ken Skinner, Winifred Cockey, Carl Herziger, Robert Munro, and his son, Pat Burns, had become major partners in his shopping centers, industrial parks, and hotels. Fritz Burns had known and worked with many of them for astounding lengths of time: Charles Getchell for 55 years by 1979, Winifred Cockey for 44 years, William Hannon for 42 years, Ken Skinner for 31 years, and Joseph Rawlinson for 26 years. He could be assured his business ventures would remain properly managed under the control of these associates, all of whom had financially benefited during their long partnership with Fritz Burns.[31]

Greg Dillon, Fritz Burns, Barron Hilton, and Bob Munro sail past the Kona Hilton, circa 1968.
Courtesy of Ken Skinner.

Burns had managed his many philanthropic endeavors since 1955 through a not-for-profit fund, the Burns Foundation, to which he would normally transfer the necessary assets from one of his companies before distributing them to the intended beneficiaries. He had long since resolved to dedicate the bulk of his considerable fortune after his death to philanthropy, with a specific focus on local educational and religious charities. Toward that end, in 1975 he created the Fritz B. Burns Trust, later renamed the Fritz B. Burns Foundation, and made it the major beneficiary of his estate upon his death. Burns served as President until his death and was succeeded by his son Patrick. He had asked Joseph Rawlinson to serve as President after he and Patrick died, in part because Burns, an increasingly devout Catholic in his later years, had always admired Rawlinson's commitment to the values and the moral strictures of his Mormon faith. Other officers between 1975 and 2000 included Gladys and Patrick Burns, Charles Getchell, Edward Schulte, William Hannon, Ken Skinner, and Lorraine Perry. Directors of the Foundation have included all of the above, as well as Edmund Schneiders, Reverend Charles Casassa, S.J., Donald Freeberg, Edward Slattery, Richard Dunn, and J. Robert Vaughan.

In 1975, Fritz Burns also created an updated will and made provisions for his surviving family, including Gladys and Patrick, and a number of close friends. The varied slate of assets included in that will serve as a testament to the diversity of Burns' economic activities over the course of his life. Still extant from 1937 was Marlow-Burns & Company, his original home-building enterprise with Fred Marlow, as well as a later development company formed with Marlow to develop and sell commercial properties. In addition, there were his real estate and commercial holdings in the Hilton Hawaiian Village; his diversified holdings in

Hawaii, including a lumber operation and a construction company; commercial properties in Panorama City, Pasadena, Westchester and Playa Del Rey, Fremont, and San Fernando; and real estate in Playa Del Rey, Westchester, the San Fernando Valley, Riverside County, and Hollywood.

The 1977 sale of Burns' interest in Hilton-Burns Hotels also increased Burns' financial holdings. By the time of his death in 1979, the total value of his estate was over one hundred million dollars. After an out-of-court settlement between the Fritz B. Burns Foundation and the children of Gladys Burns, she received a substantial portion of Fritz Burns' estate in addition to the amount stipulated in the will.[32] The Fritz B. Burns Foundation received the bulk of Burns' fortune, an amount that had grown in value by September 1984 to slightly more than one hundred million dollars.

His enormous wealth and financial interests aside, Fritz Burns still arrived daily at the office with his two briefcases, overflowing with the minutiae of his multiple businesses, until his faltering health made it impossible a few years before his death. He entered the final chapter of his life with the same desire to conquer each new and exciting task that had been a hallmark of his fifty-year career as a businessman. Al Kerwin, who had worked for an enthusiastic builder and salesman by the name of Fritz Burns at Toluca Wood in 1940 and become partners with him again in La Quinta thirty years later, once offered this summary of the man: "Burns believed in accomplishment instead of making money. If you accomplish something, the money follows . . . Burns went through life seeking accomplishments. He used money to accomplish things."[33] After a lifetime of chasing those accomplishments, Fritz Burns found himself in the final years of his life with far more money than he could ever need and an ever-shorter amount of time in which to "accomplish things." Ever the sensible businessman, he created the Fritz B. Burns Foundation to insure his money would be used to build on those accomplishments long after his own death.

CHAPTER TEN

The Long Shadow

> *DEATH-BED*
> *So now he lay there*
> *with withered shank*
> *perpetrator of a thousand pranks*
> *when I was young and*
> *virile and spry*
> *and now it comes the time to die*
> *God made a time for everything:*
> *Accept it.*
> *Fritz Burns, 1978.*[1]

By Fritz Burns' seventy-sixth birthday in October 1975, he and his associates were divesting the company of many of its most time-consuming projects, including the Hilton-Burns Hotels partnership in Hawaii and the building program in La Quinta. Nevertheless, the firm's holdings were still substantial, and Burns maintained his heavy work schedule. For that reason, his secretary Jackie Sanborn expressed surprise when Burns emerged from his office at three in the afternoon one Friday. "He had both his briefcases with him, and he looked like he was going to leave work early," Sanborn remembered. "I had never seen him do that before. He said to me 'I don't feel well,' and went home. It was so unlike him to leave early or be ill, I was really surprised. The next thing we knew, he called us and told us he had pneumonia."[2]

Burns continued to work from home while recovering from his illness, but the physical vigor he had maintained through years of exercise began to diminish. Soon after, he suffered a minor heart attack and a small stroke; while they did not incapacitate him mentally, both contributed to his physical decline. By that summer, Burns began to experience heart trouble and edema. Gladys also was beginning to show symptoms of Alzheimer's disease, and Burns' son Patrick was also in declining health after suffering from hepatitis for almost a decade. Gladys' daughters Frances and Maria came daily to care for Fritz and Gladys, and Burns' associates traveled often from the Wilshire office to meet with him and keep him updated on his business affairs.[3]

Burns approached his illness with the same management style and attention to detail that had marked his business career. With Jackie Sanborn, he began sorting through the enormous collection of documents and mementos he had saved over his lifetime. "He wanted to stay active and keep his mind busy, because he couldn't stand to do nothing," Sanborn remembered. "We started to go through his file cabinets one by one. There were so many of them—he always filed anything he received, and he had never thrown any of it away. He still had everything, including the love letters he had written to Gladys when they were dating."[4]

Aware of his increasing infirmity, Burns recognized it was no longer necessary or prudent to maintain the strenuous pace that had so defined his work career. In a personal note, he admonished himself: "Be more careful about your health and physical exertions. Don't do or think about anything you don't have to. It's time for you to be lazy. Don't feel as though you have to do something every day in order to justify living."[5] Unable to remain motionless, Burns abandoned this relaxed regimen as quickly as it began. He undertook several personal projects in addition to his continued business meetings, such as assembling notes for his autobiography and working with his son Pat to publish his poems as a Christmas present for his family and friends.[6]

By Christmas 1978, Burns was confined to a hospital bed. While his rapid decline distressed his family and friends, his

personal papers suggest Fritz Burns himself was more prepared. He had begun to make arrangements for the disposal
of his personal possessions. Unable to shake the lessons
learned in a lifetime of leadership and authority, Burns
managed even the smallest of these somber details. "Start
giving a thousand dollars to every relative I can think of," he
noted to himself, and in a note to his son, asked "Pat, when I
die, as we all do, where should I be buried? Should we get a
family plot now, in order to save a lot of rushing around at
the last minute?"[7]

On the morning of February 19, 1979, Burns awoke before
dawn in his house on South Hudson Avenue with an unusual
tightness in his chest. Assuming the discomfort was caused
by hunger, he asked for an early breakfast. Within the hour,
his heart failed. By the time he was discovered, he had died
silently in his bed, eight months shy of eighty years.[8] Among
his personal possessions was found a final poem, accepting
the inevitable approach of death as the final chapter of a
divinely ordered existence.

Fritz Burns' funeral was held on February 21, 1979 at St.
Basil Roman Catholic Church on Wilshire Boulevard, his
home parish since 1940. Cardinal Timothy Manning, Arch-
bishop of Los Angeles, presided over the ceremony, and
Burns' longtime friend and pastor of St. Basil's, Monsignor
Benjamin Hawkes, spoke at length of Burns' modesty and
simplicity in his eulogy. The twenty-two honorary pallbear-
ers represented friends and business partners from the entire
span of Burns' career, including A. H. Clarke, Greg Dillon,
Charles Getchell, Barron Hilton, William B. Hannon, Al
Kerwin, Fred Marlow, Robert Munro, Joseph E. Rawlinson,
N.S. Ridgeway, Ken Skinner, Dick Schulte, and Edwin
Pauley, Sr. Four motor escorts followed his coffin to Calvary
Cemetery in East Los Angeles, where he was buried in the
Carson family plot. Six years later, Gladys Carson Burns was
buried next to him.[9]

Fritz Burns' circle of acquaintances had grown so large by the end of his life that he sent over two thousand Christmas cards every year. For months after Burns' death, his family received condolences from many of these former employees, colleagues from the building and hotel industries, business and political figures, and longtime friends. A testament to Burns' hiring practices and personal convictions, they represented leaders in every field and a broad diversity of ethnicity, religion, and background. Burns' stepdaughter Frances Morehart, who responded to the letters, recalled that many condolences came from unexpected sources. A Zeta Psi fraternity brother of Burns' from the University of Minnesota in 1917 remembered Burns more than sixty years later. A number of letters were from former associates who credited Burns with giving them their start in business. "Your father was probably the most influential man that I ever met," Ed Hogan wrote to Patrick Burns. "He was always willing to share his knowledge and was much more humble than most people of lower stature. I've never met a finer man and thank God for the privilege of knowing your father."[10]

Eulogies and obituaries for Fritz Burns stressed his business accomplishments and pioneering efforts in the home building field, public achievements by whose high visibility Burns had become a renowned figure deserving of such recognition. Less prominent, however, was his devotion to philanthropic causes. Burns had been discreet about his charitable contributions, and had limited his time and efforts to select causes he felt would benefit from his attention. "I have a bad habit about becoming tenacious about projects in which I take an initial interest," he wrote to a friend in 1970, "and invariably they grow into bigger and better and more expensive things."[11] Among a number of organizations he aided, three in particular benefited from Burns' generosity: Loyola Marymount University, Loyola Law School, and St. Anne's Maternity Home, all in Los Angeles. Each institution enjoyed several decades of Burns' generosity and stewardship.

Fritz Burns' affiliation with Loyola Marymount University began in 1927, when he worked with Harry Culver to bring Loyola College to the Del Rey Hills during the development of Palisades Del Rey. During the school's move from downtown Los Angeles in 1928, Burns volunteered as one of six "generals" of the school's fundraising effort to construct a new campus. He renewed his relationship with Loyola in the 1940s, when the Marlow-Burns development in Westchester brought him within walking distance of the campus. One of Burns' top salesmen at the time, William Hannon, had graduated from the University in 1937, and Burns' son, Patrick, attended the school in 1948. During and after World War Two, Burns had also formed friendships with several members of the Society of Jesus, the Jesuits, who operated the institution.[12] From 1950 until 1968, he served as a University Regent, and from 1945 until his death his gifts to the University totaled several million dollars. In 1963, for example, Burns joined with oil magnate Frank Seaver to fund a new science building for the University, Seaver Hall. He declined the University's offer to name the building after both men because he "didn't believe in hyphenated names."[13]

Beyond the public support Burns provided to Loyola Marymount, he was also involved for a number of years in a private endeavor to help one of the University's students. As an undergraduate at Loyola University in the 1960s, Gary Lease knew of Burns through a family friend, Fanchon Royer, whom Burns had dated in the 1930s. As he neared graduation, Lease was seeking funding for further studies in theology in Munich, Germany. After he wrote Burns a letter explaining his financial needs and intellectual goals, Lease was surprised to find himself summoned to Burns' offices at Wilshire and Highland for a meeting.

For the next five years, unbeknownst to his colleagues,

Burns funded Lease's tuition and expenses in Munich. Burns also enjoyed a long correspondence with Lease, in which he laughed about his own academic mishaps five decades earlier, offered advice on professional choices, and celebrated Lease's success. "I am delighted that you are doing so well," Burns wrote in 1965, "and believe me, I am being well rewarded just in the reading of your letters."[14] After earning his doctorate in Munich, Lease returned to Loyola University as a theology professor for a brief time in the early 1970s and went on to become the Chair of the Department of Religious Studies at the University of California at Santa Cruz. "In a very fundamental way I owed him much of what I am today," Lease wrote after Burns' death. "The fact that he took a chance and sent me to Germany at a time when the most treasured and most ancient ideals of a university education were still held dear by those who practiced them and who still passed them on to their students is something for which I must be forever thankful to him."[15]

After Burns' death, the Fritz B. Burns Foundation continued his public support of Loyola Marymount University. The Foundation gave over twenty million dollars to the school between 1983 and 2000, with more than thirteen million in grants for academic scholarships and financial aid for students in need. The campus' facilities have also been greatly expanded through funding from the Foundation, such as a 1983 grant for the Fritz B. Burns Fine Arts Center, a four-building complex and 212-seat recital hall that dramatically improved the University's fine arts program and facilities. In addition to these gifts, the Foundation served as the major contributor to a new eighteen-million-dollar fitness and health complex, the Fritz B. Burns Recreation Center, which opened in August 2000.[16]

Loyola Marymount has also benefited from the generosity of Burns' family, business associates and friends since his death. Individual financial support from F. Patrick Burns,

William Hannon, Ed Hogan, and Howard Drollinger, among others, has been a major factor in the University's continued growth, and a number of facilities and programs at the University bear their names. F. Patrick Burns and William Hannon rank among the University's most generous donors throughout its history. Patrick's gifts to the school totaled over twelve million dollars. Both also served as Trustees of the University during their lifetimes. In recognition of the longtime financial support of Fritz Burns, his Foundation, and his associates, the University's Westchester location was renamed the Fritz B. Burns campus in 1998.[17]

Burns' relationship with Loyola Marymount included his support of Loyola Law School, located in downtown Los Angeles. In addition to the law school's connection to the University, a personal tie also attracted Burns to the institution. Burns had first met Joseph E. Rawlinson, current President of the Fritz B. Burns Foundation, in 1952. Rawlinson was a Certified Public Accountant at Serene, Koster, & Barbour, a Los Angeles accounting firm employed by Burns. Burns' accountant and longtime friend Fred Pike had died that year, and Burns began to hire Rawlinson regularly for accounting work.[18]

Burns' legal matters had long been handled by his uncle, William Schreyer, who had forsaken real estate development for law school during the Depression and run a successful practice for many years in Los Angeles. By 1959, Schreyer's eyesight was failing, and he decided to retire. From 1954 to 1958, Rawlinson had been attending Loyola Law School's evening program, and six months after he passed the California bar in 1959, he moved into Burns' office as his regular legal counsel. "I already had great admiration for his personality before I started as his attorney," Rawlinson said. "In all the years I worked with him, I never saw him get testy with anyone or lose his temper over anything. He had a sweet way of treating everyone he worked with and dealt with."[19] The admiration was mutual, and through Rawlinson, Burns met and became friends with Father Joseph J. Donovan, S.J, Regent of Loyola Law School, in 1960.[20]

At the time, Father Donovan was seeking a new site for the law school, which had outgrown its campus on South Grand Avenue in downtown Los Angeles. Burns agreed to serve as Chairman of a fundraising campaign and made an initial gift of one million dollars to launch the drive. "The original downtown site on Grand Avenue is too small and the existing building not worth salvaging," Burns wrote to a friend in 1962. "I am very anxious to get this job done and all the money raised, then I will be through—or are we ever through?"[21] Burns arranged a sale of the existing law school property to Occidental Petroleum as well as the purchase of land owned by the Roman Catholic Archdiocese of Los Angeles on Ninth Street (now James Wood Boulevard), across the street from the former Chancery offices of the Archdiocese.[22] The Archdiocese also agreed to purchase land Burns had donated to Loyola Law School in Playa Del Rey, where the Archdiocese was building St. Bernard High School, to supplement the fundraising campaign.[23]

Moving to its new campus in 1964, Loyola Law School occupied modern facilities that represented a fivefold increase in available space. Burns continued to support the institution financially for the rest of his life, and made a major donation for further construction one year before his death. In recognition of his contributions to the Law School, Burns received an honorary Doctor of Laws degree from the institution at the June 1963 commencement exercises. He also served for a number of years as Honorary Co-Chairman of the school's Board of Visitors, and in 1978 was given the Loyola Law School Distinguished Achievement Award.[24]

After Burns' death, his Foundation continued his support of Loyola Law School and donated over fourteen million dollars over the next two decades. In addition to student

Fr. Charles Casassa, S.J., President of Loyola University from 1949 to 1969, views plans for Loyola Law School's new building with Fritz Burns in 1964. In recognition of his service to the school, Casassa honored Burns with a Doctor of Laws degree from Loyola University in 1967.
Courtesy of Loyola Law School.

financial aid, these grants allowed Loyola Law School to build a world-famous campus designed by architect Frank O. Gehry. "Almost all the buildings at the law school have been funded by Fritz Burns or the Burns Foundation," said Fr. Donald Merrifield, S.J., Chancellor of Loyola Marymount University and President of the University from 1969 to 1984. "They might have different names, such as Founders' Hall, because there's already a Fritz Burns Building, but they were all made possible by him and his Foundation." The sum of all contributions by Fritz Burns and the Fritz B. Burns Foundation to Loyola Marymount and Loyola Law School exceeds sixty million dollars, and the Foundation is the largest single contributor to both institutions.[25]

The third major beneficiary of Fritz and Gladys Burns' generosity for over forty years was St. Anne's Maternity Home, a Los Angeles philanthropy offering residential care and community-based services to pregnant and parenting young women. St. Anne's first opened in 1908 as a home for unmarried pregnant women, and for many years was one of only eight licensed maternity homes in California.[26] Gladys Burns first became involved with St. Anne's in the late 1920s, and was a founding member of the St. Anne's Ladies' Guild in 1938. In addition to financial support of the institution, members of the Guild also volunteered their time and effort. "Gladys was a very down-to-earth person in a lot of ways," commented Tom Owenson, President and Chief Executive Officer of St. Anne's since 1972. "I was told that she and Fritz had a beautiful home in Hancock Park, with a staff of house-keepers and maids to take care of their home, but she would come down to St. Anne's and be on her hands and knees, scrubbing the floors, doing the dirty work. She was very committed and very involved."[27]

Over the next several decades, Gladys made St. Anne's the primary focus of her philanthropic efforts, and served terms as president of the St. Anne's Foundation and as a member of the institution's board of directors. "It was a natural thing for me to want to do for these youngsters, I guess," she said later. "Becoming a good wife and mother myself, I just took to the whole idea; I rather extended my field, you might say."[28] In addition to Gladys' volunteer work, Fritz and Gladys Burns also provided extensive financial support to St. Anne's. Both were founding members of the St. Anne's Foundation, created in 1946 to fund the improvement and expansion of the institution's facilities, and were the principal contributors for building campaigns in 1955 and 1965. Their numerous acquaintances and prominent standing in the community gave them the opportunity to marshal many of Los Angeles' leading figures to attend fundraising events. At the gala opening of his "Home Of Tomorrow" in 1951, for example, Fritz Burns promised half the proceeds from admission prices to St. Anne's. Attendees included political figures, business associates, religious leaders, and a number of high-ranking entertainment industry stars, such as Ethel Barrymore, Bob and Dolores Hope, Mr. and Mrs. Ricardo Montalban, Archbishop James Francis McIntyre, Mr. and Mrs. Welton Becket, theater magnate Charles P. Skouras, and actress Loretta Young, a close friend of Gladys Burns and a longtime supporter of St. Anne's.[29]

As he did with Loyola Law School, Fritz Burns also creatively utilized his land holdings to benefit St. Anne's. During the development of West Westchester, Burns donated a large parcel of property zoned for commercial use on the south side of Manchester Avenue in Playa Del Rey to St. Anne's. He then arranged for his son Pat and his associates Charles Getchell and William Hannon to purchase the property, where they built a bank and family restaurant. As with Burns' earlier donations of land, the complicated transaction benefited all parties. Burns received a tax write-off for his donation of the property, St. Anne's received a large sum of cash, and Burns' associates acquired what they knew would become valuable commercial property when West Westchester developed.[30]

St. Anne's has continued to benefit from Fritz and Gladys Burns' generosity since their deaths. Since the Fritz B. Burns Foundation began distributing grants in 1983, St. Anne's has received over three million dollars in funding. In 1992, when the institution sought funds to construct a residential building to care for wards of the Los Angeles County Department of Children and Family Services, the Foundation was the principal contributor to the fundraising campaign. St. Anne's Maternity Home now offers shelter, parenting services, and educational programs to over two hundred pregnant and parenting adolescents each year through an on-site residential program. Outreach programs annually serve over a thousand adolescent parents in Los Angeles County, while school-based educational programs reach ten thousand more students throughout the county.[31]

While Loyola Marymount University, Loyola Law School, and St. Anne's Maternity Home are the three primary beneficiaries of the Fritz B. Burns Foundation, numerous other institutions receive grants from the organization. In keeping with Fritz Burns' intent and practice during his life, the Foundation assists institutions across the religious, social, and political spectrum. Under the stewardship of Burns' family, friends, and business associates, it has distributed over one hundred million dollars since 1983 for education, medical care, and social services.[32]

Besides Loyola Marymount and Loyola Law School, the Fritz B. Burns Foundation has supported over thirty educational institutions. These include the Roman Catholic Archdiocese of Los Angeles, Brigham Young University, Claremont McKenna College, Immaculate Heart High School, Loyola High School, Mount St. Mary's College, Notre Dame Academy, St. Bernard High School, and St. Genevieve High School. Other recipients include Los Angeles-area preschools, elementary schools, and secondary schools of numerous religious denominations, as well a number of colleges and universities in California and the western United States. The Foundation has focused on institutions serving the population of areas Fritz Burns helped to develop, such as schools in Westchester, Playa Del Rey, Panorama City, Burbank, and North Hollywood. The sum of these gifts surpasses sixty million dollars, and makes the Fritz B. Burns Foundation one of the largest educational philanthropies in Southern California.[33]

Over twenty-five hospitals, medical research facilities, and retirement and nursing homes have also received grants from the Fritz B. Burns Foundation. Primary beneficiaries include the Braille Institute, Children's Hospital of Los Angeles, Daniel Freeman Hospital, the Holy Cross Hospital Foundation, the Little Company of Mary Foundation, Queen of Angels/Hollywood Presbyterian Hospital, the Salk Institute, St. John of God Retirement Care, St. Joseph Medical Center, and Valley Presbyterian Hospital. Total grants for institutions in these fields are in excess of twenty million dollars.[34]

A third focus of the Foundation, social services, accounts for a plethora of grants to organizations ranging from counseling services to libraries to food banks. The combined value of these grants is over ten million dollars since 1983. Primary beneficiaries include the American Red Cross, Los Angeles Mission, M.E.N.D., the Salvation Army, San Fernando Mission, St. Joseph Center, Union Rescue Mission, United Way, the Westside Food Bank, the Boy Scouts of America, and the YMCA.[35]

Among his many accomplishments in business and philanthropy, Fritz Burns exerted a profound influence on America's shift from a nation of urban renters to suburban homeowners between 1935 and 1965. His founding role in the National Association of Home Builders, as well as his life-long defense of America' private housing industry, alone make him an important figure in the history of private housing in the United States. His most significant contribution to the housing industry and the nation as a whole remains his pioneering role in the introduction of the mass-produced, low-cost home. Burns built them by the thousands. Those who came after him, both in Southern California and across the nation, built them by the millions. Frank Lloyd Wright may have inspired the modern ranch house, but Fritz Burns and his more famous successors made it a ubiquitous American institution.

Comparison with his more widely known contemporaries illustrates Fritz Burns' significance in the development of the archetypal American suburb. In Long Island, New York, William Levitt reached national prominence in the postwar era in Levittown, where he incorporated principles of on-site mass construction and standardized floor plans to build seventeen thousand homes between 1947 and 1951. His accomplishments earned the builder numerous accolades and his portrait on the cover of *Time* magazine in July 1950.[36] One half century later, Levittown has become emblematic of both suburbia and American culture of the 1950s. The early aerial view of its stark curvilinear streets, treeless yards, and endless rows of nearly identical houses has been reproduced so often as to become a cliché, the "American Gothic" of its century. Accordingly, William Levitt is widely recognized as the source of the mass-pro-duced ranch home and the postwar suburb, as well as their attendant effects on American culture. In December 1998, William Levitt again graced the cover of *Time*, which dared to call Levittown "as much an achievement of its cultural moment as Venice or Jerusalem."[37]

On the opposite coast, Ben Weingart, Louis Boyar, and Mark Taper built on a similar scale in Southern California from 1949 to 1953. On beet fields near Long Beach, the three partners created the self-contained city of Lakewood, with over seventeen thousand homes around a commercial center. Assembly-line production techniques and standardized floor plans again allowed the developers to produce enormous numbers of homes in a brief period of time. Generous federal financing through the G.I. Bill brought war veterans en masse to the new community, which grew to over fifty thou-sand residents by 1954. As in Levittown, a majority of Lake-wood's residents worked outside the area and commuted to defense and industrial plants in Long Beach.[38]

Fritz Burns never attempted a unified housing project as large as Lakewood or Levittown. Even in the Westchester/Playa Del Rey area of Los Angeles, where Burns operated homebuilding firms almost continuously from 1940 to 1965, he produced fewer than four thousand homes. Though less than one fourth the total built in Levittown or Lakewood, these numbers only tell part of the story.

The first home Fritz Burns built with assembly-line methods on a standardized floor plan was completed at Westside Village. He built 787 more around it, refining his new methods of field construction in the process. In an industry noted for its conservatism and incremental change, Burns startled his peers by simultaneously pouring hundreds of concrete foundations, stockpiling mountains of shingles and lumber, shattering construction records, and building entire communities at once when his fellow builders were constructing ten or twenty homes at a time. He exploited new federal funding opportunities to finance his mass housing projects and recognized the potential market in housing defense workers. In these respects, the story of Westside Village is all but identical to that of Levittown and Lakewood—except that Westside Village opened in 1939.

Two years before America's entry into World War Two, five years before the introduction of the G.I. Bill, eight years before the first home was built in Levittown and a full decade before the developers of Lakewood were able to do the same, Fritz Burns had finished his first substantial tract of inexpensive, mass-produced homes. In this unprecedented endeavor, Burns used large-scale construction methods for housing that are incorrectly acknowledged to have been "introduced" in more famous postwar developments. In the eight years before other builders began to match Burns' output, he produced another four hundred homes in Toluca Wood, a thousand more in Westchester during World War Two, and another five thousand throughout the various developments of Kaiser Community Homes. By 1952, he had built more than three thousand more in Panorama City, and by 1965, a thousand more in West Westchester. At the very moment *Time* hailed William Levitt as the pioneer of mass housing construction and on-site assembly methods, Fritz Burns was putting the finishing touches on his ten thousandth mass-produced home.

In the first twenty-five years after the end of World War Two, private builders in the United States built close to thirty million new residences, almost all of them detached single-family homes.[40] Triple supports facilitated their construction and sale: generous federal financing, efficient methods of mass construction, and an eager population of middle-class buyers. The aspiring homeowners were willing to accept the deficiencies of these new communities in exchange for what Fritz Burns had called in 1943 "their own 'vine and fig tree,' their own bit of this earth, where they are at least to some extent masters of their fate."[41] Besides providing housing for more than fifteen million World War Two veterans, these homes ushered in a new era of widespread home ownership in America. In 1944, less than half of American households owned the house in which they lived; by 1999, two out of every three American homes was owned by its occupants.[42]

Fritz Burns' important role in the early years of this notable transformation in American life involved politics as well as "lumber and nails." Through his organization of the National Association of Home Builders and extensive campaigning on behalf of the private housing industry during and after World War Two, Burns assisted in the creation of federal policies favorable to the private home builder that included the G.I. Bill and the National Housing Act of 1949. In the undeveloped fields of Los Angeles, he offered a more tangible contribution in home sales and construction. Through radically new methods of on-site development at Westside Village and Toluca Wood before World War Two, Burns introduced home builders to the efficient construction practices that made the mass-produced housing of the post-war era possible.

In addition to the national impact of Fritz Burns' home building practices and innovations, an important element of his legacy remains his physical contribution to the built environment of Southern California. The total number of houses constructed by Burns and his associates from 1935 to 1975 stands in excess of twelve thousand. More than a hundred thousand residents of Southern California have lived in these neighborhoods in Panorama City, Westchester, North Hollywood, Playa Del Rey, Monterey Park, Ontario, Compton, Echo Park, Sylmar, Burbank, Torrance, and Windsor Hills. While individualizing their identical houses, they created the communities Burns envisioned more than a half century ago. The fortunes of these neighborhoods have risen and fallen over the years, and the homes have been remodeled, expanded, and altered to fit the needs of second and third generations of homeowners. Underlying the superficial alterations of almost every single home, however, is a variation on that one simple floor plan Burns introduced at Westside Village in 1939.

Despite a lifetime of pioneering work in multiple industries, and despite a Foundation continuing his generosity on a remarkable scale, these homes stand as the greatest accomplishment of Fritz B. Burns. They reflect not only his primary passion but also his most significant impact on the city in which he lived a long and fruitful life. The man once honored as "Mr. Housing, U.S.A." was at heart a builder of communities, a visionary with the rare ability to conjure two hundred homes out of a bean field and a neighborhood out of a cow pasture. From the first house he built in Windsor Hills to the final home in West Westchester, home building remained at the heart of his professional interests throughout his life.

The substantial and far-reaching impact of Fritz Burns' career as a home builder crowns his achievements as a realtor, industrialist, salesman, hotelier, civic leader, politician, retailer, philanthropist, and his personal favorite title, "merchandiser." That this litany of accomplishment describes a man who also experienced serious adversity and devastating failure in his lifetime makes his story even more remarkable. Such a chronicle of success was entirely unfamiliar to the penniless man living on the beach in Playa Del Rey in 1934, a man who knew the life of Job as well as the life of Riley. What insight did Fritz Burns have in that lonely tent, years removed from the profits of his past and the compound successes of his future? A decade after he worked his way up from that humble dwelling, Burns wrote a note to himself that simultaneously reflected both the ambition and humility that enabled him to return from adversity in each of his endeavors: "My knowledge is quite limited. In business, I know nothing except how to make money. In speaking, nothing except how to get across my idea. In society, nothing except how to make people like me. In organization, nothing except how to be president."[43]

The facts of Fritz Burns' life suggest that he knew a great deal more. The multiplicity of roles he sought out and excelled in over the course of that life proves a singular and indisputable fact: in that lonely tent on a windswept beach in 1934, over a thousand miles from his Midwestern home, accompanied by little more than the ocean's roar and the meager remainders of failed ambitions, lived a man of extraordinary vision.

APPENDIX

Officers and Directors of the
Fritz B. Burns Foundation, 1955-2001

OFFICERS

Fritz B. Burns	1955–1979
F. Patrick Burns	1955–1980
Gladys C. Burns	1955–1982
Edward A. Schulte	1955–1983
C.W. Getchell	1979–1983
William H. Hannon	1979–1994
Joseph E. Rawlinson	1979–
W.K. Skinner	1979–
Lorraine F. Perry	1995–

DIRECTORS

Fritz B. Burns	1955–1979
F. Patrick Burns	1955–1980
Gladys C. Burns	1955–1983
C.W. Getchell	1978–1987
William H. Hannon	1978–1994
Joseph E. Rawlinson	1978–
W.K. Skinner	1978–
Charles S. Casassa, S.J.	1982–1989
Edmund F. Schneiders	1982–1986
Richard Dunn	1983–1994
J. Robert Vaughan	1986–2001
Don Freeberg	1987–
Edward F. Slattery	1989–

Endnotes

The following abbreviations are used in the notes:

DF Collection   Dockweiler Family Collection, Charles Von der Ahe Library, Loyola Marymount University, Los Angeles, California.

EET Collection   Eugene E. Trefethen Collection, Bancroft Library, University of California, Berkeley, California.

FBB Collection   Fritz B. Burns Collection, Charles Von der Ahe Library, Loyola Marymount University, Los Angeles, California.

HJK Collection   Henry J. Kaiser Collection, Bancroft Library, University of California, Berkeley, California.

LA Archives   Los Angeles City Council minutes, 1944–46, Los Angeles City Archives, Piper Technical Center, Los Angeles, California.

Morehart Collection   Fritz B. Burns' personal notebooks, in the possession of John and Frances Morehart, Carpinteria, California.

WHS   Holdings of the Westchester/Playa Del Rey Historical Society, Charles Von der Ahe Library, Loyola Marymount University, Los Angeles, California.

All newspapers cited were published in Los Angeles, unless otherwise noted.

Chapter One

[1]Author's interviews with Winifred Cockey, July 24, 2000, Honolulu, Hawaii, Joseph Rawlinson, May 31, 2000, Burbank, California, and Ken Skinner, June 7, 2000, Burbank, California; Dickinson & Gillespie promotional brochures, FBB Collection, uncatalogued materials.

[2]Dickinson & Gillespie promotional brochures, FBB Collection, uncatalogued materials; and Cockey interview, July 24, 2000.

[3]"House-Warming Is Attended by Hundreds," *Palisades Del Rey Press*, January 16, 1926; "Playa Del Rey Beach History is Recalled," *Westchester Citizen*, July 11, 1963; and "Nostalgic Farewell Set for Red Cars," *Los Angeles Times*, April 7, 1961.

[4]Interview of William Hannon by Michael Engh, May 30, 1997, Los Angeles, California; and letter, Fritz Burns to Marie Theilen, June 20, 1933, Los Angeles, California, FBB Collection, CSLA–4, Series 2, Box 4, Folder 4.

[5]Dickinson & Gillespie promotional brochures, FBB Collection, uncatalogued materials; Cockey interview, July 24, 2000; and "The Sheltering Skyline," *Los Angeles Magazine*, (March 2000), 28–9.

[6]"Fritz Burns Enthused Over Plans," *Palisades Del Rey Press*, December 10, 1927.

[7]"Memorandum regarding Del Rey property," March 15, 1933, FBB Collection, CSLA–4, Series 2, Box 4, Folder 7.

[8]Jack Tobin, "Under All Is The Land," 16, unpublished 1987 biography of Fritz Burns, FBB Collection, uncatalogued materials; Rawlinson interview, May 31, 2000; and lease agreement between Fritz Burns and Lou Somers for Del Rey Beach Club, March 1, 1931, FBB Collection, CSLA–4, Series 2, Box 4, Folder 1.

[9]Framed copy of check from Monarch Refineries to Herndon Development Company, December 20, 1934, FBB Collection, uncatalogued materials.

[10]Tobin, 7; and author's interview with Ken Skinner, May 19, 2000, Burbank, California.

Chapter Two

[1]"Mr. Housing, U.S.A.," *Los Angeles Mirror*, November 18, 1952.

[2]Burns autobiographical notes [n.p], FBB Collection, CSLA–4, Series 1, Box 2, Folder 37.

[3]Letter, Fritz Burns to Robert Burns, June 8, 1943, Los Angeles, California, FBB Collection, CSLA–2, Series 2, Box 6, Folder 1; and speech honoring Fritz Burns by James Doherty to the Friendly Sons of St. Patrick, March 17, 1964, text in FBB Collection, uncatalogued materials.

[4]Letter, Fritz Burns to Gary Lease, September 24, 1962, Los Angeles, California. FBB Collection, uncatalogued materials.

[5]Burns autobiographical notes, FBB Collection, CSLA–4, Series 1, Box 2, Folder 37.

[6]Burns autobiographical notes, FBB Collection.

[7]Speech honoring Fritz Burns by James Doherty to the Friendly Sons of St. Patrick, March 17, 1964, text in FBB Collection, uncatalogued materials.

[8]Letter, Burns to Lease, September 24, 1962. FBB Collection, uncatalogued materials.

[9]Letter, Fritz Burns to William Schreyer, December 13, 1919, Philadelphia, Pennsylvania, FBB Collection, CSLA–4, Series 1, Box 1, Folder 1.

[10]Burns autobiographical notes, FBB Collection.

[11]Tobin, 2; 1915–16 academic transcript for Fritz Burns from De La Salle Institute, Minneapolis, Minnesota, FBB Collection, uncatalogued materials; and Burns autobiographical notes, FBB Collection.

[12]"Fritz B. Burns: Mr. Housing, U.S.A." *Los Angeles Mirror*, November 18, 1952.

[13]Dickinson & Gillespie promotional brochures, FBB Collection, uncatalogued materials.

[14]University of Minnesota 1917 academic transcript for Fritz B. Burns, FBB Collection, uncatalogued materials.

[15]Letters, Fritz Burns to William Schreyer, July 29, 1918, Fort Sheridan, Illinois, and December 23, 1918, New Orleans, Louisiana, FBB Collection, CSLA–4, Series 1, Box 1, Folder 1.

[16]Burns autobiographical notes, FBB Collection.

[17]Author's interview with Frances Morehart, July 6, 2000, Carpinteria, California.

[18]Letter, Fritz Burns to William Schreyer, December 23, 1918, FBB Collection, CSLA–4, Series 1, Box 2, Folder 37.

[19]Letter, Burns to Schreyer, December 23, 1918, FBB Collection, CSLA–4, Series 1, Box 2, Folder 37.

[20]Letter, Burns to Lease, September 24, 1962. FBB Collection, uncatalogued materials; and Morehart interview, July 6, 2000.

[21]Letter, Burns to Schreyer, December 13, 1919, Philadelphia, Pennsylvania, FBB Collection, CSLA–4, Series 1, Box 2, Folder 37.

[22]Letter, Burns to Lease, September 24, 1962. FBB Collection, uncatalogued materials.

[23]Letter, Burns to Schreyer, December 13, 1919, FBB Collection, CSLA–4, Series 1, Box 2, Folder 37.

[24]Letter, Fritz Burns to Robert Burns, April 2, 1924, Los Angeles, California, FBB Collection, CSLA–4, Series 1, Box 1, Folder 1.

[25]"High Jinks Spark Burns' Career," *Los Angeles Mirror*, November 19, 1952; and Burns autobiographical notes, FBB Collection, CSLA–4, Series 1, Box 2, Folder 37.

[26]Dickinson & Gillespie promotional brochures, FBB Collection, uncatalogued materials.

[27]Letter, Clifford Gillespie to Fritz Burns, December 7, 1921, Los Angeles, California, FBB Collection, CSLA–4, Series 1, Box 1, Folder 1.

[28]Kenneth Jackson, *Crabgrass Frontier: The Suburbanization of The United States* (New York: Oxford University Press, 1985), 178–9.

[29]Marc Weiss, *The Rise of The Community Builders: The American Real Estate Industry and Urban Land Planning* (New York: Columbia University Press, 1987), 98–9; and Robert Fishman, *Bourgeois Utopias: The Rise And Fall of Suburbia* (New York: Basic Books, 1987), 158–162. One of Dickinson & Gillespie's earliest real estate subdivisions in southern California was on land owned by the Huntington Land Company.

[30]List of Dickinson & Gillespie real estate subdivisions, FBB Collection, CSLA–4, Series 1, Box 1, Folder 12.

[31]Fred Marlow, *Memoirs And Perceptions*, 22, privately printed 1981 biography, FBB Collection, uncatalogued materials.

[32]"L.A. Developers Recall Early Days," *Los Angeles Times*, March 22, 1987.

[33]Dickinson & Gillespie promotional brochures, FBB Collection, uncatalogued materials; "Memorandum re: Del Rey property," March 15, 1933, FBB Collection, CSLA–4, Series 2, Box 4, Folder 7; and Michael Engh, S.J., "'A Multiplicity and Diversity of Faiths': Religion's Impact on Los Angeles And the Urban West, 1890–1940," *Western Historical Quarterly* 28 (Winter 1997), 467–9.

[34]Marlow, 23.

[35]Letter, Clifford Gillespie to Fritz Burns, 1923, Los Angeles, California, quoted in Tobin, 26.

[36]Burns autobiographical notes, FBB Collection; and Hannon interview, May 30, 1997.

[37]List of Dickinson & Gillespie real estate subdivisions, FBB Collection, CSLA–2, Series 2, Box 6, Folder 5; and Dickinson & Gillespie promotional brochures, FBB Collection, uncatalogued materials.

[38]Tobin, 8; and letter, Fritz Burns to Robert Burns, February 1, 1923, Los Angeles, California, FBB Collection, CSLA–4, Series 1, Box 1, Folder 1.

[39]Biographical fact sheet for Fritz Burns, *American Catholic Who's Who*, 1977, FBB Collection, CSLA–4, Series 1, Box 1, Folder 39.

[40]Cockey interview, July 25, 2000, and Rawlinson interview, May 31, 2000.

[41]"L.A.'s First National Pro Eleven Had Storybook Year," *Los Angeles Times*, September 21, 1959.

[42]Fishman, 162.

[43]*Palisades Del Rey Press*, June 1, 1926 and September 30, 1926.

[44]*Palisades Del Rey Press*, June 15, 1926; and Tobin, 6.

[45]Author's interview with Herb Lightfoot, April 26, 2000, Westlake Village, California; and "High Jinks Spark Burns' Career," *Los Angeles Mirror*, November 18, 1952.

[46]*Palisades Del Rey Press*, June 15, 1926.

[47]Dickinson & Gillespie promotional brochure, FBB Collection, CSLA–4, Series 1, Box 1, Folder 5.

[48]Kevin Starr, *Material Dreams: Southern California Through The 1920s* (New York: Oxford University Press, 1990), 72.

[49]Tobin, 26; and Dickinson & Gillespie promotional brochure, FBB Collection, CSLA–4, Series 1, Box 1, Folder 5.

[50]Dickinson & Gillespie promotional brochure, FBB Collection, CSLA–4, Series 1, Box 1, Folder 5.

[51]Dickinson & Gillespie promotional brochure, FBB Collection, CSLA–4, Series 1, Box 1, Folder 5.

[52]*Palisades Del Rey Press*, May 15, 1927.

[53]*Palisades Del Rey Press*, April 12, 1927 and April 20, 1928.

[54]*Palisades Del Rey Press*, June 1, 1926.

[55]*Palisades Del Rey Press*, December 10, 1927.

[56]*Palisades Del Rey Press*, May 12, 1928; and Loyola University Building Fund Campaign documents, FBB Collection, CSLA–4, Series 2, Box 4, Folder 2.

[57]Loyola University Building Fund Campaign documents, FBB Collection, CSLA–4, Series 2, Box 4, Folder 2; and "Burns Receives Loyola Law School Distinguished Achievement Award," Loyola Law School press release, Los Angeles, California, April 19, 1978, FBB Collection, CSLA–2, Series 2, Box 6, Folder 1.

[58]1929 Del Rey Investment Corporation pamphlet, FBB Collection, CSLA–2, Series 2, Box 6, Folder 1.

[59]*Palisades Del Rey Press*, December 1, 1928 and December 22, 1928; and Tobin, 6.

[60]Letter, Fritz Burns to C.C. Young, March 28, 1930, Los Angeles, California, FBB Collection, CSLA–4, Series 2, Box 4, Folder 1.

[61]Starr, 70.

[62]Fishman, 164; and Jackson, 187.

[63]Jackson, 193.

[64]Tobin, 8; and Hannon interview, May 30, 1997.

[65]Rawlinson interview, May 31, 2000.

[66]Letter, William Schreyer to Fritz Burns, May 22, 1931, Los Angeles, California, FBB Collection, CSLA–4, Series 2, Box 4, Folder 5; and Tobin, 16.

[67]Fritz Burns, *Poems & Parodies By Burns*, privately published book of poetry, 1978, FBB Collection, uncatalogued materials.

[68]"High Jinks Spark Burns' Career," *Los Angeles Mirror*, November 19, 1952.

[69]Rawlinson interview, May 31, 2000.

[70]Letter, Fritz Burns to Marie Theilen, June 30, 1933, Los Angeles, California, FBB Collection, CSLA–4, Series 2, Box 4, Folder 5.

[71]*Palisades Del Rey Press*, December 1, 1926; and Tobin, 7.

[72]Burns, *Poems & Parodies By Burns*.

[73]Postcard, Fritz Burns to Marie Theilen, October 20, 1934, Los Angeles, California, FBB Collection, uncatalogued materials; and Tobin, 17.

[74]Cockey interview, July 25, 2000; Rawlinson interview, May 31, 2000; and Tobin, 8 and 29–32.

Chapter Three

[1]Sales lecture by Fritz Burns, May 3, 1941, FBB Collection, CSLA–4, Series 1, Box 1, Folder 17.

[2]Jackson, 195–230; Fishman, 175–8; and Rosalyn Baxandall and Elizabeth Ewen, *Picture Windows: How the Suburbs Happened* (New York: Basic Books, 2000), 56–7.

[3]Marlow, 24–5.

[4]*Housing Construction: Statistics from 1889 to 1963* (Washington, D.C.: U.S. Department of Commerce, 1968), 1; and Jackson, 195–6.

[5]Marlow, 25.

[6]Marlow, 25.

[7]Letter, Clifford Gillespie to Fritz Burns, October 6, 1921, Los Angeles, California, FBB Collection, CSLA–4, Series 1, Box 1, Folder 7.

[8]Fishman, 175.

[9]Hise, 141. Hise notes that Burns and Fred Marlow were in the top tenth of one percent of Los Angeles builders in terms of volume of housing produced in 1939.

[10]Marlow, 1–20.

[11]Marlow, 18.

[12]*Los Angeles Evening Herald–Express*, August 15, 1934.

[13]Marlow, 26; and Windsor Hills promotional brochure, FBB Collection, CSLA–2, Series 3, Box 2, Folder 1.

[14]Marlow, 27–28.

[15]Carl Glasscock. *Lucky Baldwin: The Story of An Unconventional Success* (New York: Burt, 1933); Sandra Snider. *Elias Jackson "Lucky" Baldwin: California Visionary* (Los Angeles: Stairwell, 1987).

[16]Windsor Hills promotional brochure, FBB Collection, CSLA–2, Series 3, Box 2, Folder 1.

[17]Windsor Hills street map, FBB Collection, CSLA–2, Series 3, Box 1, Folder 1.

[18]Marlow, 28.

[19]Windsor Hills promotional brochure, FBB Collection, CSLA–2, Series 3, Box 2, Folder 1.

[20]Marlow, 28.

[21]Tobin, 11.

[22]Windsor Hills street map, FBB Collection, CSLA–4, Series 3, Box 1, Folder 1.

[23]Wardell Engineering home floorplans, FBB Collection, CSLA–4, Series 3, Box 2, Folder 1.

[24]Windsor Hills promotional brochures, FBB Collection, CSLA–4, Series 3, Box 2, Folder 1; and Marlow, 28.

[25]Sales lecture by Fritz Burns, October 4, 1941, FBB Collection, CSLA–4, Series 1, Box 1, Folder 17.

[26]"20 Pointers for Selecting Your Home Site," 1938 Marlow–Burns brochure, FBB Collection, uncatalogued materials.

[27]Windsor Hills promotional brochure, FBB Collection, CSLA–4, Series 1, Box 3, Folder 48.

[28]List of Windsor Hills property restrictions, FBB Collection, CSLA–2, Series 3, Box 2, Folder 1.

[29]H.G. Bissinger. *A Prayer For The City* (New York: Random House, 1997), 203–8; Fishman, 175–8; Jackson, 203–30; and Baxandall and Ewen, 56–7.

[30]Bissinger, 203–8, Jackson, 208.

[31]*Postwar Housing in California* (Sacramento: State Reconstruction and Reemployment Commission, 1945), 38. Burns served as chairman of the Southern California committee for this report. Restrictive covenants are not addressed in the text. Herb Lightfoot, a salesman for Burns' later development in Panorama City, noted that by 1949 Burns' sales crews did not enforce racial restrictions. Lightfoot interview, April 26, 2000.

[32]Hannon interview, May 30, 1997.

[33]Cockey interview, July 24, 2000.

[34]Robert Gillingham, *The Rancho San Pedro* (New York: Cole-Holmquist, 1983).

[35]Gladys Carson Burns' first husband, Edward Scheller, had died in 1928. Morehart interview, July 6, 2000.

[36]Morehart interview, July 6, 2000.

[37]Cockey interview, July 24, 2000; and marriage certificate for Fritz B. Burns and Gladys C. Scheller, St. Joan of Arc Roman Catholic Church, Las Vegas, Nevada, November 6, 1940, FBB Collection, uncatalogued materials. In the eyes of the Catholic Church, Fritz Burns was free to marry Gladys Carson Scheller because his marriage to Lucille Robinson had been in a civil ceremony which the Church did not recognize.

[38]Morehart interview, July 6, 2000.

[39]Skinner interview, May 19, 2000.

[40]Listed survey results for private home builders, FBB Collection, CSLA–2, Series 3, Box 2, Folder 1.

[41]"Westside Village Reveals Rustic Past," *Los Angeles Times*, January 7, 1996.

[42]Skinner interview, May 19, 2000.

[43]Fritz Burns, "Livable Homes For Those Who Love Living," 1944 real estate brochure produced and distributed by Marlow-Burns and Revere Copper and Brass Incorporated, FBB Collection, uncatalogued materials; Hise, 137–141; "Diversity is Key Word for Burns," *Los Angeles Examiner*, October 15, 1961;

[44]Burns, "Livable Homes," FBB Collection, uncatalogued materials; and "Diversity is Key Word for Burns," *Los Angeles Examiner*, October 15, 1961. Beginning in February 1941, Los Angeles municipal codes required builders of new subdivisions to install sidewalks and curbs "acceptable for public use" or compensate the Bureau of Engineering for such improvements. City of Los Angeles Municipal Code, Ordinance #83,881, LA Archives, Los Angeles, California.

[45]1941 Toluca Wood newspaper advertisement, FBB Collection, uncatalogued materials.

[46]"Toluca Wood Homes Meet Quick Favor," *Los Angeles Evening Herald & Express*, December 14, 1940; "Beautiful Setting Adds to Appeal of Cape Cod Home in Toluca Wood," *Los Angeles Downtown Shopping News*, June 14, 1941; and Burns, "Livable Homes."

[47]Toluca Wood floor plans and photographs, HJK Collections, Container 274, Folder 5; and "Beautiful Setting Adds to Appeal of Cape Cod Home in Toluca Wood," *Los Angeles Downtown Shopping News*, June 14, 1941.

[48]Hise, 141.

[49]Riverside Ranchos promotional brochures, FBB Collection, uncatalogued materials.

[50]1941 Toluca Wood newspaper advertisement, FBB Collection, uncatalogued materials.

Chapter Four

[1]Sales lecture by Fritz Burns, July 7, 1941, FBB Collection, CSLA–4, Series 1, Box 1, Folder 17.

[2]Baxandall and Ewen, 78; Hise, 120–1; and "Burns Sees Better Days for Builders," *Los Angeles Herald-Express*, October 27, 1943.

[3] Morehart interview, July 6, 2000.

[4]"Westchester—Born in Time for Space Age Boom," *Los Angeles Herald-Examiner*, April 12, 1963.

[5]"Westchester—Born in Time for Space Age Boom."

[6]Author's interview with Greg Hise, Associate Professor, School of Policy, Planning, and Development, University of Southern California, May 12, 2000, Los Angeles, California.

[7]"From Line-up to Job at Busy Aircraft Factories," *Los Angeles Times*, November 12, 1939; "Westchester is Expanding Swiftly" and "War Housing Essential," *Los Angeles Herald-Express*, September 5, 1942; and "Burbank Has Become a Hive of Aerial Industry," *Los Angeles Herald-Express*, February 17, 1941.

[8]"Growing Pains of a Great City," *Los Angeles Daily News*, October 19, 1951; *Los Angeles Herald-Examiner*, April 12, 1963; and Hise, 143.

[9]"Business Center Begun in Westchester District," *Los Angeles Times*, August 2, 1942.

[10]Sales lecture by Fred Marlow, February 14, 1942, FBB Collection, CSLA–4, Series 1, Box 1, Folder 17.

[11]Burns, "Livable Homes," FBB Collection, uncatalogued materials.

[12]"Westside Village: Living for Young Homemakers," 1947 real estate brochure, FBB Collection, CSLA–2, Series 2, Box 6, Folder 1; and Tobin, 13–14.

[13]Sales lecture by Fritz Burns, January 21, 1942, FBB Collection, CSLA–4, Series 1, Box 1, Folder 17.

[14]1942 Marlow-Burns newspaper advertisement for Westchester, FBB Collection, CSLA–4, Series 4, Box 1, Folder 9; and Burns, "Livable Homes," FBB Collection, uncatalogued materials.

[15]Burns, "Livable Homes," FBB Collection, uncatalogued materials.

[16]Sales lecture by Fritz Burns, January 21, 1942, FBB Collection, CSLA–4, Series 1, Box 1, Folder 17; and *Los Angeles Times* real estate advertisements, August 2, 1942;

[17]Tobin, 19. Will Rogers Junior High School was later condemned and demolished during an expansion of Los Angeles International Airport.

[18]Tobin, 19.

[19]Sales lecture by Fritz Burns, August 5, 1941, FBB Collection, CSLA–4, Series 1, Box 1, Folder 17.

[20]Sales lecture by Fritz Burns, October 25, 1941, FBB Collection, CSLA–4, Series 1, Box 1, Folder 17.

[21]Marlow, 28.

[22]"Westchester—Born in Time for Space Age Boom," *Los Angeles Herald-Examiner*, April 12, 1963.

[23]*Housing Construction: Statistics from 1889 to 1963* (Washington, D.C.: U.S. Department of Commerce, 1968), 1.

[24]Sales lecture by Fred Marlow, May 16, 1942, FBB Collection, CSLA–4, Series 1, Box 1, Folder 17.

[25]Sales lecture by Fritz Burns, January 21, 1942, FBB Collection, CSLA–4, Series 1, Box 1, Folder 17.

[26]Marlow, 28.

[27]*Valley Times*, March 30, 1944; and *Burbank News*, July 29, 1943.

[28]*Burbank News*, July 1943; *Aircraft Times*, April 6, 1944; and "Double Bungalows," *Los Angeles Herald*, April 1, 1944.

[29]Fishman, 178. Fishman calls all of postwar Los Angeles a "shock city."

[30]Carey McWilliams, "Look What's Happened to California," *Harper's Magazine*, (October 1949), 21–9.

[31]"Westchester Draws Crowds," *Los Angeles Daily News*, December 25, 1942; and Burns, "Livable Homes," FBB Collection, uncatalogued materials.

[32]"Growing Pains of a Great City," *Los Angeles Daily News*, October 19, 1951.

[33]Carey McWilliams. *California: The Great Exception* (A.J. Wyn: New York, 1949), 13–17; and "Growing Pains of a Great City," *Los Angeles Daily News*, October 19, 1951.

[34]"Manchester Village," *Aircraft Times*, April 6, 1944.

[35] The Fritz Burns Story," *Los Angeles Herald-Examiner*, July 4, 1965; *Los Angeles Realtor*, December 23, 1939; and Tobin, 19.

[36]Certificate honoring Fritz Burns as a charter member of the Home Builders Institute of America, January 31, 1941, FBB Collection, CSLA–4, Series 1, Box 1, Folder 16; and sales lecture by Fred Marlow, January 27, 1941, FBB Collection, CSLA–4, Series 1, Box 1, Folder 17.

[37]Hise interview, May 12, 2000; and Atkinson, W.P., ed. *Housing…U.S.A.: As Industry Leaders See It* (New York: Simmons, 1954), 1.

[38]Joseph Mason. *History of Housing in the U.S., 1930–1980* (Houston: Gulf Publishing, 1982), 32–4.

[39]Baxandall and Ewen, 81.

[40]*Los Angeles Building News*, July 16, 1953.

[41]Notes for talk by Fritz Burns to the Home Builders Institute, January 13, 1942, FBB Collection, CSLA–4, Series 1, Box 1, Folder 15.

[42]Mason, 33; "Burns Heads New Building Group Setup," *Los Angeles Daily News*, September 10, 1943; and Burns autobiographical notes, FBB Collection, CSLA–4, Series 1, Box 2, Folder 37.

[43]"Builders Wire FDR Plea Against Public 'Housers'," *Los Angeles Examiner*, September 21, 1943.

[44]Dion Neutra, "The Neutra Genius: Innovations and Vision." *Modernism* 1, (December 1998), 26–33.

[45]Thomas Hines, "Housing, Baseball, and Creeping Socialism." *Journal of Urban History* 8, (February 1982), 123–145.

[46]"Channel Heights Housing Project," *Architectural Forum* 80, (March 1944), 65–74; and Baxandall and Ewen, 80–1.

[47]Baxandall and Ewen, 101; and "Encouraging News for Builders," *Los Angeles Herald-Express*, October 23, 1943.

[48]Baxandall and Ewen, 81.

[49]"Burns Sees Better Days for Builders," *Los Angeles Herald-Express*, October 27, 1943.

[50]"Burns Urges Builders to Be Ready for Coming Elections," *Los Angeles Daily News*, November 5, 1943.

[51]Fritz Burns, "To Own—Certainly," *Tomorrow's Town* (New York: National Committee on Housing, Inc., 1943), 2.

[52]Fritz Burns, "We're the Suicide Troopers of the War Building Industry," *American Builder*, (December 1942), 36–9.

[53]"Burns Hits Public Housing, "*Los Angeles Herald*, May 21, 1943.

[54]Tobin, 19.

[55]Burns, "Livable Homes," FBB Collection, uncatalogued materials.

Chapter Five

[1]1947 Kaiser Community Homes brochure, FBB Collection, uncatalogued materials.

[2]"F. Patrick Burns Joins Board of Trustees," Loyola Marymount University press release, April 19, 1979, FBB Collection, uncatalogued materials.

[3]McWilliams, 8–24; and Hise 152–5.

[4]*Victory Bulletin*, October 1943, National Housing Agency, Washington. D.C. Cited in Burns, "Livable Homes," FBB Collection, uncatalogued materials.

[5]Jackson, 231–33; "Kaiser Proposes Mass Housing Plan," *New York Times*, March 9, 1944; and Burns, "Livable Homes," FBB Collection, uncatalogued materials.

[6]"Comments by Henry J. Kaiser on President Truman's Housing Program," February 10, 1946, HJK Collection, Carton 263, Folder 8; and Jackson, 233.

[7]*Housing Construction*, 1.

[8]"Burns Urges Builders to Be Ready for Coming Elections, "*Los Angeles Daily News*, November 5, 1943.

[9]"Comments by Henry J. Kaiser on President Truman's Housing Program," February 10, 1946, HJK Collection, Carton 263, Folder 8; "Wyatt Gets Firsthand Facts on Housing Crisis," *Los Angeles Times*, September 29, 1946; and "Kaiser, Burns to Start Mass Production of Homes When L.A. Plant Opens March 20," *Los Angeles Daily News*, February 16, 1946.

[10]Tobin, 20.

[11]"Fix It Yourself," 1944 brochure by the Fritz B. Burns Research Division, FBB Collection, uncatalogued materials.

[12]"The Post-War House," *House Beautiful* 88, (May 1946).

[13]"Home of Tomorrow, Wilshire Showplace, Open To Public," *Los Angeles Evening Herald and Express*, March 24, 1951; "New Residential Showplace Will Open March 17," *Los Angeles Times*, March 1, 1951. In Burns' self-published book of poetry, he included a short poem recited at a party at Welton and Fay Becket's home. Burns, *Poems & Parodies by Burns*, FBB Collection, uncatalogued materials.

[14]Burns, "Livable Homes," FBB Collection, uncatalogued materials.

[15]"Home of Tomorrow," *Building News*, March 29, 1951; and "Inside and Out of $175,000 Postwar Dream Home," *The New York Post*, March 11, 1946.

[16]"The Post-War House," *House Beautiful* 88, May 1946.

[17]Advertisement in *The Saturday Evening Post*, January 22, 1944.

[18]"The Greatest House-Building Show on Earth," *Architectural Forum* 86, (March 1947), 105–13.

[19]"Home of Tomorrow, Wilshire Showplace, Open To Public," *Los Angeles Evening*

Herald and Express, March 24, 1951; and "New Residential Showplace Will Open March 17," *Los Angeles Times*, March 1, 1951.

[20]"New Residential Showplace Will Open March 17," *Los Angeles Times*, March 1, 1951.

[21]"The Post-War House," *House Beautiful* 88, May 1946. For a further analysis of Burns' Postwar House and Home of Tomorrow, see Dana Cuff, *The Provisional City: Los Angeles Stories of Architecture And Urbanism* (Cambridge: MIT Press, 2000), 228–37.

[22]Baxandall and Ewen, 126–135.

[23]"Kaisercraft Homes Report," April 1945, HJK Collection, Container 274, Folder 6. Kaiser officials stressed that Burns "became intimately acquainted with the leading builders from every city of importance throughout the United States."

[24]Greg Hise showed me the substance of this point in an interview on May 12, 2000.

[25]"City Spurs Action on Chavez Ravine," *Los Angeles Herald and Express*, July 9, 1959.

[26]"The Long Island Builders' House," *Architectural Forum*, (July 1950), cited in Baxandall and Ewen, 124.

[27]"Suggested Remarks for Mr. Kaiser at Opening of Press Conference—Kaiser Community Homes," HJK Collection, Container 263, Folder 18.

[28]Mark Foster. *Henry J. Kaiser: Builder in The Modern American West* (Austin: University of Texas Press, 1989), 48–67; and Albert Heiner, *Henry J. Kaiser: Western Colossus* (San Francisco: Halo, 1991), 51–73.

[29]Morehart interview, July 6, 2000; and Marlow, 36.

[30]Foster, 82.

[31]*Colliers*, February 27, 1943, 62. Reprinted in Foster 1989.

[32]Foster, 118.

[33]*The Kaiser Story* (Oakland: Kaiser Industries Corporation, 1968), 8.

[34]"Kaiser Proposes Mass Housing Plan," *New York Times*, March 9, 1945; and "Kaiser Tells of Dream City Built for His Richmond Workers," *Los Angeles Herald-Tribune*, March 9, 1945.

[35]"Kaiser, Burns to Start Mass Production of Homes When L.A. Plant Opens March 20," *Los Angeles Daily News*, February 16, 1946.

[36]Tobin, 19–20; and Hise, 166.

[37]Morehart interview, July 6, 2000; and Marlow, 36.

[38]Heiner, 151. Kaiser considered the process of selecting sponsors and the logistics of creating a special ceremony for each christening important enough to necessitate the creation at both Richmond and Portland of full time departments to handle such events.

[39]Morehart interview, July 6, 2000.

[40]Burns' close friend Alex Clarke remembered in 1957 a promising east coast land deal some associates had asked Burns to evaluate three decades earlier: "It is unnecessary to set down all the details of Burns' procedure upon arriving at the scene of action. 'I believe I know what to do,' he said. He procured old and current maps, asked many questions, toured the area thoroughly and studied population trends, potential transportation extensions, costs, popular preferences, and so on. In a few days he arrived at a conviction…and advised against the deal. Members of the group were not overpleased—but they had reason to be later. Burns knew what to do—and does yet." Speech by Alex Clarke, July 24, 1957, FBB Collection, CSLA–2, Series 2, Box 6, Folder 1.

[41]Rawlinson interview, May 31, 2000.

[42]Marlow, 36.

[43]*The Kaiser Story*, (Oakland: Kaiser Industries Corporation, 1968), 8.

[44]"Vanport: Oregon's Second Largest City," *Western Construction News*, (August 1943). 351–54, cited in Foster, 76.

[45]"Kaiser Tells of Dream City Built for Richmond Workers," *Los Angeles Herald-Tribune*, March 9, 1945.

[46]"Steel and Sonotherm Construction," April 1945 internal Kaiser Industries report, HJK Collection, Container 275, Folder 6.

[47]"Prefabricated Plastic Houses," January 1945 internal Kaiser Industries report, HJK Collection, Container 274, Folder 10.

[48]"Notes on Housing," HJK Collection, Container 274, Folder 10; and "Kaisercraft Homes Report," April 1945, HJK Collection, Container 274, Folder 6.

[49]"Kaisercraft Homes Report," April 1945, HJK Collection, Container 274, Folder 6.

[50]Internal Kaiser Industries memorandum suggesting partners, EET Collection, Container 11, Folder 1.

[51]"Kaisercraft Homes Report," April 1945, HJK Collection, Container 274, Folder 6.

[52]"Kaiser Community Homes: The First Program," HJK Collection, Container 274, Folder 1.

[53]"Councilman Hits Airport Land Purchase," *Los Angeles Daily News*, February 27, 1946; "Bond Issues Approved for Airport," *Los Angeles Times*, April 6, 1945; Tobin 7; and Rawlinson interview, May 31, 2000. Burns also appeared before the Los Angeles City Council in 1945 to argue against the city's condemnation of the Section 35 property. Los Angeles City Council minutes for September 9, 1945, LA Archives.

[54]"Forecast for 1946," speech by Henry J. Kaiser, January 1, 1946, HJK Collection, Container 263, Folder 3.

[55]"The Greatest House-Building Show on Earth," *Architectural Forum* 86, (March 1947), 105–13.

[56]"Kaiser Community Homes: The First Program," HJK Collection, Container 274, Folder 1.

[57]Kaiser Community Homes corporate files, EET Collection, Container 11, Folder 1.

[58]"Greatest House-Building," *Architectural Forum*, 106.

[59]"Greatest House-Building," *Architectural Forum*, 109.

[60]"Suggested Remarks for Mr. Kaiser at Opening of Press Conference—Kaiser Community Homes," HJK Collection, Container 263, Folder 18.

[61] kinner interview, June 7, 2000.

[62]Skinner interview, June 7, 2000.

[63]Skinner interview, June 7, 2000; also Heiner, 325.

[64]"Kaiser, Burns to Start Mass Production of Homes When L.A. Plant Opens March 20," *Los Angeles Daily News*, February 16, 1946.

[65]Letter, Fritz Burns to T.M. Price, May 2, 1946. Burns reported severe problems acquiring the necessary materials to continue KCH's building program. EET Collection, Container 11, Folder 1.

[66]"Kaiser, Burns to Start Mass Production of Homes When L.A. Plant Opens March 20," *Los Angeles Daily News*, February 16, 1946; "Housing-Material Studies," HJK Collection, Container 274, Folder 1.

[67]Skinner interview, June 7, 2000. In a February 1952 letter, Kaiser employee J.G. Stollerty noted "As I recall, [the Manchester plant] was only in operation for about six months when the entire building operation was moved to the tract site, where it was found that more economies could be effected due to our large building program."

[68]Kaiser Community Homes promotional brochures, FBB Collection, uncatalogued materials.

[69]Kaiser Community Homes promotional brochures, FBB Collection, uncatalogued materials.

[70]"Greatest House-Building," *Architectural Forum*, 113; and "Kaiser Homes," HJK Collection, Container 274, Folder 3. Burns considered the psychological equity a family held in its home "a more powerful influence than the monetary equities, in holding them to their homes regardless of what circumstances may arise."

[71]"Greatest House-Building," *Architectural Forum*, 105.

[72]"Panorama City: Sweet Song of Success," *The San Fernando Valley Realtor* 4, (December 1960), 18–20.

[73]"First Kaiser Home Finished," *Los Angeles Examiner*, September 17, 1946; HJK Collection, Container 263, Folder 18; and "40 GI Families Move into New Kaiser Houses," *Los Angeles Examiner*, February 22, 1947.

[74]"Kaiser Community Homes Projects And Achievements," HJK Collection, Container 274, Folder 3.

[75]Figures supplied by Ken Skinner, Fritz B. Burns Foundation, Burbank, California.

[76]Morehart interview, July 6, 2000.

[77]Jackson, 233.

[78]1947 Kaiser Community Homes promotional brochure, FBB Collection, uncatalogued materials.

[79]Kaiser Community Homes interoffice memorandum, Fred Pike to E.E. Trefethen, May 13, 1946, EET Collection, Container 11, Folder 1.

Chapter Six

[1]"Fritz Burns Is Ranked Among Top Developers," *Honolulu Star-Bulletin*, June 1, 1965.

[2]"Westchester—Born in Time for Space Age Boom," *Los Angeles Herald-Examiner*, April 12, 1963.

[3]Kaiser Community Homes interoffice memo, Fred Pike to Eugene Trefethen, May 13, 1946, EET Collection, Container 11, Folder 1.

[4]"Panorama City: Jewel of The Valley," *Los Angeles Mirror-News*, March 19, 1957.

[5]Skinner interview, June 7, 2000.

[6]"Mushroom City: When General Motors Built a Chevrolet Plant, A City Followed," *Fortnight Magazine*, (July 1955), 55; and "L.A. Chevrolet Assembly Plant Opens This Week," *Los Angeles Examiner*, February 15, 1948.

[7]In his personal notebooks, Fritz Burns mentions a number of meetings with Henri de Roulet concerning the purchase of the Panorama Ranch from August 1944 to April 1946. Morehart Collection [n.p.], August 1944 through April 1946.

[8]"830,000 Residents in The Valley," *Los Angeles Herald-Examiner*, May 10, 1963.

[9]Kaiser Community Homes interoffice memo, Fred Pike to Eugene Trefethen, May 13, 1946, EET Collection, Container 11, Folder 1; and letter, Fred Pike to F.A. Ferrogiaro, June 27, 1952, Los Angeles, California, EET Collection, Container 11, Folder 8.

[10]"Greatest House-Building," *Architectural Forum*, 107.

[11]Letter, Fred Pike to F.A. Ferrogiaro, June 27, 1952, Los Angeles, California, EET Collection, Container 11, Folder 8.

[12]Kaiser Community Homes property maps, EET Collection, Container 11, Folders 9 and 10; and Skinner interview, June 7, 2000.

[13]Fritz Burns' personal notebook from November 1949, Morehart Collection.

[14]"Dream of Community Triumphantly Realized," *Los Angeles Examiner*, January 3, 1955.

[15]"Burns Attributes Continued Growth of Panorama City to Conversion of Greenbelt Areas to New Apartments," undated Kaiser Community Homes press release, HJK Collection, Container 274, Folder 13.

[16]"Planned City in Eleven-Year Progress," *Valley Times*, January 20, 1959.

[17]Undated program for "Panorama City Shoppers" Pee Wee baseball team, FBB Collection, CSLA–2, Series 3, Box 4, Folder 1.

[18]"Burns A Sponsor For The YMCA Fund Drive," *Los Angeles Times*, January 10, 1955.

[19]"Mushroom City," *Fortnight Magazine*, (July 1955), 55.

[20]"Drag Strip Races on San Fernando Valley Air Strip Prove Effective Aid in Reducing Juvenile Delinquency," *Home Builder's Journal*, 1956; and "Fritz Burns Honored By Kiwanians," *Van Nuys News*, May 21, 1964.

[21]"Contest Winner Starts New Future in Southern California," undated Kaiser Community Homes press release, HJK Collection, Container 274, Folder 13; "Building a Future in 1948," *Los Angeles Times*, September 4, 1999; Hise interview, May 12, 2000; and Rawlinson interview, May 31, 2000.

[22]Panorama City promotional brochure, FBB Collection, uncatalogued materials.

[23]"830,000 Residents in The Valley," *Los Angeles Herald-Examiner*, May 10, 1963.

[24]Lightfoot interview, April 26, 2000.

[25]"Panorama City: Sweet Song of Success," *San Fernando Valley Realtor* 4, (December, 1960), 18–20; and Panorama City promotional brochures, FBB Collection, uncatalogued materials.

[26]"Keeping Up With The Joneses," 1947 Kaiser Community Homes brochure, FBB Collection, uncatalogued materials.

[27]Kaiser Community Homes supplement for trade papers and magazines, September 16, 1946, HJK Collection, Container 263, Folder 18.

[28]1949 Panorama City Shopping Center brochure, HJK Collection, Container 274, Folder 12.

[29]Lightfoot interview, April 26, 2000.

[30]Lightfoot interview, April 26, 2000.

[31]Infant of Valley, Panorama City Giant in Business," *Los Angeles Mirror-News*, September 30, 1960.

[32]"Mart Opening Fills Need in Panorama City," undated Kaiser Community Homes press release, FBB Collection, CSLA–4, Series 4, Folder 11; and Skinner interview, June 7, 2000.

[33]"Panorama City Continues Its Rapid Growth," *Los Angeles Herald & Express*, March 9, 1956.

[34]Hise, 206.

[35]"Infant of Valley, Panorama City Giant in Business," *Los Angeles Mirror-News*, September 30, 1960, and "Panorama City Continues Its Rapid Growth," *Los Angeles Herald & Express*, March 9, 1956.

[36]"Panorama City: Sweet Song of Success," *San Fernando Valley Realtor* 4, (December, 1960), 18–20.

[37]"The Fritz Burns Story," *Los Angeles Herald Examiner*, July 4, 1965.

[38]Author's interview with Ed Hogan, June 2, 2000, Westlake Village, California.

[39]Hogan interview, June 2, 2000.

[40]Tobin, 22; and "Celebrity Ranch," *Los Angeles Times*, August 28, 1975.

[41]"Goldwater Republicans Whoopin' It Up," *Los Angeles Herald-Examiner*, May 10, 1964; and "The Fritz Burns Story," *Los Angeles Herald-Examiner*, July 4, 1965.

[42]Tobin, 23.

[43]"Famed Builder F.B. Burns Dies," *Valley News*, February 20, 1979.

[44]Letter, Eugene Trefethen to Henry J. Kaiser, May 12, 1951, EET Collection, Carton 11, Folder 5.

[45]"Summary Report of Kaiser Community Homes in Los Angeles Area," April 24, 1951, EET Collection, Carton 11, Folder 5.

[46]"Panorama City Flourishing on Historic Site," *Los Angeles Examiner*, January 3, 1955; "Panorama City," *Life Magazine*, (October 7, 1957), 163.

[47]"High Jinks Spark Burns' Career," *Los Angeles Mirror*, November 19, 1952.

[48]"High Jinks Spark Burns' Career," *Los Angeles Mirror*, November 19, 1952; and "Panorama City Flourishing on Historic Site," *Los Angeles Examiner*, January 3, 1955.

Chapter Seven

[1]"Call Socialized Housing Trend in U.S. 'Appalling'," *Valley Times*, May 11, 1951.

[2]Peter Drier, "Labor's Love Lost? Rebuilding Union's' Involvement in Federal Housing Policy," *Housing Policy Debate* 11, (April 2000), 327–92; and "Remarks Before State Housing Committee," HJK Collection, Container 263, Folder 24.

[3]Alexander von Hoffman, "A Study in Contradictions: The Origins and Legacy of the Housing Act of 1949," *Housing Policy Debate* 11, (April 2000), 299–326.

[4]Dreier, 345.

[5]"Housing Act of 1949," *Architectural Forum*, 1949, vol. 91(2), 83–5; and *A Handbook of Information on Provisions of The Housing Act of 1949* (Washington, D.C.: Housing and Home Finance Agency, 1949).

[6]Von Hoffman, 307; and Dreier, 330.

[7]"The Case Against Socialized Housing," National Association of Home Builders brochure, DF Collection, CSLA–12, Series 2, Box 2, Folder 10; Mason, 47–54; and Von Hoffman, 307.

[8]In 1948, Burns had written a letter to every house owner in a Kaiser Community Homes development and called federally-funded public housing "an attempt . . . to make you pay for someone else's rent in addition to your own monthly payment and taxes." HJK Collection, Container 274, Folder 3.

[9]Cockey interview, July 25, 2000.

[10]Letter, Fritz Burns to Winifred Cockey, June 4, 1954. FBB Collection, uncatalogued materials.

[11]Don Parson, "Los Angeles' 'Headline-Happy Public Housing War'," *Southern California Quarterly* 65, (Fall 1983), 251–85; Thomas Hines, "Housing, Baseball, And Creeping Socialism," *Journal of Urban History* 8, (February 1982), 123–43; and "Mayor Challenges Housing Foes to Present Arguments," *Los Angeles Times*, May 23, 1952.

[12]Hines, 137; and author's interview with Frank Wilkinson, June 5, 2000, Los Angeles, California.

[13]*Postwar Housing in California* (Sacramento: State Reconstruction and Reemployment Commission, 1945), v.

[14]"Public Housing," *Wall Street Journal*, July 17, 1951; and *Los Angeles Times*, August 9, 1951.

[15]Frank Wilkinson, "And Now The Bill Comes Due," *Frontier* 15, (October 1965), 1–2.

[16]"The Chavez Ravine Incident," *Los Angeles Times*, May 13, 1959; and Cary Henderson, "Los Angeles And The Dodger War, 1957–1962," *Southern California Quarterly* 62, (Fall 1980), 264.

[17]Hines, 128. In a further irony, Frank Wilkinson's home in nearby Windsor Hills was part of Burns' first large housing development. In addition, Wilkinson years later gave an account of his career as part of a lecture series at Loyola Law School funded by the Fritz B. Burns Foundation.

[18]Hines, 134.

[19]"Council Votes to Cancel Public Housing Project," *Los Angeles Times*, December 27, 1951; and Parson, 258.

[20]"Creeping Socialism Called U.S. Menace," *Los Angeles Times*, September 8, 1951: and "Where's The Housing Shortage?" *Los Angeles Times*, October 3, 1951.

[21]Parson, 277.

[22]"Public Housing," *Wall Street Journal*, July 17, 1951; "Group Will Fight City Housing Plan," *Los Angeles Times*, February 17, 1952; and "Group Hits L.A. Housing," *Los Angeles Evening Herald & Express*, February 18, 1952.

[23]Wilkinson, "And Now The Bill Comes Due," *Frontier*, 2.

[24]Wilkinson interview, June 5, 2000; Parson, 260–1; and "City Housing Official Accused as Party Red in Court Quiz," *Los Angeles Times*, September 3, 1952. For a substantially different perspective on Fritz Burns, Frank Wilkinson, and their involvement in the Los Angeles public housing debate, see Dana Cuff's *Provisional City*, 272–94.

[25]*Los Angeles Examiner* and *Los Angeles Herald & Express*, September 3, 4, and 5, 1952; Wilkinson interview, June 5, 2000.

[26]Morehart interview, July 6, 2000, Carpinteria, California.

[27]Wilkinson interview, June 5, 2000. F. Patrick Burns testified against Wilkinson before the California State House Un-American Activities Committee. He had met Wilkinson at USC in 1949.

[28]"F. Burns' Reply to Local Group Is Made Public," *The Burbank News*, July 29, 1943.

[29]Parson, 257; and Drier, 327–92.

[30]"San Fernando Valley Has Answer to Low-Cost Housing," *Valley Times*, May 11, 1951.

[31]"Short Cut To Low Rents," *Business Week*, July 28, 1951.

[32]"San Fernando Valley Has Answer to Low-Cost Housing," *Valley Times*, May 11, 1951.

[33]Skinner interview, July 5, 2000.

[34]Jon Teaford, "Urban Renewal and Its Aftermath," *Housing Policy Debate* 11, (April 2000), 443–65.

[35]"Los Angeles Builder Leader in National Fight Against Slums," *Los Angeles Building News*, July 16, 1953.

[36]Fritz Burns' personal notebooks, October 1953. Morehart Collection.

[37]"Let's Rebuild America," *California Savings and Loan League Journal*, (December 1953), in FBB Collection, CSLA–2, Series 3, Box 2, Folder 1.

[38]Cockey interview, July 25, 2000.

[39]Von Hoffman, 313–4.

[40]"Slum Clearance Progress Told," *Los Angeles Times*, October 25, 1953.

[41]"Chronological Background of Fritz B. Burns," September 26, 1952, FBB Collection, CSLA–2, Series 2, Box 6, Folder 1; "Builder Host to Better Housing Group Leaders," *Los Angeles Times*, November 24, 1954; and Cockey interview, July 25, 2000.

[42]"Bunker Hill Remodeling," *Los Angeles Times Home Magazine*, February 13, 1955.

[43]"The Modernization Battle of Bunker Hill," *Practical Builder*, (October 1955), in FBB Collection, CSLA–2, Series 3, Box 3, Folder 1.

[44]"Mayor Studies Buying of Abandoned Housing Sites," *Los Angeles Daily News*, October 15, 1953.

[45]"Present New Six-Year Housing Plan Without U.S. Aid," *Los Angeles Herald & Express*, May 28, 1952.

[46]*Los Angeles Times*, May 28, 1957.

[47]Skinner interview, July 5, 2000. Ken Skinner recalled an exchange between Walter O'Malley and Charles Getchell, one of Burns' senior associates, at a Los Angeles Realty

Board banquet after Dodger Stadium opened. Getchell told O'Malley that Burns had considered the Chavez Ravine transaction an unfair deal. O'Malley replied, "If they had offered it to Fritz, wouldn't he have taken it?"

[48]Henderson, "Los Angeles And The Dodger War," 282–3; Thomas Hines, "Housing, Baseball, And Creeping Socialism," 123–43; and "Post Chavez Ravine Notices of Eviction," *Los Angeles Herald & Express*, April 10, 1959.

[49]Neil J. Sullivan, *The Dodgers Move West* (New York: Oxford, 1987), 182; "Chavez Ravine Purchase By City Momentarily Held up in Council," *Valley Times*, November 14, 1957; and Skinner interview, July 5, 2000.

Chapter Eight

[1]Burns, *Poems & Parodies*, FBB Collection, uncatalogued materials.

[2]Heiner, 312; Foster, 273–4.

[3]Tobin, 26.

[4]Heiner, 317.

[5]Morehart interview, July 6, 2000.

[6]Noel Kent, *Hawaii: Islands Under The Influence* (New York: Monthly Review, 1983), 104–21.

[7]H. Brett Melendy, *Walter Francis Dillingham, 1875–1963, Hawaiian Entrepreneur And Statesman* (Lewiston, NY: Mellen, 1996), 257–83; and Lawrence Fuchs, *Hawaii Pono* (Honolulu: Bess, 2000), 384.

[8]Tobin, 26.

[9]Cockey interview, July 25, 2000; and "The Fritz Burns Story," *Los Angeles Herald-Examiner*, July 4, 1965.

[10]Program notes for "A Night at A Hawaiian Village," HJK Collection, Container 280, Folder 18.

[11]"Hawaii's A'Poppin'," *Fortune*, (June 1960), 282–4; and "Hawaii," *Holiday Magazine*, (July 1960), 52.

[12]Untitled Kaiser Services press release, April 23, 1954, EET Collection, Container 11, Folder 6.

[13]"Hawaiian Village Opens Today," *Los Angeles Realtor*, September 15, 1955.

[14]"Hawaii," *Holiday Magazine*, (July 1960), 52; and Skinner interview, June 7, 2000.

[15]Cockey interview, July 25, 2000; and Heiner, 319.

[16]"Hawaii Building Has Problems, Surprises," *Los Angeles Examiner*, July 31, 1955.

[17]Tobin, 28.

[18]Heiner, 332.

[19]Hannon interview, May 30, 1997.

[20]Heiner, 332.

[21]"Kaiser-Burns Line Up Ten Major Projects for the Waikiki Area," *Waikiki Beach-Press*, November 22, 1955.

[22]Burns, *Poems & Parodies*, FBB Collection, uncatalogued materials.

[23]Program notes for "A Night at A Hawaiian Village," HJK Collection, Container 280, Folder 18; "Memories of a Legend of Waikiki," *Honolulu Advertiser*, April 30, 2000; and Foster, 257.

[24]"Rites Open New Hotel," *Honolulu Advertiser*, September 19, 1955; Cockey interview, July 25, 2000; and Tobin, 29.

[25]Tobin, 28–29.

[26]Hawaiian Village Hotel promotional brochures, FBB Collection, uncatalogued materials.

[27]Letter, Fritz Burns to Henry J. Kaiser, December 28, 1955, Los Angeles, California, EET Collection, Container 11, Folder 6; and Foster, 257.

[28]Foster, 257.

[29]Tobin, 29.

[30]Heiner, 332.

[31]Informational brochure on Kaiser Aluminum Dome, HJK Collection, Container 280, Folder 12; and Heiner, 348.

[32]Tobin, 33.

[33]Hogan interview, June 2, 2000.

[34]Foster, 268–9.

[35]Heiner, 346.

[36]Tobin, 33; Skinner interview, June 14, 2000; and Cockey interview, July 25, 2000.

[37] Hawaii's A'Poppin'," *Fortune*, (June 1960), 282–4.

[38]Foster, 261.

[39]"$100 Fare to Hawaii Seen Attracting The Top-Drawer Tourists," Hawaiian Village Hotel press release, May 21, 1959, HJK Collection, Container 274, Folder 13.

[40]"Luau New High in Reveling," *Los Angeles Examiner*, October 10, 1956; and "Honolulu Parties Set to Fete Pinkie Scheller," June 12, 1958; and *Honolulu Star-Bulletin*, June 10, 1958.

[41]"Priest Controls Vast Power As Fund Caretaker," *Los Angeles Times*, October 18, 1982. Fritz Burns stipulated that Hawkes be allowed use of the Hawaii home as a vacation retreat after Burns' death.

[42]"Maria (Pinkie) Scheller, George Hartman's Bride," *Los Angeles Examiner*, June 16, 1958.

[43]Skinner interview, June 7, 2000.

[44]Author's interview with Greg Dillon, April 27, 2000, Beverly Hills, California.

[45]Tobin, 33.

[46]Dillon interview, April 27, 2000; and Tobin, 33.

[47]Kaiser Community Homes memoranda, from Henry J. Kaiser, Jr. to Fritz Burns, January 14, 1946, and from Henry J. Kaiser, Jr. to Eugene Trefethen, January 14, 1946. EET Collection, Container 11, Folder 1.

[48]Foster, 279.

[49]Foster, 261–2.

[50]"Ground is Broken For Kona Hilton," *Waikiki Beach Press*, September 16, 1966.

[51]"Village Announces $27 Million Project," *Honolulu Star-Bulletin*, June 1, 1965.

[52]Tobin, 34; and Cockey interview, July 25, 2000.

[53]Dillon interview, April 27, 2000.

[54]Dillon interview, April 27, 2000.

[55]"Hilton Hotels Selects New Board Member," *New York Times*, February 19, 1962.

[56]Skinner interview, June 14, 2000.

[57]Tobin, 35; and Skinner interview, June 7, 2000.

Chapter Nine

[1]Hogan interview, June 2, 2000.

[2]Author's interview with Jacqueline Sanborn, December 13, 2000, Los Angeles, California; Morehart interview, July 6, 2000; and Skinner interview, May 19, 2000.

[3]Sanborn interview, December 13, 2000.

[4]Skinner interview, May 19, 2000.

[5]Morehart interview, July 6, 2000.

[6]Hannon interview, May 30, 1997.

[7]Hannon interview, May 30, 1997.

[8]Skinner interview, June 7, 2000.

[9]Dickinson & Gillespie subdivision map for Del Rey Hills, FBB Collection, uncatalogued materials.

[10]Tobin, 7.

[11]Letter, Fritz Burns to Charles Casassa, S.J., February 1, 1963, Los Angeles, California, FBB Collection, uncatalogued materials; and Skinner interview, May 19, 2000.

[12]Hannon interview, May 30, 1997.

[13]Hannon interview, May 30, 1997.

[14]"Garden Hotel to Key New Center," *Los Angeles Examiner*, January 12, 1958.

[15]Hogan interview, June 2, 2000.

[16]"Burns Had The Golden Touch," *The Argonaut*, February 2, 1979.

[17]Skinner interview, June 14, 2000.

[18]"Airport-Marina Hotel Opens in Westchester," *Los Angeles Herald-Examiner*, January 13, 1962.

[19]"Burns buys 551 Acres in Heart of Fremont to Build A Planned Community," Fritz B. Burns & Associates press release, December 20, 1963, HJK Collection, Container 274, Folder 3.

[20]Skinner interview, May 19, 2000.

[21]Marlow, 31–2.

[22]Press biography of Fritz Burns, July 1, 1963, FBB Collection, CSLA–2, Series 2, Box 6, Folder 1.

[23]"From Farmland to Industrial Park," *Sunnyvale Daily Standard*, May 28, 1965.

[24]"Farmland to Industrial Park."

[25]"He Loves Land, Hotels, Reindeer," *Los Angeles Herald Examiner*, July 4, 1965; and author's interview with Richard Dunn, August 30, 2000, Los Angeles, California.

[26]Tobin, 34–5.

[27]Skinner interview, July 5, 2000; and Tobin, 34–5.

[28]"Mr. F. Patrick Burns," *Los Angeles Herald-Examiner*, April 19, 1974; and Skinner interview, May 19, 2000.

[29]Skinner interview, July 5, 2000.

[30]Skinner interview, July 5, 2000.

[31]Burns never offered his employees a retirement plan; instead, he allowed them to invest in his projects. Many of his close associates saw small investments grow substantially over the course of their employment. Skinner interview, May 19, 2000.

[32]Rawlinson interview, May 31, 2000; and Fritz B. Burns Foundation internal funding schedules.

[33]Tobin, 35.

Chapter Ten

[1]Burns autobiographical notes, FBB Collection, CSLA–4, Series 1, Box 2, Folder 37.

[2]Sanborn interview, December 14, 2000.

[3]Morehart interview, July 6, 2000; Rawlinson interview, May 31, 2000; and Sanborn interview, December 20, 2000.

[4]Sanborn interview, December 20, 2000.

[5]Burns autobiographical notes, FBB Collection.

[6]Burns autobiographical notes, FBB Collection.

[7]Burns autobiographical notes, FBB Collection.

[8]Sanborn interview, December 14, 2000.

[9]Fritz B. Burns & Associates interoffice memo, Charles Getchell to Gladys Carson Burns and Frances Morehart, February 20, 1979, FBB Collection, CSLA–2, Series 2, Box 6, Folder 5.

[10]Letter, Ed Hogan to F. Patrick Burns, March 21, 1979, Los Angeles, California, FBB Collection, CSLA–2, Series 2, Box 2, Folder 5.

[11]Letter, Fritz Burns to Gary Lease, July 31, 1970, Los Angeles, California. FBB Collection, uncatalogued materials.

[12]Morehart interview, July 6, 2000. The "Loyola Victory" ship that Gladys Burns christened at Henry J. Kaiser's shipyards in 1945 was named after Loyola University in Chicago. Gladys and Fritz Burns had toured that institution two years earlier.

[13]"Fritz Burns Resigns; New Regent Selected," *Los Angeles Loyolan*, January 22, 1968. In 1974, after a merger with Marymount College resulted in the newly coeducational Loyola Marymount University, the institution honored Burns for his generosity and achievements by naming him a Regent Emeritus.

[14]Letter, Burns to Lease, April 5, 1965, Los Angeles, California. FBB Collection, uncatalogued materials.

[15]Lease interview, September 6, 2000; and letter, Gary Lease to Fanchon Royer, March 16, 1979, Santa Cruz, California, FBB Collection, uncatalogued materials.

[16]"Loyola Marymount Opens $7.5 Million Arts Center," *Los Angeles Times*, June 23, 1985; and "Eighteen Million Dollar Recreation Center Opens," Loyola Marymount University press release, August 28, 2000, FBB Collection, uncatalogued materials.

[17]Loyola Marymount University internal memorandum, Robert Bride to James Loughran, S.J., July 24, 1989, FBB Collection, uncatalogued materials.

[18]Rawlinson interview, May 31, 2000.

[19]Rawlinson interview, May 31, 2000.

[20]Gerald McLaughlin, *Loyola Law School: A Sense of Purpose and A Sense Of Mission*, (Los Angeles: Loyola Marymount University, 2000), 52–3.

[21]Letter, Burns to Lease, September 24, 1962, Los Angeles, California. FBB Collection, uncatalogued materials.

[22]McLaughlin, 62.

[23]"3,600 Get Diplomas at Rites in Southland," *Los Angeles Times*, June 10, 1963; and testimony of Theodore Bruinsma, *Gladys Carson Burns Trust v. Joseph Rawlinson*, January 15, 1981, FBB Collection, uncatalogued materials.

[24]"Rites in Southland," June 10, 1963; and "Burns Receives Loyola Law School Distinguished Achievement Award," Loyola Law School press release, Los Angeles, California, April 19, 1978, FBB Collection, uncatalogued materials.

[25]Author's interview with Fr. Donald Merrifield, S.J., May 15, 2000, Los Angeles, California.

[26]"New St. Anne's Maternity Hospital Given Blessing," *Los Angeles Times*, September 12, 1955.

[27]Interview with Tom Owenson, President & CEO, St. Anne's, January 18, 2001, Los Angeles, California.

[28]"Generations Serve St. Anne's," *Los Angeles Herald-Examiner*, November 7, 1941.

[29]"Home Of Tomorrow's Premiere Announced," *Los Angeles Times*, March 9, 1951.

[30]Skinner interview, January 7, 2001.

[31]Owenson interview, January 18, 2001; and Fritz B. Burns Foundation internal funding schedules.

[32]Fritz B. Burns Foundation internal funding schedules.

[33]Fritz B. Burns Foundation internal funding schedules.

[34]Fritz B. Burns Foundation internal funding schedules.

[35]Fritz B. Burns Foundation internal funding schedules.

[36]"William Levitt" *Time*, July 3, 1950, 67.

[37]"William Levitt," *Time*, December 7, 1998, 48.

[38]Fishman, 179.

[39]Figures supplied by Ken Skinner, Fritz B. Burns Foundation, Burbank, California.

[40]*Housing Construction: Statistics from 1889 to 1963*, (Washington, D.C.: U.S. Department of Commerce, 1968), 1; and Fishman, 192.

[41]Fritz Burns, "To Own—Certainly," *Tomorrow's Town*, (New York: National Committee on Housing, Inc., 1943), 2.

[42]Drier, "Labor's Love Lost?" 351.

[43]March 1949 personal notebook for Fritz Burns. Morehart Collection.

Sources

COLLECTIONS

Dockweiler Family Collection, Charles Von der Ahe Library, Loyola Marymount University, Los Angeles, California.

Eugene E. Trefethen Collection, Bancroft Library, University of California, Berkeley, California.

Fritz B. Burns Collection, Charles Von der Ahe Library, Loyola Marymount University, Los Angeles, California.

Henry J. Kaiser Collection, Bancroft Library, University of California, Berkeley, California.

Los Angeles City Council minutes, 1944–46, Los Angeles City Archives, Piper Technical Center, Los Angeles, California.

Morehart Collection, holdings of John and Frances Morehart, Carpinteria, California.

Westchester/Playa Del Rey Historical Society, Charles Von der Ahe Library, Loyola Marymount University, Los Angeles, California.

PUBLISHED MATERIALS

Atkinson, W.P., David D. Bohannon, Milton J. Brock, et al, eds. *Housing ... U.S.A.: As Industry Leaders See It.* New York: Simmons-Boardman, 1954.

Baxandall, Rosalyn, and Elizabeth Ewen, *Picture Windows: How the Suburbs Happened.* New York: Basic Books, 2000.

Baur, John E. "William Paul Whitsett: A Biographical Sketch." *Southern California Quarterly 76*, Spring 1994: 5–30.

Bissinger, H.G. *A Prayer For The City.* New York: Random House, 1997.

Brodsly, David. *L.A. Freeway: An Appreciative Essay.* Berkeley: University of California Press, 1981.

Buck, Elizabeth. *Paradise Remade.* Philadelphia: Temple University Press, 1993.

Burns, Fritz. *Livable Homes for Those Who Love Living.* Los Angeles: Marlow-Burns & Company, 1944.

——. *Poems & Parodies By Burns.* Los Angeles: Privately published, 1978.

———. "To Own—Certainly." *Tomorrow's Town*. New York: National Committee on Housing, Inc., 1943.

———. "We're the Suicide Troopers of the War Building Industry," *American Builder*, December 1942: 36–9.

California State Reconstruction and Reemployment Commission. *Postwar Housing in California*. Sacramento: California State Reconstruction and Reemployment Commission, 1945.

Cuff, Dana. *The Provisional City: Los Angeles Stories of Architecture And Urbanism*. Cambridge: MIT Press, 2000.

Davis, Sam. *The Architecture of Affordable Housing*. Berkeley: University of California Press, 1995.

Daws, Gavan. *Shoal of Time: A History of the Hawaiian Islands*. Honolulu: University of Hawaii Press, 1974.

Drier, Peter. "Labor's Love Lost? Rebuilding Union's' Involvement in Federal Housing Policy," *Housing Policy Debate* 11, April 2000: 327–92.

Duany, Andres, Elizabeth Plater-Zyberk, and Jeff Speck. *Suburban Nation: The Rise of Sprawl And The Decline of The American Dream*. New York: North Point Press, 2000.

Engh, Michael. "'A Multiplicity And Diversity of Faiths': Religion's Impact on Los Angeles And The Urban West, 1890–1940," *Western Historical Quarterly* 28, Winter 1997: 463–92.

Fishman, Robert. *Bourgeois Utopias: The Rise And Fall of Suburbia*. New York: Basic Books, 1987.

Fogelson, Robert. *The Fragmented Metropolis: Los Angeles, 1850–1930*. Rep. ed. Berkeley, University of California Press, 1993.

Foster, Mark. *Henry J. Kaiser: Builder in The Modern American West*. Austin: University of Texas Press, 1989.

Friedricks, William B. *Henry E. Huntington And The Creation of Southern California*. Columbus: Ohio State University Press, 1992.

Fuchs, Lawrence. *Hawaii Pono*. Honolulu: Bess, 2000.

Gillingham, Robert. *The Rancho San Pedro*. New York: Cole-Holmquist, 1983.

Glasscock, Carl. *Lucky Baldwin: The Story of An Unconventional Success*. New York: Burt, 1933.

Grenier, Judson A. and Robert C. Gillingham. *California Legacy: The James Alexander Watson-María Dolores Domínguez de Watson Family, 1820–1980*. Los Angeles: Watson Land Company, 1987.

Hays, R. Allen. *The Federal Government And Urban Housing: Ideology And Change in Public Policy*. Albany: State University of New York Press, 1985.

Henderson, Cary. "Los Angeles And The Dodger War, 1957–1962," *Southern California Quarterly* 62, Fall 1980: 261–89.

Heiner, Albert. *Henry J. Kaiser: Western Colossus*. San Francisco: Halo, 1991.

Hines, Thomas. "Housing, Baseball, and Creeping Socialism." *Journal of Urban History* 8, February 1982: 123–43.

Hise, Greg. *Magnetic Los Angeles: Planning The Twentieth-Century Metropolis*. Baltimore: Johns Hopkins University Press, 1997.

Hitch, Thomas Kemper. *Islands in Transition*. Honolulu: University of Hawaii Press, 1992.

Housing And Home Finance Agency. *A Handbook of Information on Provisions of The Housing Act of 1949*. Washington, D.C.: Housing And Home Finance Agency, 1949.

Jackson, Kenneth. *Crabgrass Frontier: The Suburbanization of The United States*. New York: Oxford University Press, 1985.

Jacobs, Jane. *The Death and Life of Great American Cities*. New York: Vintage Books, 1961.

The Kaiser Story. Oakland: Kaiser Industries Corporation, 1968.

Kelly, Barbara M. *Expanding The American Dream: Building And Rebuilding Levittown*. Albany: State University of New York Press, 1993.

Kent, Noel. *Hawaii: Islands Under The Influence*. New York: Monthly Review, 1983.

Langdon, Philip. *A Better Place to Live: Reshaping The American Suburb*. Amherst: University of Massachusetts Press, 1994.

Long, Raphael F. *Red Car Days: Memories of The Pacific Electric*. Glendale: Interurban Press, 1993.

Marlow, Fred. *Memoirs and Perceptions*. Los Angeles: privately printed, 1981.

Mason, Joseph B. *History of Housing in the U.S., 1930–1980*. Houston: Gulf, 1982.

McClung, William Alexander. *Landscapes of Desire: Anglo Mythologies of Los Angeles*. Berkeley: University of California Press, 2000.

McLaughlin, Gerald. *Loyola Law School: A Sense of Purpose and A Sense Of Mission*, Los Angeles: Loyola Marymount University, 2000.

McWilliams, Carey. *California: The Great Exception*. A.J. Wyn: New York, 1949.

———. "Look What's Happened to California," *Harper's Magazine*, October 1949: 21–9.

National Housing Agency. *Victory Bulletin*. Washington. D.C.: National Housing Agency, October 1943.

Melendy, H. Brett. *Walter Francis Dillingham, 1875–1963, Hawaiian Entrepreneur And Statesman*. Lewiston, NY: Mellen, 1996.

Mulholland, Catherine. *William Mulholland And The Rise of Los Angeles*. Berkeley: University of California Press, 2000.

Mullins, William H. *The Depression And The Urban West Coast, 1929–1933 : Los Angeles, San Francisco, Seattle, and Portland*. Bloomington: Indiana University Press, 1991.

Neutra, Dion. "The Neutra Genius: Innovations and Vision," *Modernism* 1, December 1998: 26–33.

Parson, Don. "Los Angeles' 'Headline-Happy Public Housing War'," *Southern California Quarterly* 65, Fall 1983: 251–85.

Paulus, Virginia. *Housing: A Bibliography, 1960–1972*. New York: AMS, 1974.

Sies, Mary Corbin, and Christopher Silver, eds. *Planning The Twentieth-Century American City*. Baltimore: Johns Hopkins University Press, 1996.

Snider, Sandra. *Elias Jackson "Lucky" Baldwin: California Visionary*. Los Angeles: Stairwell, 1987.

Starr, Kevin. *Material Dreams: Southern California Through The 1920s*. New York: Oxford University Press, 1990.

——. *Endangered Dreams: The Great Depression in California*. New York: Oxford University Press, 1996.

——. *The Dream Endures: California Enters The 1940s*. New York: Oxford University Press, 1997.

Stilgoe, John R. *Borderland: Origins of The American Suburb, 1820–1939*. New Haven: Yale University Press, 1988.

Sullivan, Neil J. *The Dodgers Move West*. New York: Oxford University Press, 1987.

Teaford, Jon. "Urban Renewal and Its Aftermath," *Housing Policy Debate* 11, April 2000: 443–65.

Thorpe, James. *Henry Edwards Huntington: A Biography*. Berkeley: University of California Press, 1994.

Tygiel, Jules. *The Great Los Angeles Swindle: Oil, Stocks, and Scandal During The Roaring 1920s*. New York: Oxford University Press, 1994.

United States Department of Commerce. *Housing Construction: Statistics from 1889 to 1963*. Washington, D.C.: U.S. Department of Commerce, 1968.

Verge, Arthur C. *Paradise Transformed: Los Angeles During The Second World War*. Dubuque: Kendall/Hunt, 1993.

von Hoffman, Alexander. "A Study in Contradictions: The Origins and

Legacy of the Housing Act of 1949," *Housing Policy Debate* 11, April 2000: 299–326.

Waldie, D.J. *Holy Land: A Suburban Memoir*. New York: W.W. Norton, 1996.

Weber, Francis J. *His Eminence of Los Angeles: James Francis Cardinal McIntyre*. Mission Hills: St. Francis Historical Society, 1997.

Weiss, Marc. *The Rise of The Community Builders: The American Real Estate Industry and Urban Land Planning*. New York: Columbia University Press, 1987.

Welfeld, Irving H. *Where We Live: A Social History of American Housing*. New York: Simon and Schuster, 1988.

Wilkinson, Frank. "And Now The Bill Comes Due," *Frontier* 15, October 1965: 1–2.

Wright, Gwendolyn. *Building The Dream: A Social History of Housing in America*. Cambridge: MIT Press, 1983.

INTERVIEWS

All interviews conducted by author unless otherwise noted.

Cockey, Winifred: July 24 and 25, 2000, Honolulu, Hawaii.

Dillon, Gregory: April 27, 2000, Beverly Hills, California.

Dunn, Richard: August 30, 2000, Los Angeles, California.

Hannon, William: by Michael Engh, S.J., May 30, 1997, Los Angeles, California.

Hise, Greg: May 12, 2000, Los Angeles, California.

Hogan, Ed: June 2, 2000, Westlake Village, California.

Lightfoot, Herb: April 26, 2000, Westlake Village, California.

Merrifield, S.J., Donald: May 15, 2000, Los Angeles, California.

Morehart, Frances: July 6, 2000, Carpinteria, California.

Owenson, Tom: January 18, 2001, Los Angeles, California.

Rawlinson, Joseph E.: May 31, 2000, Burbank, California.

Sanborn, Jacqueline: December 13, 14, and 20, 2000, Los Angeles, California.

Skinner, W.K.: May 19, June 7, June 14, July 5, 2000, and January 7, 2001, Burbank, California.

Wilkinson, Frank: June 5, 2000, Los Angeles, California.

Index

James Thomas Keane is a Research Fellow for
the Thomas and Dorothy Leavey Center for the
Study of Los Angeles at Loyola Marymount
University. A native of Los Angeles, he graduated from Loyola Marymount in 1996 with
degrees in Classics and Philosophy, after which
he pursued graduate studies at the University of
Pennsylvania and worked as a freelance writer in
Philadelphia. He now lives in Playa Del Rey, on
land originally subdivided by Fritz B. Burns.